* more than a footnote

Toni Kief

– Other Books by Toni Kief –

FICTION

Old Baggage, Never too Late for a New Beginning
    www.amazon.com/dp/1530424887

MILDRED UNCHAINED SERIES
    www.amazon.com/dp/B07WZLPJSL

Mildred in Disguise with Diamonds

Mildred, Romancing the Odds

Mildred, Raising the Ante

Mildred, Doubles Down

Mildred, Aces and Eights

HISTORICAL FICTION

Saints, Strangers and Rosehip Tea
    www.amazon.com/dp/B08J26FZXL

WRITING & SHORT STORIES

Dare to Write in a Flash
    www.amazon.com/dp/1731244746/

All available on Amazon and www.tonikief.com

*more than a footnote
Women neglected by history

Toni Kief

The Writers Cooperative of the Pacific Northwest
Snohomish County, Washington 2022

The Writers Cooperative of the Pacific Northwest
Snohomish County, Washington 2022

Copyright © 2022 Toni Kief

All rights reserved. Except for use in any review, the reproduction or utilization of this work in whole or in part in any form by any electronic, mechanical or other means now known or hereafter invented, including xerography, photocopying, and recording, or in any information storage or retrieval system is forbidden without the written permission of the author.

ISBN: 9798835258208

Toni Kief's website: www.tonikief.com

Cover design: Heather McIntyre, www.coverandlayout.com
Cover photos from commons.wikimedia.org
Interior design: Heather McIntyre, www.coverandlayout.com

This book is dedicated to my father,
Robert (Bob) Kief

(May 26, 1926, To October 19, 2013).

He was a brilliant man, fascinated by history, and would twirl his hair when lost in a book. I will never forget laying on the floor reading as he read in the recliner chair. Every book I have written, I hope you are proud.

Special Acknowledgment

Barbara Vericker, thanks for the
support and all of your help.

Colette and Jim Johnson, if it weren't for you two,
I would have read more books and written none.

* more than a footnote

Toni Kief

Contents

Artists
Guan Daosheng — 3
Fede Galizia — 7
Artemisia Gentileschi — 10
Louise Élisabeth Vigée Le Brun — 15
Mary Cassatt — 18
Hilma af Klint — 21
Margaret Bourke-White — 25
Judy Chicago — 31

Composers & Musicians
Hildegard von Bingen — 39
Barbara Strozzi — 43
Ethel Smyth — 47
Ma Rainey — 51
Ellie Greenwich — 55
Yoko Ono — 60

Dieties
Great Mother — 67
Venus of Willendorf — 69
Tiamat — 70
Lilith — 72
Kali the Destroyer — 74

Ninkasi	76
Circe	79
Mami Wata	81
Inanna	84
Neith	88
Triple Goddess: Maiden/Mother/Crone	90
Cihuacōātl - La Llorona - Weeping Woman	93

Educators

Aspasia	101
Fatima Al-Fihri	104
Nana Asma'u	108
Mary Lucinda Bonney Rambault	111
Anne Sullivan	115
Anna "Annie" Julia Haywood Cooper	124
Eve Ball	128

Emperors

Queen Pu-abi	135
Kandake	139
Sigrid the Haughty	142
Wu Zetian	144
Philippa of Hainault (Queen Philippa)	152

Enslaved

Doña Marina / La Malinche	159
Tituba	162
Mum Bett	166
Sojourner Truth	169

Harriet Ann Jacobs	174
Mary Fields	179
Johana July	182

Explorers

Aud Ketilsdatter	189
Jeanne Baret	193
Mary Henrietta Kingsley	198
Gertrude Bell	201
Osa Johnson	205
Valentina Tereshkova	210

Innovators

Lady Elizabeth Wilbraham	217
Tabitha Babbitt	221
Sarah E. Goode	224
Mary Anderson	226
Beulah Louise Henry	229
Dr. Patricia E. Bath	234
Dr. Shirley Ann Jackson	237

Maybe a Pope

Joanna Papissa	245

Medicine

Dr. Agnodice	251
Susan La Flesche Picotte	254
Dr. Alice Ball	260
Florence Sabin	263

Gertrude Elion — 267
Simona Kossak — 271

Political / Activists
Florence Kelley — 277
Victoria Claflin Woodhull — 281
Mary Soutar-Brooksbank — 287
Eunice Hunton-Carter — 291
Felisa Rincón de Gautier — 295
Christine Granville — 299
Shirley (Mum Shirl) Smith — 303
Phoolan Devi — 305

Scientists
Hypatia — 311
Maria Sibylla Merian — 315
Caroline Herschel — 319
Ada Byron Lovelace — 325
Annie Jump Cannon — 328
Lise Meitner — 331

Villains
Erzsébet (Elizabeth) Báthory — 337
Anne Bonney — 342
Mary Read — 342
Cheng I Sao — 346
Belle Paulsdatter Gunnes — 350
Jane Toppan — 353
Laura Bullion — 356

Warriors

Fu Hao	363
Triệu Thị Chinh	366
Jeanne des Armoises	369
Queen Nanny	372
Bartolina Sisa Vargas	375
Mary Ludwig Hays	377
Margaret Cochran-Corbin	380
Lozen	384
Gouyen	387
Maria Bochkareva	391
Milunka Savić	395
Sarah Keyes-Evans	398
Dolores Fernandez-Huerta	401

Writers

Enheduanna	407
Murasaki Shikibu	412
Margaret Lucas Cavendish	415
Olympe de Gouges	420
Carolina Louisa Waring Atkinson	424
Sarah Winnemucca	428
Mary Johnston	432
Mary Crow Dog	435

Bibliography	441
About the Author	447

Artists

There are no records of who the artists of the prehistoric eras were. Still, studies by ethnographers and cultural anthropologists indicate that women often were the principal artists in Neolithic cultures. They created pottery, textiles, baskets, painted surfaces, and jewelry. Collaboration on large projects was typical. Further research into the artwork and skills of the Paleolithic era suggests that these cultures were similar.

Even cave paintings often have human handprints. 75% are identifiable as women, and it wasn't the long nails that tipped them off.

In ancient India, it is said that the women – and only the women – of Mithila made the devotional paintings of the Hindu gods and goddesses for more than a thousand years.

We must also acknowledge the fantastic skills that make survival demands into art: pottery, tapestries, quilting, needle arts, painting, and cloth making. Women have often been considered a belonging with few rights. Most of the names have been lost, and sometimes the fathers, spouses, or co-workers were given credit.

* more than a footnote

Guan Daosheng

b: 1262 C.E. *d:1319 C.E.*
China

Guan Daosheng, also known as **Guan Zhongji** or **Lady Zhongji** (her courtesy name – I want a courtesy name), was born into a landed family in Huzhou, China. Her name translates to "Way of Righteousness Rising as the Sun." Guan grew up on her family's ancestral lands, nicknamed "The Roost of the Esteemed." Her father recognized her possibilities, so she was surprisingly well-educated and, not surprisingly, highly talented.

In 1286, at age twenty-four, Guan married Zhao Mengfu, a scholar, political official, and artist. He is often considered the greatest artist of the earlier Yuan period. Guan and Zhao were highly regarded and rich. They established a home with gardens in Wuxing and a retreat in Dongheng village near Deqing. Together (duh), they had four children, and they also raised his children from a previous marriage.

Zhao worked for the Imperial court, making her travel possible. Guan used this opportunity to meet with many of the leading artists and associate with the upper classes, as wealthy folks tend to do.

In 1279, Kublai Khan and the Mongol invasion was completed, and they founded the Yuan Dynasty.

To establish cultural control over the Chinese, he searched for the most talented scholars to serve at his court. This was when Zhao joined the highest offices of state, and he was honored as a great artist as well as a man of letters. He was assigned the task of recording the emperor's activities. Her husband's success allowed Guan to display her talents.

Guan and Zhao followed the Buddhist faith and made friends with monks, connecting with Zhongfeng Mingben, who would become their teacher. They also met other monks and teachers that resided in the monasteries in the Tianmu Mountains.

Guan's paintings started to appear around 1296, followed by her calligraphy in 1299. Her paintings were made with ink, bamboo, and plum with delicate strokes. It is suggested that Guan and her husband painted together. Her calligraphy with Zhao and one of their sons, Zhao Yong, was collected in a scroll by the Yuan Emperor Ayurbarwada, also known as Emperor Ren. "The imperial seal was applied to their work, and they became part of the Imperial Archives collection.

Guan's work on bamboo painting was atypical for a female artist, as the subject was culturally considered to represent masculine qualities. She also depicted bodies of water alongside bamboo in her work which suggested a feminine association with the plant.

A bamboo scroll of Guan's from 1301 was discovered in her husband's studio, and it demonstrated her knowledge of working bamboo. The scroll stated: "To play with brush and ink is a masculine sort of thing to do, yet I made this painting. Wouldn't someone say that I have transgressed? How despicable; how despicable." Guan's bamboo paintings were widely praised by critics who often voiced surprise that a woman could produce such masculine solid brushstrokes and did not betray that a woman made them. In 1317, the recognition helped Guan receive the title "Madam of the Wei Kingdom" from the imperial court. Her work received many honors and was housed in the imperial archives collection. The emperor commissioned Guan to copy the famous Thousand Character Classic. Her art became popular at court, and at the same time, she was painting Buddhist murals for Yuan temples.

In Guan's bamboo paintings, she often depicted the subject as part of a landscape, and the previous trend had been to paint the stalks individually. As seen in Bamboo Groves in Mist and Rain, attributed to Guan, the bamboo was depicted as part of the thickets where it naturally grows.

Guan included poems in her paintings and used a poetry style that women rarely used. Her poetry indicates a concern for her husband and children but humorously does this. At one time, her husband considered taking a concubine, and he wrote a short poem to Guan about what he was contemplating to assure her she would remain as the official wife. Guan wrote *Song of You and Me* in response. She left it for him to find, and the subject was reportedly never raised again; even after her death, he did not remarry.

Much of Guan's work has a dedication to high-ranking female patrons. That action suggests she may have been promoting the influence of women at the imperial court.

Guan was on her way home aboard the official boat when she died in 1319 at fifty-eight. She had been suffering a long illness, possibly Beriberi. Zhao had sought permission for passage due to Guan's illness. He sent a letter to a relative informing them of her death and the pain of his loss. He described her disease as 'Zuimeng tie' (Alcoholic delirium, now imagined as escape drinking, social or medicinal).

Today, Guan's home and garden in Huzhou, Lianhuazhuang, has been restored. Guan and Zhao are buried together, and the tomb is in the country at Dongcheng. A small museum was built in her husband's, Zhao Mengfu's, honor.

Fede Galizia

b: (1574) 1578 C.E.   d: 1630 C.E.
Milan, Italy

Who was **Fede Galizia**? She was born in either Trent or Milan between 1574 and 1578. Given her gender and the many problems with the Italian historical archives, it is not easy to find any documentation regarding the painter and her life. So here we go...

Fede Galizia's father was Nunzio Galizia, a renowned painter of miniatures. The success of Sofonisba Anguissola likely drove his decision to break the norms and teach his daughter. Sofonisba was from Cremona, around fifty miles from Milan, and she had been allowed to study by her father and gained significant recognition for her art. By the age of twelve, Fede was mentioned by Gian Paolo Lomazzo, a painter and art theorist friend of her father. He wrote, "This girl dedicates herself to imitate the most extraordinary of our art."

She was already an established portrait artist in her teen years with an international reputation. Undoubtedly, her father's work as a miniaturist led to Fede's profound attention to detail, such as glasses, jewels, and clothing, which made her a very realistic and desired portrait painter. Often commissioned for religious and secular themes, some of her work has survived. Perhaps her most recognizable work was Judith with the Head of Holofernes, painted in 1596, which is now in Sarasota, Florida, at the Ringling Museum of Art.

Fede is often considered a pioneer of the still life genre. The disappearance of Fede from the historical record has less to do with her talent, recognized by major artists and collectors of the 16th and 17th centuries, and more to do with how history systematically presents women as "flower painters." Fede's work shouldn't be reduced to a single style. One of her signed still-life paintings of 1602 is the first dated still-life by an Italian artist. Given the recognition by her contemporaries, it is difficult to understand how such a famous artist during her lifetime could have fallen into oblivion. Although she was never entirely erased by the city guides of Milano. Sixty-three works have been cataloged as hers, of which forty-four are still-lifes.

Jesuit scholar and historian Paolo Morigia was one of Fede's early patrons. In a collection of short biographies published in 1595, he wrote that she showed signs of "becoming a truly noble painter." He praised one of her portraits of him, declaring this work "of such excellence, and such a good likeness, that one could not desire anything more." Although that particular portrait was lost, another of him was painted a year later and survives to this day.

Fede never married, and the exact date of her death is unknown. She drafted a will in 1630, which we used as a clue. This was during the time of an

Italian plague sweeping the country – it is assumed she fell victim to the disease and died around that time.

Artemisia Gentileschi

b: *July 8, 1593*
Rome, Italy

d: *circa* 1656
Naples, Italy

Artemisia Gentileschi was born on July 8, 1593. Artemisia was the daughter of painter Orazio Lomi Gentileschi and Prudenzia di Ottaviano Gentileschi. Her mother died when Artemisia was eight years old. Considering Artemisia was the first of six children and eight when her mother died, I'm not surprised to see it was during childbirth. Her father, Orazio, was an accomplished artist and follower of Michelangelo Merisi da Caravaggio, better known as Caravaggio. Her father's studio was very successful, and there was an endless stream of artists and models. This made it possible for Artemisia to nurture her talent. As her art developed, she never lost the influence of the dark and shadow of her father's original inspiration. She has often been called "Caravaggista."

In this era, women were not invited into the art community. Artemisia had an in with her father's influence and successful studio, a familiar story for the distinguished women artists of the time. She was able to study in this community of men. Hoping to help the seventeen-year-old Artemisia refine her painting technique, her father hired Agostino Tassi to tutor her. This gave Tassi one-to-one access to

Artemisia, and during one of their tutoring sessions, he raped her.

Initially, she continued to work with Tassi as he convinced her they would wed. When her father learned of this, he brought charges against Tassi. Artemisia was tortured with thumbscrews to test her truthfulness. This test must have been even more devastating for an artist, but miraculously, Artemisia escaped permanent damage to her hands. Tassi denied having sexual relations with her in court and brought many witnesses to testify that Artemisia was "an insatiable whore." The testimony was refuted by Orazio (who sued him for perjury). Artemisia's accusations against Tassi were corroborated by a former friend of his, who recounted Tassi's boasting about his sexual exploits at Artemisia's expense. It came out that Tassi had been imprisoned earlier for incest with his sister-in-law and was charged with arranging the murder of his previous wife. Orazio, her father, sought justice for his daughter, and Tassi was convicted of raping Artemisia. He was sentenced to less than a year in prison and exiled from Rome. Tassi avoided this punishment by involving the Pope to protect him due to his art. Later Tassi was invited back to the Gentileschi studio.

Artemisia left her father's studio, moving away from Rome. During this transition, Artemisia married a fellow artist, Pietro Antonio di Vicenzo Stiattesi, and they settled in his home province of Florence. Her marriage was more for convenience than passion, but it was vital in progressing her art.

Artemisia had impressive and wealthy connections from her time in Rome, such as King Philip IV of Spain, Cosimo de' Medici, and Galileo Galilei, yes, that guy, the astronomer. This was key in promoting her career when she received one of her first major commissions. Artemisia was hired to paint a fresco at the Casa Buonarotti, the home of Michelangelo. It was being turned into a monument and museum to the great master. With this support, she continued to develop her distinctive style.

In 1618, Artemisia and her husband had a daughter, Prudentia, named after Artemisia's deceased mother. Financial problems, alongside widespread rumors regarding Artemisia's affair with a Florentine nobleman called Francesco Maria di Niccolò Maringhi, caused her to leave for Rome without her husband. She was not as successful in Rome as in Florence, and toward the end of the decade, she spent some time in Venice.

Continuing her nomadic lifestyle without her husband, Artemisia and her daughter moved to Naples in 1630, where she worked with many well-known artists. It was 1638 when Artemisia was invited to the court of Charles I of England, and her father had been the court painter since 1626. While in London, Artemisia painted some of her most famous works, including her *Self-Portrait as the Allegory of Painting* (1638). She may have worked alongside her father on an allegorical fresco for the Greenwich residence of Charles I's wife, Queen Henrietta Maria. Her father died in 1639 at the age of seventy-five, so

Artemisia's work was probably necessary to complete this significant project.

Artemisia appears to have stayed in London for a couple of years. Little is known of her later movements, although some correspondence dated as late as 1650 suggests that she returned to Naples and was still actively working.

Her date of death is uncertain, but speculations suggest she may have died of the plague which devastated Naples in 1656. However, the precise date has been questioned for centuries, and some argued that she passed away earlier, but commissions have been uncovered after that date.

She was both praised and disdained by the contemporary critical opinion of the time, but there was no denying her genius. How dare a woman exercise such creative talent previously considered exclusively male. In the words of Mary D. Garrard, she "has suffered a scholarly neglect that is almost unthinkable for an artist of her caliber." Although respected and well-known during her lifetime, Artemisia was nearly omitted from art historical accounts. Due to her style being often similar to her father's, many of her works were misattributed to him.

Artemisia's work was rediscovered in the early 1900s and was championed by the Caravaggio scholar Roberto Longhi. Her life and painting accounts were colored by exaggeration and sexualized interpretations. This is partly due to a sensationalized novel about Artemisia published by Longhi's wife, Anna Banti, in 1947.

In the 1970s and 1980s, feminist art historians such as Mary Garrard and Linda Nochlin began to study Artemisia Gentileschi, leading to changes and discoveries. They focused on her artistic achievements and her influence on the course of art history rather than on her biography. In the 1976 "Women Artists 1550-1950 Exhibition catalog, the art historian Ann Sutherland Harris argued that Artemisia Gentileschi was "the first woman in the history of western art to make a significant and undeniably important contribution to the art of her time."

Louise Élisabeth Vigée Le Brun

b: *April 16, 1755*   d: *March 30, 1842*
Paris, France

Élisabeth Louise Vigée Le Brun was best known as a portrait painter during the Rococo period. She was the daughter of Jeanne Maissin, a hairdresser, and Louis Vigée, a portraitist and fan painter who was her first art teacher. In 1760, at the age of five, Élisabeth was sent to a convent, where she remained for six years. Her father died when she was twelve years old, and his influence on Élisabeth's art was only a few years.

Her mother remarried a wealthy jeweler, Jacques-François Le Sèvre. The family moved to the Rue Saint-Honoré, close to the Royal Palace.

In her book, *Memoirs of Madame Vigée Lebrun*, Élisabeth directly stated her feelings about her stepfather: "I hated this man; even more so since he made use of my father's possessions. He wore his clothes, just as they were, without altering them to fit his figure." There may have been more sins, but this could be enough for a child.

By the time she was in her early teens, Élisabeth was painting portraits professionally. In 1774, the city seized her studio, and Élisabeth was charged with practicing without a license. She then took the opportunity and applied to the Académie de Saint-Luc.

On January 11, 1776, she married Jean-Baptiste-Pierre Le Brun, a painter and art dealer. Élisabeth began exhibiting her work at the Hôtel de Lubert near where they lived in Paris. Attending the various Salons helped her gain many important contacts necessary for success. Her husband's great-great-uncle was Charles Le Brun, the first director of the French Academy under Louis XIV, which was a handy connection. Élisabeth soon found herself in a position to paint portraits of nobility.

Her artistic legacy isn't recognized today, but she was Marie Antoinette's portrait painter. If you have seen Marie, you've probably seen Élisabeth's work. Élisabeth painted the queen and her family more than thirty times, and her massive legacy was more than six hundred and sixty portraits and over two hundred landscapes. Unlike most women in art at that time, Élisabeth was incredibly well known.

When the French Revolution began, she escaped to Paris with her daughter. They traveled throughout Europe, welcomed by aristocrats, and Élisabeth's artwork was hardly interrupted. They made it to Russia, where Élisabeth painted portraits of Queen Catherine and her daughters. Élisabeth had incredible patronage of European aristocrats, actors, and writers. In ten different cities, she was elected to art academies. She demonstrated elements of an adopted Neoclassical style.

Between 1835 and 1837, when Élisabeth was in her eighties, she published her memoirs, *Souvenirs*, in three volumes (it is available on Amazon in English and French). Throughout her life, Élisabeth never stopped painting, and due to her connections, talent, and passion, she was able to provide for herself. Élisabeth's entire life was her art. Her work is displayed in major museums, such as the Louvre, Hermitage Museum, National Gallery in London, Metropolitan Museum of Art in New York, and other collections in continental Europe and the United States.

Élisabeth Louise Vigée Le Brun died in Paris on March 30, 1842, aged eighty-six. She was buried at the Cimetière de Louveciennes near her old home. Her tombstone epitaph says, "Ici, enfin, je repose…" (Here, at last, I rest…).

Mary Cassatt

b: May 22, 1844
Allegheny City, PA, USA

d: June 14, 1926
Paris France

Chances are you're familiar with some of the women in this chapter, and **Mary Cassatt** may be one of the few. Mary was born May 22, 1844, in Allegheny City, Pennsylvania, and the family moved shortly after her birth to Philadelphia, Pennsylvania.

    She was in her early teens when she became determined to make a career in art. Mary studied painting at the Pennsylvania Academy of Fine Arts. In 1866, she moved to France to further her work and study. At the time, women still couldn't attend art school, so she pursued private lessons. Staying dedicated to her passion, it was in 1868 that her work, *A Mandolin Player*, made her one of the first American women to be accepted to show at the Paris Salon, the official art exhibition Académie des Beaux-Arts.

    The Franco-Prussian war hit her artistic career, and since her father was unsupportive, she was forced to leave France in 1870. Mary briefly considered quitting her passion due to a lack of support and inspiration. Thankfully, the archbishop of Pittsburgh commissioned her to paint copies of the master painter Correggio. So, she was off to Parma, Italy. While still in Europe, Mary's work took on an impressionistic style. Mary met and connected with Edgar Degas during this trip, a fellow impressionist and well-known pastel artist. It's this friendship that inspired her to continue. She joined his circle of friends and spoke that this was when she first "began to live."

Her parents and sister moved to Paris in 1877, and her brothers and their families visited frequently. Even though Mary never married, she had a close tie to her family, adding to her vision. Mary is best known as an impressionist who focused on women, children, and motherhood. She often exhibited with other artists such as Monet, Pissarro, and Degas. They all shared an independent spirit.

Mary refused throughout her life to be associated with any art academy or designated style. She never accepted any prizes and stands alone in her depictions of women's activities in their tasks of caring for children, reading, crocheting, pouring tea, and enjoying the company of other women. Cassatt pursued her painting in the remaining decades of the 19th century, and the 1890s became her most creative period.

She lived in Paris for most of her life but considered herself an American and was proud of her Philadelphia roots. A trip to Egypt in 1910 impressed Mary with the beauty of ancient art. This led her into a crisis of creativity; not only had the trip exhausted her, she said, "I fought against it, but it conquered, it is surely the greatest Art the past has left us … how are my feeble hands to ever paint the effect on me."

She was diagnosed with diabetes, rheumatism, neuralgia, and cataracts in 1911. She struggled to continue, but in 1914, Mary was forced to stop painting as her vision was nearly gone. Mary Cassatt died on June 14, 1926 at Château de Beaufresne, near Paris, and was buried in the family vault at Le Mesnil-Théribus, France.

Hilma af Klint

b: October 26, 1862 *d: October 21, 1944*
Solna, Sweden *Sjursholm, Sweden*

Hilma af Klint was born in 1862, in Solna, Sweden, as the fourth of five children. Her parents were a Protestant couple, Mathilda af Klint, and her father, Victor af Klint, was an admiral and a mathematician. Her father was based at Karlberg castle for most of her childhood. During the summer, they would travel to Hanmora, in Adelso, an island in Lake Malaren. This was where Hilma's fascination with nature and organic life began.

In 1892, at the age of twenty, Hilma was one of the first women to attend the Royal Academy of Fine Arts in Stockholm. She spent the next five years studying drawing, portraiture, and landscape painting. Graduating with honors, Hilma was awarded a studio in the Academy's "Atelier Building" in the cultural center of Stockholm.

Her studio was in the same building as Blanch's Café and Art Gallery. This was where the traditional academic art clashed with the Artists Association's ideas of the French plein-air painting, where the 19th century style of painting outdoors originated. There was a trend to a sense of the open air and nature that became a central feature of impressionism.

Hilma sought spiritual knowledge, like many of her contemporaries. As a teenager, she had participated in spiritistic séances, and for a period in her thirties, she was a member of the Edelweiss Society and the Rosicrucian Order. These connections were a source of inspiration. However, her major influence was the Theosophical Society, which she joined at its inception in Sweden in 1889.

In 1896, Hilma joined with four other like-minded women artists and left the Edelweiss Society to found the "Friday Group." They were also known as "The Five." Every Friday, they gathered for spiritual meetings, including prayers, studies of the New Testament, meditation, and séances. The medium of the group exercised automatic writing and mediumistic drawing. Eventually, they established contact with spiritual beings called "The High Ones." In 1896, the five women began taking meticulous notes of the messages from the spirits. In time, Hilma felt she was meant for more meaningful work.

After ten years with "The Five," she accepted a critical assignment of Paintings for the Temple. Hilma worked on this commission from 1906 to 1915, and it had changed direction, as things do in nine years. Hilma then left the studio for another nine years to care for her blind mother. That same year, Rudolf Steiner, leader of the German Theosophical Society, held lectures in Stockholm. While there, he visited Hilma's studio and saw some of her early Paintings for the Temple. In 1913, Steiner founded the Anthroposophical Society, which Hilma joined in

1920 and remained a member for the rest of her life. The Society was a gathering of people who wished to nurture the soul's life, both in the individual and human society, based on actual knowledge of the spiritual world.

Her Paintings for the Temple encompasses 193 works, divided into series and sub-groups. It is one of the first examples of abstract art in the west. Hilma had shared an interest in the spiritual with many other pioneers of abstract art. This trend is to surpass the restrictions of the physical world. Many of the artists of this group were drawn to Theosophy, a new religious movement, and as part of the occultist stream of Western esotericism. It uses both older European philosophies such as Neoplatonism and Asian religions such as Hinduism and Buddhism. It was a tool to attempt to build an attractive alternative to the static principles of academic art. The abstract, non-figurative art opened up a radically new means of expression toward a spiritual reality.

In 1917, Hilma opened a new studio on the island of Munsö in Lake Mälaren, close to her family's estate on the island of Adelsö. Her mother passed away in 1920, and Hilma relocated to Helsingborg in Sweden soon after.

Hilma was convinced that reality was not confined to the physical and material worlds, and she believed there was an inner realm. Hilma employed dualistic symbols to express that "Everything is Unity" to convey this message. She developed an artistic approach to expressing her beliefs in her paintings.

A solid education and more than twenty years of professional creative experience are part of her art at this time.

Hilma was well aware of the uniqueness of her art. The overshadowing question was: "What is the message that the paintings convey?" Hilma envisioned her work would contribute to influencing people's consciousness in general and society itself. Although, she was convinced that her contemporaries were not ready to understand her art. Hilma received strict orders from the "High Ones," her spiritual leaders, not to show the paintings to anyone. She believed that her art belonged to the future, and only then would it be understood.

After celebrating her eightieth birthday, Hilma returned to Stockholm and was soon injured in a traffic accident. Hilma died in the autumn of 1944, at the age of eighty-one.

One of her wishes was her work should not be publicly displayed until twenty years after her death. She left more than 1300 works and 125 notebooks, which a selected few have seen. Additionally, she expressed her desire to keep the 193 paintings for the Temple together.

The Hilma af Klint Foundation owns and administers her work in Stockholm, Sweden. Hilma af Klimt was buried at the Galärvarvskyrkogården (literally Galley Shipyard Cemetery) on the island of Djurgården in Stockholm, Sweden.

Margaret Bourke-White

b: June 14, 1904
Bronx, NY, USA

d: August 27, 1971
Stamford, CT, USA

Margaret White was born in the Bronx, New York, to Joseph White, a non-practicing Jew whose father came from Poland, and Minnie Bourke, of Irish Catholic descent. Margaret grew up near Bound Brook, New Jersey, and attended and graduated from Plainfield High School in Union County. She often claimed that she learned perfectionism from her naturalist father, an engineer, and an inventor. Margaret credits her mother for her developed and unapologetic desire for self-improvement.

Roger Bourke White, Margaret's younger brother, became a prominent Cleveland businessman and high-tech industry founder. Her older sister, Ruth White, was known for working at the American Bar Association in Chicago, Illinois. Clearly, her "Free-thinking" parents work to succeed and advance humanity through personal achievement, which is carried on with their children.

While Margaret was still young, she developed an interest in photography. Her father had a passion for cameras and encouraged her. Margaret enrolled at Columbia University, and she started her studies in herpetology. After one semester, she left the University due to her father's death. Not one to give up on education, Margaret enrolled at the University of Michigan. This was when her interest in photography rekindled as she worked on the school paper. She also attended Purdue University, Western Reserve University in Cleveland, Ohio, and finally graduated from Cornell University with a Bachelor of Arts degree in 1927.

Margaret wasn't all education and college transfers; in 1924, she married Everett Chapman, and the marriage lasted only two years. In 1927 Margaret officially added her mother's surname, "Bourke," to her autograph.

A year later, Margaret moved from Ithaca, New York, to Cleveland, Ohio, where she started a commercial photography studio. She started out concentrating on architectural and industrial photography.

One of her first clients at the studio was Otis Steel Company. Her association with them wasn't easy. The Otis security people were reluctant to let her shoot freely for several reasons. One of the reasons was that steel-making was part of the national defense industry. Second, she was a woman, and as we know, "men in power often worry a frail woman and her delicate cameras couldn't tolerate the intense heat, hazards, and conditions inside a steel mill. When Margaret finally got permission, there were technical issues. The black-and-white film was sensitive to blue light, not the reds and oranges of hot steel, and the photos came out all black. Margaret described that nothing was recognizable other than a half-dollar-sized disk marking where the molten metal had churned up in the ladle. "The glory had withered."

Her associate, Mr. Bemis, stated, "We're woefully underexposed. That red light from the molten metal looks as though it's illuminating the whole place. But it's all heat and no light. No actinic value."

Margaret didn't let that stop her and brought in a new style of a magnesium flare. The flare produces a white light, and with assistants holding the flares to illuminate her scenes resulted in some of the best steel-factory photographs of that era. This innovation brought her national attention.

In 1929, Margaret accepted a job as associate editor and staff photographer for Fortune magazine. The following year she became the first Western photographer allowed to enter the Soviet Union. In 1936, Henry Luce hired her as the first female photojournalist for Life magazine. Her first photographs of the construction of the Fort Peck Dam were featured in Life's first issue, dated November 23, 1936. This included the magazine cover, which became such a favorite that it was the 1930s' United States Postal Service's Celebrate the Century commemorative postage stamp.

During the mid-1930s, like Dorothea Lange, Margaret photographed drought victims of the Dust Bowl. The Life magazine issue of February 15, 1937, published her now-famous photograph of black, flood-victims standing in front of a sign, "World's Highest Standard of Living," showing it to a white family. The picture later would become the basis for the artwork of Curtis Mayfield's 1975 album, *There's No Place Like America Today.*

She married the novelist Erskine Caldwell from 1939 to their divorce in 1942. Margaret and Erskine collaborated on *You Have Seen Their Faces* (1937), a book about conditions in the South during the Great Depression.

Not one to stay close to home, Margaret traveled to Europe to record how Germany, Austria, and Czechoslovakia were faring under Nazism as the first known female war correspondent. Also, as the first woman allowed to work in combat zones during World War II. In 1941 she traveled to the Soviet Union just as Germany broke its pact of non-aggression. She was the only foreign photographer in Moscow when German forces invaded. Forced to take refuge in the U.S. Embassy, she captured the ensuing firestorms on camera.

Margaret was attached to the U.S. Army Air Force in North Africa, then to the U.S. Army in Italy, and later in Germany. She repeatedly came under fire in Italy in the areas of fierce fighting. On January 22, 1943, Major Rudolph Emil Flack, Squadron and Mission Commander, piloted the lead aircraft with Margaret on board. Margaret became the first female photographer/writer to fly on a combat mission. Another time she describes the field of 130 enemy planes as "one bright orange flash."

At *Life* magazine, Margaret was called "Maggie the Indestructible." She was also aboard a ship torpedoed in the Mediterranean, the sinking of the England-

Africa bound British troopship SS Strathallan that she recorded in an article, "Women in Lifeboats," in Life, February 22, 1943. In addition, Margaret was strafed by the Luftwaffe, stranded on an Arctic island, bombarded in Moscow, and pulled out of the Chesapeake Bay when her chopper crashed. I wonder if *Life* magazine had insurance benefits.

In the spring of 1945, she traveled throughout a collapsing Germany with Gen. George S. Patton. Upon her arrival at Buchenwald, the notorious concentration camp, she said, "Using a camera was almost a relief. It interposed a slight barrier between myself and the horror in front of me."

After the war, she produced a book entitled Dear Fatherland, Rest Quietly, a project that helped her come to grips with the brutality and horror she had witnessed during and after the war.

In 1953, Margaret developed her first symptoms of Parkinson's disease. It wasn't boredom that forced her to slow her career. Due to progressing paralysis, Margaret had to undergo several operations. They were able to end her tremors, but her speech was still affected. Not one to rest on her laurels, Margaret published an autobiography, *Portrait of Myself*, in 1963, which became a bestseller.

Her health issues continued, and she isolated herself in her home in Darien, Connecticut. Her living room "was wallpapered in one huge, floor-to-ceiling, perfectly-stitched-together black-and-white photograph of an evergreen forest that she had shot in Czechoslovakia in 1938".

A pension plan set up in the 1950s, considered generous at the time, was insufficient for her growing healthcare costs.

In 1971 she died at Stamford Hospital in Stamford, Connecticut, aged sixty-seven, about eighteen years after developing Parkinson's. Margaret Bourke-White, an American photographer and documentary photographer, firsts from the beginning of her career to the end.

It was hard to decide which chapter Margaret fit in: an artist, warrior, and writer.

Judy Chicago

b: July 20, 1939
Chicago, IL, USA

Judy Chicago was born Judy Cohen in 1939 in Chicago, Illinois. She grew up in a liberal environment, unusual for the time. Her intellectual Jewish parents worked to support their children and openly articulated their left-wing politics. Judy began drawing at the age of three and attended classes at the Institute of Chicago starting in 1947. In 1948, her father, Arthur Cohen, left his union job amid the McCarthy blacklist and the controversy surrounding the family's "Communist" leanings. Two years later, he died from a massive stomach ulcer.

Having attended art classes at the Art Institute throughout her teens, Judy went to UCLA, where she received her M.F.A. in 1964. Her early paintings were bold depictions of female sexual expression, but her peers did not accept them. Judy then turned her attention to sculpture. In 1961 Judy wed Jerry Gerowitz, and during this time, she began gaining recognition for her Minimalist geometric works. However, Judy felt these works were a bland version of her original vision and feared she had bent to a male-dominated aesthetic.

Her relationship with her husband, Jerry, was a stormy one; he died two years after they married in a car crash. Judy's use of imagery in the aftermath of this tragedy became more expressive and personal. The female body re-emerged as a theme and inspiration in an abstract form. Her art in the subsequent years reflects Judy's attempt to reconcile her identity as a woman and an artist. She continued to attend graduate school and later auto-body classes. She studied both sculptural and spray-painting techniques. Judy continued to challenge with her increasingly symbolic depiction of the vulva.

Her first solo exhibition in 1965 was largely Minimalist. Through the mid-1960s and 1970s, her work became dominated by explicitly feminist themes. In 1969, Judy married the sculptor Lloyd Hamrol, but this time she rejected the tradition of taking her husband's name and instead adopted a new surname, Chicago. It was her statement of independence as well as a tribute to her hometown.

In 1970, Judy pioneered a radical educational experiment tied to the emerging women's movement. Judy joined with artist Miriam Schapiro, and together they established a women-only art course at California State University in Fresno. Soon the class was moved to the California Institute of Arts in Valencia. The study focused on expressionism through the process of "consciousness-raising." This practice recognized and respected the female identity and independence through the group's art practice. They combined object-making, installation, and performance. The Womanhouse Art Space began for teaching, performance, exhibition, discussion, and expression.

Although successful, the project was frequently beset with tension over leadership. Judy resisted the inequality of the educational institution where the project was based, and she felt the need to create an "alternative system" far from Cal Arts. In 1973 she founded the Feminist Studio workshop in an entirely separate location in Los Angeles.

Womanhouse expanded to become the Woman's Building, where numerous other creative feminist organizations developed. The female art community in Los Angeles was established and has become a significant symbol of the 1970s feminist movement.

In 1974, Judy began her most significant and controversial work. In her drive to recognize women's stories and bring them into the historical narrative, she began art-making techniques dismissed by the fine art world, such as ceramic decoration and embroidery. Working as a collaboration, Judy used needlework and glass-based practices of artisans. *The Dinner Party* (1979) is a monumental thirty-nine place dinner table presented in a triangular form with a plate to mark each guest's place. Many of the place settings are inscribed with symbols of the vulva. The Dinner Party opened in March 1979 at the San Francisco Museum to over five thousand attendees and much discussion. Dismissed as "kitsch," "bad art," and "obscene" by some art critics, the piece was famously dismantled and stored away, and it was seldom seen as art institutions rejected it throughout the country.

Three decades of protest and controversy surrounding the piece followed until it was finally reinstalled in 2007 at the Elizabeth Sackler Center for Feminist Art in Brooklyn, New York. The Dinner Party remains an essential symbol of the women's movement and a work of contention. The Dinner Party rests upon the Heritage Floor, an equilateral triangle forty-eight feet on each side. This monumental floor comprises 2300 hand-cast porcelain tiles and provides structural and metaphorical support for The Dinner Party table. Inscribed in gold luster are the names of 999 mythical and historical women of achievement, selected to contextualize the thirty-nine women represented in the place settings and to demonstrate how many women struggled to make their ideas known – sometimes in the face of overwhelming obstacles – only (like the women on the table) to have their hard-earned achievements marginalized or erased. Not to sit and wait, Judy's focus shifted from a solely feminist perspective to a broader concern with the underrepresentation of female experience in visual media. The Birth Project followed the Dinner Party. From 1980 to 1985, Judy worked with women worldwide to create needlework pieces in response to a perceived absence of birth imagery in historical narratives and the visual arts. Then Judy turned her attention to exploring the manifestations of masculinity in a series of large-scale paintings entitled Powerplay.

Judy then explored her identity as a woman of the Jewish faith and began working with the photographer, soon-to-be third husband, Donald Woodman. Judy directed an eight-year-long project dedicated to unearthing Holocaust imagery and culminating in a multimedia installation, *The Holocaust Project: From Darkness into Light*. *The Holocaust Project* toured the U.S. to widespread acclaim and controversy.

1994 to 2001, Judy joined with needle artists in creating *Resolutions: A Stitch in Time*, which reinvented traditional proverbs to promote lost social values for a contemporary multicultural society. In 1999, she returned to teaching, expanding her approach significantly from the 1970s to incorporate a male influence.

Judy's three most recent projects have seen her documenting her cats in a humorous book, developing glass-blowing techniques, and engaging in a piece entitled Atmospheres, which recalls a project she began back in the 1970s. Using pyrotechnics, Atmospheres is a smoke-and-firework piece shown as part of Pacific Standard Time, an exhibition documenting and celebrating southern California art from 1945 to 1980.

Judy's work is significant in conjunction with the feminist movement of the 1960s through the 1980s and on. She helped recognize and reinstate women's roles throughout history and in the hierarchies of fine art and craft. She is instrumental in the rediscovery of forgotten or undervalued art. When women couldn't study painting, they continued with needles and weaving. Her celebration of the female has inspired several generations of contemporary artists. The celebration of "female" art forms such as needlework and embroidery, ceramic, and textile art, has built her legacy. In her spare time, Judy has written several books documenting her and other female artists' work.

Composers & Musicians

The historical development and presence of music from prehistoric times to the present day have existed worldwide. Though definitions of music vary wildly, every known culture partakes in it, and music is considered a cultural universal. I am confident the discovery of rhythm was the earliest gatherer tapping her foot, waiting for the hunters to return with the possibility of meat in the casserole

Hildegard von Bingen

b: circa 1098   *d: September 17, 1179*
Germany

Hildegard of Bingen (German: **Hildegard von Bingen**; Latin: **Hildegardis**; also known as **Saint Hildegard** and **the Sibyl of the Rhine**) was a German Benedictine abbess and a Christian mystic, writer, composer, philosopher, mystic, herbologist, visionary, and as a medical writer and practitioner. Summed up, she was an all-around stunning genius during the High Middle Ages. Hildegard was one of the rare individuals whose knowledge spans a substantial number of subjects and is known to draw on complex bodies of knowledge for her work. She refused to be defined by the patriarchal hierarchy of the church, and, although she abided by its strictures, she pushed the established boundaries for women expanding and exploring the limits.

Hildegard was born around 1098, although the exact date is uncertain. Her parents were Mechtild of Merxheim-Nahet and Hildebert of Bermersheim. They were of a lower nobility status in the service of Count Meginhard of Sponheim. Sickly from birth, Hildegard is traditionally considered their youngest and tenth child, although the records are sketchy on the other siblings. Hildegard stated that from a very young age, she had visions.

Her parents offered her as an oblate to the Benedictine monastery at Disibodenberg reformed in the Palatinate Forest. The date of Hilde's enclosure at the monastery is debated. Her Vita says she was eight years old when she was professed with Jutta, the daughter of Count Stephan II of Sponheim. However, Jutta's date of enclosure is known to have been in 1112, when Hildegard would have been fourteen. By 1136, Hildegard was elected as mother superior. She went on to found the monastery of Rupertsberg in 1150 and, in 1165, the monastery of Eibingen. She also wrote theological, botanical, and medicinal works, knocked out letters, hymns, and antiphons for the liturgy.

The vision of "The Shade of the Living Light" Hildegard claimed to have first seen at the age of three, and by five, she understood that she was experiencing visions. She recognized that it was a gift she could not explain to others. Much later, Hildegard explained that she saw all things in the light of God through the five senses: sight, hearing, taste, smell, and touch. Hildegard was hesitant to share her vision experience and only confided to Jutta, who told Volmar, Hildegard's tutor and, later, secretary. Throughout her life, she continued to have the visions, and in 1141, at the age of forty-two, Hildegard received one she considered to be an instruction from God, to "write down that which you see and hear." She was still hesitant to record her visions.

Furthermore, she wrote poems while supervising miniature illuminations in the Rupertsberg manuscript of her first work, *Scivias*. The illustrations recorded in *Scivias* were visions that Hildegard experienced, causing her great suffering and tribulations. There are more surviving chants by Hildegard than by any other composer from the entire Middle Ages, and she is one of the few known composers to have written both the music and the lyrics. One of her works, the *Ordo Virtutum*, is an early example of liturgical drama and arguably the oldest surviving morality play.

In her first theological text, *Scivias* ("Know the Ways"), Hildegard describes her internal struggles. In her spare time, Hildegard was considered by many in Europe to be the founder of scientific natural history in Germany.

Pope Eugenius heard about Hildegard's writings between November 1147 and February 1148 at the synod in Trier. From this, she received Papal approval to document her visions as revelations from the Holy Spirit, giving her instant credence.

September 17, 1179, as Hildegard was dying, the sisters claimed they saw two streams of light appear in the skies and cross over the room. Although the history of her formal canonization is complicated, the Roman Catholic church has listed her as a saint for centuries. On May 10, 2012, Pope Benedict XVI extended the liturgical cult of Hildegard to the entire Catholic Church in a process known as "equivalent canonization." On October 7, 2012, he named her a Doctor of the Church in recognition of "her holiness of life and the originality of her teaching."

Hildegard Von Bengin died on September 17, 1179 (aged eighty or eighty-one) at Bingen am Rhein, Landkreis Mainz-Bingen, Rheinland-Pfalz, Germany. She was initially buried at the graveyard of the convent of Disibodenberg. Her remains were moved to the parish church of Eibergen (Germany) in 1642, where she is commemorated with a beautiful shrine. It seems she should be in nearly every chapter of this book

Barbara Strozzi

b: *circa* July 1619   d: November 11, 1677
Venice, Italy

Born in 1619 in Venice, **Barbara Strozzi** (also called **Barbara Valle**) was baptized on August 6 at the Santa Sofia parish. At that time, Venice was a city of wealth, peace, culture, academic curiosity, and musical innovation. Barbara was the adopted daughter of poet Giulio Strozzi, most likely his natural daughter, as she was recognized or 'legitimized' in his will of 1628. Her mother, Isabella lived in the same household and was assumed to be one of the household servants; Giulio named her his principal heir until Barbara came of age.

Little is known about Barbara's childhood and musical training, but she grew up in a household frequented by the age's most significant literary and musical minds. The Strozzi name was recognized far and wide as her father founded and was involved with several groups of creative intellectuals. He was an influential member of the Accademia degli Incogniti, formed by the writer Giovanni Francesco Loredano in Venice. This group was almost single-handedly responsible for the 'invention' and spread of music and theater, what was to become known as Opera. This new art form flourished in Venice throughout the 17th century.

The Incogniti counted famous authors, poets, philosophers, and musicians among its members. It was into this community of artists that young Barbara was introduced as a singer and composer. In the dedication of a group of songs called *Bizzarrie poetiche*, composer Nicolò Fontei in 1635 said that his songs were inspired by "principally the most kind and virtuosic damsel, Signora Barbara."

Her performances and participation in the academy activities were of sufficient interest, even scandal since women were rarely included in such gatherings. The book *Satire, e lter raccolte per l'Academia de gl'Unisoni in casa di Giulio Strozzi* (1637) contains the oft-quoted slur against Barbara "It is a fine thing to distribute the flowers after having already surrendered the fruit." The talk around town suggested she was a courtesan and not a chaste young woman with a liberal upbringing. Often musical inclinations were credited to courtesans. No matter the gossip, she continued to concentrate on music. Without her father's connections and involvement in the musical activities of Venice, it is unlikely that Barbara would have been able to launch a career as a composer. She made it official in 1644 with the publication of a volume of madrigals, *Il primo libro de' madrigali* ("First Book of Madrigals").

Between 1644 and 1664, she published eight music collections, of which one – her Opus 4 – is now lost. The preface to her second collection cites Francesco Cavalli, one of the most prominent and historically significant composers of 17th century Venice, as her teacher. Although Barbara was Giulio's sole heir, she seems not to have gained financially when he died in 1652. That may have been her inspiration to publish several books in quick succession, perhaps in search of a steady patron. Her effort was unsuccessful, and her financial situation remained tenuous throughout the remainder of her career.

Barbara published multiple volumes of music, which suggests it was well received. Her compositional output following her first volume of madrigals mainly was arias, cantatas, and ariettas, no rap. The arias are generally short pieces, and every stanza is sung to the same music. Cantatas are mostly longer works in which the music changes to suit the story's meaning. Ariettas are even shorter arias. Most of the poetry was usually love-themed.

In the mid-17th century, the musical trend valued wit, virtuosity, and (wink wink) erotic imagery. Barbara even had a collection of sacred music, the *Sacri musicali affetti*, which represents the church as a loving mother.

Although never married, Barbara had four children, at least three of which were with Giovanni Paolo Vidman. Giovanni was a colleague of her father and a prominent supporter of the opera. This was not uncommon during this period, where aristocratic patrimony was of higher importance than the legality of marriage. The Vidman family nonetheless provided an inheritance for three of her children.

Barbara lived with her parents until their deaths and remained in the house, which was rented from a Vidman brother. To consider her a courtesan or prostitute is unlikely. Clearly, she was too busy writing, composing, and attending to her parents and children to have had an outside profession. Two of her daughters joined a convent, and one of her sons became a monk.

Barbara was honored as the most prolific composer – man or woman – of printed secular vocal music in Venice. Her unique output was varied and voluminous with vocal music, except for just one volume of sacred songs.

As an Italian composer and singer of the Baroque Period, Strozzi published eight volumes of her music during her lifetime and had more secular music in print than any other composer of the era. She achieved this with no support from the Church and no consistent patronage from the nobility.

Barbara Strozzi died in Padua, Italy, in 1677, aged fifty-eight. She did not leave a will, so her son Giulio Pietro claimed her inheritance. Barbara was a passionate and extraordinary talent, leaving 125 published vocal music pieces. I can only imagine what may have been in progress when she died. She is believed to have been buried at The Church of the Eremitani in Veneto, Italy.

Ethel Smyth

b: April 22, 1858 *d: 1944*
England

Ethel Smyth was the fourth of eight children. She was born in Sidcup, Kent, which is now in the London Borough of Bexley. While April 22 is the actual day of her birth, Smyth often stated it was April 23, William Shakespeare's birthday. Her family celebrated the connection. Her father, John Hall Smyth, was a major general in the Royal Artillery, and her mother was Emma Struth Smythe. Her father was very strict and objected to Ethel's career in music, so she moved on to become a 20th century British composer and a champion of women's rights and female musicians.

Ethel had high regard for her father, but her mother introduced her to music. Around 1870, under the influence of a governess who had studied at the Leipzig Conservatory, Ethel began to explore her passion. Initially homeschooled with her five sisters, until 1872 to 1875, she was allowed to attend Putney School. Despite musical activities at school, she did not develop her talent until she returned to Frimley, a town in the Borough of Surrey Heath in Surrey, England, approximately thirty miles southwest of central London. This was when she received tuition from Alexander Ewing. Ewing became more of a friend and mentor, encouraging her musical aspirations. At the same time, his wife, Juliana Ewing, encouraged Ethel to pursue an author's career. General Smyth's distrust of Ewing brought this relationship to an end. It was too late. Ethel was already on her way to study composition in Leipzig.

Ethel specialized in the romantic lyrical and classical music style developed by the German composer Brahms and the music theory while at Leipzig Conservatory in Germany. Her sophisticated music received rave reviews early on. She returned to London in 1889 and continued her work in multiple areas of composition. Ethel produced orchestral pieces, choral arrangements, chamber music, and six operas. Despite her initial success and talent, Ethel struggled to find musicians to perform due to her gender.

It was 1910 when Ethel met Emmeline Pankhurst, a founder of the British suffrage movement and head of the Women's Social and Political Union. Pankhurst led an all-women's activist group that campaigned for women's suffrage since 1903. Due to Pankhurst's influence, Ethel took two years off from her music and devoted herself to the women's rights movement. During her political activism, she didn't leave music completely. Ethel wrote *The March of Women*, 1911, which later became the battle cry for the British Women's Movement. In 1912, Ethel, along with Pankhurst and a hundred other suffragists, were arrested in London for throwing stones at the houses of the opponents of women's rights.

Ethel was sentenced to Holloway Prison for two months. One day conductor Thomas Beecham went to visit her. When he arrived, he found suffragists singing in the yard, and he looked up to see Ethel leaning out of a window conducting with her toothbrush. This rousing rendition of *The March of Women* became the most famous performance of the song.

In 1912, Ethel began to lose her hearing. After visiting a specialist in Paris, she went to Egypt to work on *The Boatswain's Mate*, a comic opera. This became one of the most revolutionary pieces. The opera's first half contained both words and music, but the second half was entirely instrumental. The Boatswain's Mate is a more accessible and light-hearted piece for the general public, a break from the Grand Opera style.

By 1919, Ethel had given up her music career due to her continued hearing loss. This was when she made Julia Ewing, her childhood teacher's wife, right in foreseeing an author's life for her. Ethel wrote several biographies, including *Impressions that Remained* and the memoir, *Streaks of Life*, which captured her experiences in music, activism, and as a lesbian. She openly wrote her romantic involvements with famous women of her time, including Lady Pauline Trevelyan; the Empress Eugénie; heiress Winnaretta Singer; Lady Mary Ponsonby; writer Edith Somerville; and writer Virginia Woolf. I wonder what the General would say if he were still alive.

Ethel died in England in 1944 at the age of eighty-six. She remains a highly regarded composer, author, and political voice of the early 20th century.

Ma Rainey
aka
Gertrude Pridgett

b: April 26, 1886   d: December 22, 1939
Columbus, GA, USA

Gertrude Malissa Nix Pridgett was born April 26, 1886, to minstrel troupers Thomas Pridgett, Sr. and Ella Allen-Pridgett. As early as 1900, at the age of fourteen, she worked at the Springer Opera House as a singer and dancer in the local talent show, "A Bunch of Blackberries."

On February 2, 1904, Gertrude married comedy songster William "Pa" Rainey, and she changed her name appropriately. "Ma" and "Pa" Rainey toured with various African-American minstrel troupes and vaudeville groups, most notably the Rabbit Foot Minstrels throughout the south. Though she had not heard the blues in Columbus, the extensive traveling changed that.

It was in 1905 when Ma was introduced to authentic country blues. It didn't take long for her to write her songbook. Ma's natural ability captured the depth of the rural southern life of the 1920s. Before long, she was drawing throngs of fans throughout the South.

While performing with the Moses Stokes troupe in 1912, Ma met a new dancer, Bessie Smith. Eight years older than Bessie didn't interfere with their bond. It is often reported that Ma was Bessie's vocal coach, but true or not, they were a tremendous force that introduced the southern blues to the world. Ma certainly did share her singing experience and style with Bessie. Around 1915, the Raineys were being billed as the "Assassinators of the Blues." Her marriage was falling apart, and they separated around 1916. Ma continued to tour with her band, Madam Gertrude Ma Rainey and Her Georgia Smart Sets. She featured a chorus line and called the show the Cotton Blossoms Show.

Three years after the first blues recording by Mamie Smith, Ma recorded with Paramount records. Already a popular singer in the Southern theater circuit, Ma entered the recording industry as an experienced and stylistic talent. Her first session featured *Bo-Weevil Blues*. Fellow blues singer Victoria Spivey later said in *The Devil's Music*, "Ain't nobody in the world been able to holler 'Hey Boweevil' like her. Not like Ma. Nobody."

The same year, 1923, Ma released *Moonshine Blues* with Lovie Austin, and *Yonder Comes the Blues* with Louis Armstrong. In her spare time that same year, she recorded *See See Rider*, one of the most famous blues songs. As no fool, Ma held the copyright, and it became one of the most recorded songs, with over a hundred versions.

During Rainey's five-year recording career at Paramount, she cut nearly ninety sides, most of which dealt with the subjects of love and sexuality – themes that earned her the billing of Madam Rainey. Unlike many other blues musicians, Rainey earned a reputation as a professional on stage and in business. She was shrewd, fair, and intelligent, which was celebrated in the 1988 play *Ma Rainey's Black Bottom*. As William Barlow explained in *Looking Up at Down*, her songs were also "diverse, yet deeply rooted in day-to-day experiences of Black people from the South." Ma Rainey's blues were simple, straightforward stories about heartbreak, promiscuity, drinking binges, the odyssey of travel, the workplace, the prison road gangs, magic, and superstition – in short, the southern landscape of African Americans in the Post-Reconstruction era.

Draped in elegant gowns and covered in jewelry, Ma commanded the stage. She often opened with *Moonshine Blues* inside the cabinet of an oversized victrola, from which she emerged to greet an excited audience. She was a profound entertainer as her audience was swept away with Ma and her music.

Until 1926, Rainey performed with her Wild Jazz Cats on the Theater Owner's Booking Association circuit. She recorded with a wealth of musicians on the Paramount label. In 1927, Ma made Black Cat, Hoot Owl Blues with the Tub Jug Washboard Band. During her last sessions, held in 1928, she sang in the company of her former pianist Thomas "Georgia Tom" Dorsey and guitarist Hudson "Tampa Red" Whittaker, producing such classics as *Black Eye Blues*, *Runaway Blues*, and *Sleep Talking Blues*.

The touring circuits were declining in the 1930s, yet Ma still performed. Almost a complete cycle from when she started in tent shows. She retired from the music business in 1935 and settled in Columbus, Georgia. For the following years, she devoted her time to the ownership of two entertainment venues – the Lyric Theater and the Airdome.

Gertrude Malissa Nix Pridgett-Rainey died in Rome, Georgia, on December 22, 1939. The foundation of America's blues tradition, she brought the little-known southern music to the world. She has inspired many African American singers, poets, and writers. Sterling Brown paid tribute to her in his poem *Ma Rainey*, which appeared in his 1932 collection *Southern Road*. In 1984, August Wilson's play, *Ma Rainey's Black Bottom*, is also a movie starring Viola Davis. Alice Walker credited Ma Rainey's music as a model of African American womanhood when she wrote the Pulitzer Prize-winning novel, *The Color Purple*. The recognition and appreciation continue. Thanks, Ma; I love your music and your pride and affirmation of women and Black life.

Ellie Greenwich

b: October 23, 1940   d: August 2009
New York, USA

Eleanor Louise Greenwich was born in Brooklyn, New York, to a painter turned electrical engineer William Greenwich, and Rose Baron Greenwich, a department store manager. Both parents were of Russian descent, and she was reportedly named for Eleanor Roosevelt. Her parents often played music in the home, sparking Ellie's musical interest. She learned how to play the accordion at the age of ten.

Ellie was in her teens when she started composing songs. In a 1973 interview Elle said she had met Archie Bleyer when she was fourteen. He complimented her work and advised her to continue her education before breaking into the songwriting "jungle." While attending Levittown Memorial High School, Ellie formed a singing group with two friends called the Jivettes. Soon the group grew as they performed at local functions. This was the time Ellie began to write love songs on her accordion, inspired by a school crush.

When Ellie graduated high school, she applied to the Manhattan School of Music but was rejected. They informed her they didn't accept accordion players. This was when Ellie taught herself to play piano, leaving the accordion stowed away in her room. Ellie then moved on to Queens College; at the same time, she recorded her first single for RCA

Records, the self-written *Silly Isn't It*, with *Cha-Cha Charming* on the B side. RCA Records changed her name to Ellie Gaye.

Cha-Cha Charming was released in 1958 as she transferred to Hofstra University after a professor at Queens belittled her for recording pop music. Ellie continued to write music and was instrumental in forming and popularizing the women's groups of the 1960s. Some of her associations were the Ronettes, the Crystals, Neil Diamond, Manfred Mann, The Shangri-Las, The Raindrops, Tommy James & the Shondells, Bob B. Soxx & the Blue Jeans, and Lesley Gore, making her one of the most respected pop songwriters.

It was 1962 when she met aspiring songwriter Jeff Barry. Although it is possible, they had been acquainted as children since they shared a relative, the first time Greenwich and Jeff Barry met as adults was at a Thanksgiving dinner hosted by her maternal uncle, who was married to Barry's cousin.

Ellie and Barry recognized early on their mutual love of music. Barry was married when they met, and his wife was also at the dinner. After composing for a few months, they scored an appointment in the famed Brill Building, where multiple songwriting teams were discovered. Their relationship didn't turn romantic until a few years after he divorced. They became a songwriting duo recognized as one of the most successful and prolific Brill Building composers.

They first began writing for Phil Spector's short-lived Phillies label, and this was when Ellie co-wrote some of her most memorable songs. They also documented an album beneath the Raindrops' name, credit scoring with *The Type of Boy You Will Not Ignore*. In 1964, near the end of their marriage, they worked with Leiber and Stoller and created the Crimson Bird imprint.

After the divorce, Ellie and Barry continued writing for a while. Eventually, she went on to record as a vocalist as well as songwriting. She also served with background vocals to numerous of rock's biggest celebrities. In 1967, Ellie formed Pineywood Music with Mike Rashkow. Over the following years, the Greenwich-Rashkow team wrote and/or produced recordings for Ellie and Dusty Springfield, the Definitive Rock Chorale, the Other Voices, The fuzzy Bunnies, and the Hardy Boys. Also, in 1967, Greenwich recorded her first solo album, *Ellie Greenwich Composes, Produces and Sings*, released in 1968, which produced two chart hits, *Niki Hoeky* (number one in Japan) and *I Want You to Be My Baby*. She provided background vocals and vocal arrangements for diverse artists such as Dusty Springfield, Bobby Darin, Lou Christie, Frank Sinatra, Electric Light Orchestra, Blondie, Cyndi Lauper, and Gary U.S. Bonds. She did studio work with her ex-husband, singing backgrounds for Andy Kim, who was recording for Barry's Steed Records, and the Archies.

Eleanor "Ellie" Greenwich passed away of a coronary attack at sixty-eight in August 2009. She had been hospitalized for pneumonia at St. Luke's-

Roosevelt Hospital (now Mount Sinai West), New York City.

Music:
Be My Baby
I Can Hear Music
Maybe I Know
Today I Met the Boy I'm Gonna Marry
The Sunshine After the Rain
I Want You to Be My Baby
Wait 'Til My Bobby Gets Home
Niki Hoeky
I'll Never Need More Than This
I Don't Wanna Be Left Outside
Goodnight Goodnight
The Kind Of Boy You Can't Forget
If You Loved Me Once
Goodnight Baby – Baby I Love You
Another Boy Like Mine
Ain't That Peculiar?
Studio Chatter/Ellie In The Studio with Brooks Arthur
Oh How Happy
Big Honky Baby
Call Me His
Baby Baby Baby
Sad Old Kind of Movie
We're Gonna Make It
A Long Time Comin'
What's A Girl Supposed To Do
Couldn't You Wait

Another Boy Like Mine Demo 28
What Every Teenager Goes Through
Be A Man
Look Of Love
Beautiful People
Gettin' Together

Albums
Composes, Produces and Sings
Ellie Greenwich
Do-Wah-Diddy: Words and Music by Ellie Greenwich and Jeff Barry

Yoko Ono

February 18, 1933
Tokyo, Japan

Often remembered as the villain in the Beatles story, **Yoko Ono** (whose first name translates to "ocean child") was born in Tokyo to Eisuke and Isoko Ono, on February 18, 1933. She is the eldest of three children. Yoko is from a wealthy aristocratic family; her father was the head of a Japanese bank and transferred to San Francisco two weeks before her birth. The rest of the family eventually followed, yet Yoko didn't meet her father until she was two years old. Her father was a well-educated and, yet, a frustrated pianist.

Yoko began piano lessons from the age of four and continued until she was twelve or thirteen. She attended kabuki performances with her mother and trained and read Japanese musical scores. In 1937, the family was transferred back to Japan, and Yoko was enrolled at Tokyo's elite Gakushūin (also known as the Peers School), one of the most exclusive schools in Japan.

Three years later, the family moved to New York City. The following year, her father was transferred again to Hanoi, and the family returned to Japan. So, Yoko enrolled in Keimei Gakuen, an exclusive Christian primary school. Throughout World War

II, she remained in Tokyo and survived the firebombing of March 9, 1945. During this, her family was sheltered with other family members in a special bunker in Tokyo's Azabu district, away from the heaviest bombing.

Starvation was rampant in the destruction that followed the Tokyo bombings; the Ono family resorted to begging for food while pulling their belongings in a wheelbarrow. Yoko has stated that this time caused her aggressive pacifism and understanding of "outsider" status. During this time, her father, who had been in Vietnam, was a prisoner of war in a concentration camp in Saigon.

After the war ended in 1945, Yoko remained in Japan when her family moved to the United States and settled in Scarsdale, New York. By April 1946, the school was reopened, and Yoko enrolled. The school, located near the Tokyo Imperial Palace, wasn't damaged. Yoko was a classmate of Prince Akihito, a future emperor of Japan. She was also taking vocal lessons at this time.

It was 1953 when Yoko rejoined the family in Scarsdale, New York, USA. Her father had been appointed president of another bank in New York. Hopefully, they didn't have branches all over the world. This was when Yoko started Sarah Lawrence College in New York. There was no graduation as she dropped out to elope with Toshi Ichiyanagi.

Near the same time, she discovered the avant-garde community of artists in Greenwich Village, New York. This connection has lasted longer than all of her marriages, and Yoko's radical passion for music and art has been ridiculed and ignored for years. Her career began to change when she met with Anthony Cox, an American jazz musician/ film producer, and he was to become husband number two.

From a very turbulent relationship with Cox, Yoko had one daughter, Kyoko, born in 1963. When it came to her art, some of her significant influencers were Salvatore Dali and Andy Warhol. Yoko took her art another step and added more surrealism and a touch of absurdity. She gained a lot of attention when she produced interactive conceptual events in the early 60s, and these works demanded involvement from the observer. Her most famous piece was the "Cut piece" in 1964, where the audience cut off pieces of her clothing until she was naked. This presentation was a comment on discarding materialism for the natural. She believes that art is a two-part process that involves the artist's and the viewer's interpretation.

Her notoriety and involvement with the radical art community inspired her trip to the United Kingdom, which caused a major change in popular music. John Lennon, of The Beatles fame, visited her exhibit at the Indica Gallery in London. Not only was he a singer and songwriter, but he also had an art school background. They were "thunder struck" with each other and had an immediate intellectual connection. This would develop into not only a world-famous romance but an artistic collaboration. By 1968, their marriages were falling apart, and Yoko's husband, Anthony Cox, kidnapped their daughter during a custody visit. Yoko has not seen Kyoko again and does not know where she is. She and John had one son, Sean.

The John and Yoko story has been told many times, and they appeared to have the ideal relationship based on art, music, politics, and love. Yoko was blamed for breaking up The Beatles, but it is clear that they were all developing personal projects. Her music was extreme and mocked, but in reality, it was instrumental in the development of Punk. She and John were moving in new directions with their art when it suddenly ended. Yoko was with John when he was assassinated in front of their home in 1980.

Since John's death, Yoko has released three albums, done two concert tours, composed two off-Broadway musicals, and many movies exploring various themes. At the age of seventy-one, she hit the top of the charts with a remake of one of her earlier songs, and it is now *Every Man Has A Man Who Loves Him*, supporting gay marriages. She also awarded the first Lennon Ono Grant for Peace to Israeli Zvi Goldstein and Palestinian Khalil Rabah for their efforts to remain creative and inspirational amid the tensions of war.

Yoko was an accomplished artist and activist before John Lennon. She continues true to her politics. Yoko isn't ready to quit, and we will surely hear more from her.

Dieties

1. *A female being of supernatural powers or attributes believed in and worshiped by a people.*
2. *A female goddess believed to be the source of life and being and worshiped as the principal deity in various eras and religions.*
3. *An image of a female supernatural being, an idol.*
4. *Someone or thing with fame, beauty, grace, or wealth worshiped or idealized.*

Numerous sculptures of women have been found in the Gravettian-Aurignacian cultures of the Upper Paleolithic Age, dating as far back as 25,000 BC. Maybe even older as archeologists keep digging.

These small female figurines, made of stone, bone, or clay are often called Venus figures, have been found in areas where small communities once lived. They were often discovered lying close to the remains of the sunken walls of what were probably the earliest human-made dwellings on earth. In areas as far apart as Spain, France, Germany, Austria, Czechoslovakia, and Russia. These sites and figures appear to span at least ten thousand years. It seems highly probable that the female figurines were idols of a "great mother."

Great Mother

Before *Forever*
Everywhere

Every culture has its version of the **Earth Goddess**. The Greeks called her **Gaia**, the Incas know her as **PachaMama**, most of the worldwide goddesses relate to the Mother. In some cases, she predates writing, with ancient, pre-linguistic references to her have been found, alongside shrines, statues, and paintings of her in every corner of the globe. She is the first goddess, the primal one, the creator of all life. Archeologists and antiquarians are rediscovering the fullness of her legacy.

In ancient Middle Eastern religions, Great Mother Goddess symbolizes the earth's fertility. Her attributes vary as much as her name, and she has been known in every part of the world. Essentially, she is represented as the creative force, the beginning of all things, responsible mainly for the periodic renewal of life.

The later forms of her cult evolved into the worship of a male deity, variously considered her son, lover, or both (e.g., Adonis, Attis, and Osiris), whose death and resurrection symbolized the regenerative powers of the earth – often celebrated with fertility rites.

In Phrygia and Lydia, she was known as Cybele; among the Babylonians and Assyrians, she was identified as Ishtar; in Syria and Palestine, she appeared as Astarte; among the Egyptians, she was called Isis; in Greece, she was worshiped as Gaea, Hera, Rhea, Aphrodite, and Demeter; and in Rome, she was identified as Maia, Ops, Tellus, and Ceres. Even this list is by no means complete. Many attributes of the Virgin Mary make her the Christian equivalent of the Great Mother, particularly in her great goodness and charity; and described as both mother and virgin, with a son who is God and is resurrected.

No matter her name, the Great Mother is there.

Venus of Willendorf

30,000 to 25,000 years ago

The **Venus of Willendorf** is a 4.4-inch stone figure made approximately (give or take a couple of thousands) 25,000 years ago. On August 7, 1908, she was discovered during excavations by archaeologist Johan Veran near Willendorf, a village in Lower Austria.

She is carved from an oolitic limestone that is not local to the area and tinted with red ochre. The figure is associated with the Upper Paleolithic Gravettian, between 33,000 and 20,000 years ago. With radiocarbon dating from the surrounding earth, she was left buried around 25,000 years ago. No one dares to ask her true age.

She was named the Venus (after a Roman deity of a much later time in a town that didn't exist yet.) We can only imagine her original name, title, and gifts. She is similar to other recovered icons, stressing her reproductive parts. Her face isn't depicted, and there are several guesses on why. So, I chose she was of such great power that her face is too sacred to replicate.

There is a multitude of other carved icons of the Great Mother before written language, and we can only make guesses about the beliefs. We must recognize that her worship lasted more than 30,000 years.

The original figurine is in the Natural History Museum in Vienna, Austria.

Tiamat

Before time and Still Babylonia

Tiamat is the original Babylonian goddess of the ocean and personification of chaos. She gave birth to the first generation of gods, and later, she was killed by the storm god, Marduk. From her divided body came the heavens and the Earth.

She was first recorded in the wedges and triangles of the ancient cuniform writing. Tiamat is one of the two central protagonists of the Enuma Elish – the earliest recorded writing. In the story, Tiamat and her mate/brother Apsu/Abzu embodied primordial nothingness. As they laid together, as ancient gods do, she gave birth to gods, and from them came creation. From this beginning, the kiddos built the universe and reality. As a being of primordial nothing, the very concept of creation awakened Apsu and Tiamat from their slumber of oblivion. Tiamat rolled over and dozed at first, trying to get back to her sleep, but Apsu would not ignore the commotion of creation and attacked the gods and earth, as younger brothers do.

Well, his plan didn't work; the gods fought back, killing Apsu. Tiamat woke up cranky, and destroyed the gods and all of creation as punishment for killing her beloved. In her efforts, she spawned millions of monsters – dragons being the most celebrated.

This was when Marduk, the strongest of the gods, fought back. Only after an intense battle with the power of all the other gods together could they overcome her and the gang. In the end, Apsu was thrown to the heavens and is the void of the night sky, and his corpse became the land and is still used as a foundation for Earth.

Tiamat is the oceans and reported to have the appearance of a dragon or a serpent. Sometimes, she is multi-headed. She has been resurrected multiple times and depicted in Dungeons and Dragons. Tiamat has had as many forms as we can imagine in fiction myth.

Lilith

*First/Post everything else
Garden of Eden*

Lilith was reported as the first woman created by God simultaneously with Adam. The story goes, "On the sixth day God created man from dust, in his image, and at the same time woman was created as Lilith."

Adam and Lilith never found peace together. When he wished to lie with her (polite description), she took offense at his demanding submissive position. 'Why must I lie beneath you?' she asked. 'I also was made from dust and am therefore your equal.' Because Adam tried to compel her obedience by force, Lilith, in a rage, uttered the magic name of God, rose into the air and left.

Adam was made from dust, and after Lilith left, her start is described as from sediment and slime. Imagine what he may have said on Facebook. Lilith was the first woman to demand the Equal Rights Amendment in her refusal to submit to Adam's will. Unfortunately. The story of the First Woman is often overlooked. After Adam begs for a helpmate, Eve is made from his rib. Luckily Eve was partial to missionary position, and the rest is biblical history.

Apparently, Lilith has fallen to the curse of the "ex" wife and is known chiefly as demonic. Her true origins are obscure, but similar stories were told in Sumeria, Babylonia, and Mesopotamia. She has a single reference in the bible, but she shows up in many other places.

The dead sea scrolls give us a quote: *And I, the Sage, declare the grandeur of his radiance in order to frighten and terrify all the spirits of the ravaging angels and the bastard spirits, demons, Lilith, owls and jackals...]and those who strike unexpectedly to lead astray the spirit of knowledge...*

This breakup started the bad rap for divorce. To top it off, Lilith was cursed by God. Popular opinion is the story is "evidence" that she was initially a goddess, or at the very least an aspect of a great goddess, and was demonized for being an independent female. In Mesopotamia, she is a night demon accused of destroying children and spilling the seed of men. She has been tied to the Goddess of Way and Sexual pleasures. Don't worry, Eve; the ex is history, a myth. You are forever number one – first spouse and mother of all.

Kali the Destroyer

We were afraid to ask for dates
Southern Asia

Kali is the ferocious form of the Great Mother. She is the Hindu goddess sent to free the gods from demonic forces. These evil forces had conquered the three worlds of earth, the astral plane and the celestial plane. Kali is the goddess of time and transformation, also known as death.

Kali makes her 'official' debut in the Devi-Mahatmya, where she is said to have emanated from the brow of Goddess Durga (slayer of demons) during one of the battles between the divine and anti-divine forces. Durga's name means "Beyond Reach." She is an echo of the woman warrior's fierce virginal autonomy. In this context, Kali is considered the 'forceful' form of the goddess Durga.

Kali's blackness symbolizes her all-embracing nature because black is the color in which all other colors merge; black absorbs and dissolves them all. Black is said to represent the total absence of color and all colors at the same time. This suggests the nature of Kali symbolizes her transcendence of all forms.

Kali is the destroyer of evil spirits and the preserver of devotees. She is the consort of Shiva. She is depicted with an azure face streaked yellow, and her look is ferocious. She wears green snakes for hair (sound familiar?). She wears a necklace of human skulls, earrings of dead bodies, cobras for bracelets, and a girdle of severed arms. She is not an easy woman to shop for. She has four arms that usually hold weapons or the bodies of vanquished demons. This symbolizes both her creative and destructive nature.

Skulls, cemeteries, and blood are associated with her worship. She personifies the eternal cycle of life-death, creation-destruction. She was often celebrated as a loving and unpredictable mother. Her bad rap came from the cult of the Thugee; they took her as their primary deity and then robbed and murdered tourists as sacrifices. Kali was not happy with that turn of events, and they were dismantled by the British. We have kept the term Thug from those times.

Ninkasi
The Sumerian Goddess of Brewing

3500 B.C.E.   *Still distilling*
                 Sumeria

Ninkasi is the Sumerian goddess of brewing and beer, and she is the head brewer of the gods. Her name means "the lady who fills the mouth," She was formed of sparkling fresh water. Also referred to as *She who bakes with a lofty shovel the sprouted barley, She who mixes the bopper-malt with sweet aromatics, She who pours the fragrant beer in the Lathan-vessel that is like the Tigris and Euphrates joined*! Yes, with a capital letter, She stays busy.

    Beer was a favorite drink in ancient Mesopotamia. Although the craft of brewing would eventually be practiced across the region, it began in a small village in the Mesopotamian region dating back to 3500-3100 BCE at the Sumerian settlement of Godin Tepe. It is located in modern-day Iran and previously was a stop on the famous Silk Road. Definitely, it was brewed and cultivated by women. Beer was often a choice due to the pollution of rivers and streams, and the brewing process destroys the toxicity. Beer was the drink of choice among the ancient Sumerians, which carried over to societies around the world. In 1620 C.E., the Pilgrims left the Mayflower because they ran out of beer.

Archaeologists have discovered chemical traces of beer in a fragmented jar dating to the mid-4th century BCE. The same site also held evidence for wine-making, and they have presented the theory that brewing beer arose from baking. The fermentation process evident in grains, which may have been left out unattended, would have inspired the creation of both wine and beer. Knowing women, this is much more than a theory.

Sources indicate that the old school nomadic hunter-gatherers of some 13,000 years ago decided to settle, and Ninkasi went to work then. one of their first harvested products was grain. To keep grain from spoiling, it was often baked to be stored. Six thousand years ago, the ancient text reveals that eventually, it was formulated that the sweetest grain, if baked, left out, moistened, forgotten, then eaten, would produce an uplifting, cheerful feeling – the first beer cake.

The Hymn to Ninkasi is a song of praise to Ninkasi, celebrates the goddess, and includes an ancient recipe for brewing. First written around 1800 B.C.E., the hymn is undoubtedly much older, as evidenced by its techniques. Scholars have determined it was used at least a thousand years before the hymn was recorded. Anheuser Busch should put her on the can.

Ninkasi works today in multiple forms, and her name has not been lost to the brewing industry. If you find yourself in Eugene, Oregon, USA, check out Ninkasi Brewing Company, where our goddess toils on.

* more than a footnote

Circe

*Goddess Eternal
Aeaea, Greece*

In Greek Mythology, there was once an island called Aeaea. **Circe**, the queen of Aeaea, lived there with her many pets. She was a bit different from your average goddess/cat lady. Her pets were tame lions and wolves that had once been human. This goddess, who is likely the root of many modern Halloween witch stories, was known to fly about her island on a staff and keep a cooking cauldron of herbal potions that she could use to turn people into animals. (Not unlike our own Mothers).

Her story comes out of Homer's Odyssey, the epic tale of Odysseus and his men making a stop on their way home from the Trojan War. They dropped anchor, and many men left the ship to wander the island. Before long, they were in the clearing at Circe's mansion. Being the hostess she was, they were invited in for a feast. Once they ate her magic-laced meal, they became pigs. However, one or two men, probably vegans, were suspicious enough to leave before eating. They ran back to the ship and warned Captain Odysseus of the imminent danger. Captain O' took heed of the warnings. He left intending to learn more from some other magical gods and get the downlow on this Circe. He realized that if he ate the ancient garlic-like herb moly, he would become immune to her pork magic.

Here we see the origins of at least two more modern-day factoids. The first is the use of a garlic-like herb to fend off the magical powers of evil, and the other is this reference to the holy herb moly.

Once armed with his secret "holy-moly" immunity, Odysseus and the rest of the crew met Circe, ate her food, and did not turn into pigs. Circe was duly impressed and went on to make a lovely arrangement with O. The story goes on to be a long tale of love and transformation with rough beginnings, sailors turned into pigs, and some turned back into men again.

Odysseus and Circe ended up with a brood of three children before he returned to his travels home and his wife, Penny.

Greek Mythology uses the story of Circe to depict the fundamental and complex duality of women. There are witch-like references to her commanding dark or dangerous powers to protect herself and gain control over the people she saw as a threat. But there are also stories of her sensuality as a loving wife, nurturing healer, and protective mother who tamed dangerous beasts and controlled the elements of nature for those she loved. Circe's life still depicts a woman's life today, and though her magic herbs have lost their power, men can often still be turned into pigs quite easily with beer and a large, tasty casserole.

Mami Wata

Ivory Coast, Africa

The people who inhabit the coastal region of Benin, Ghana, and Togo, worship a vast community of water deities. **Mami Wata** is most prominent, and it appears she represents a multitude of water gods and is usually represented as a mermaid. Most scholarly sources suggest that "Mami Wata" is a pidgin English derivation of "Mother Water." Although this origination has been disputed by Africanist writers that suggest a linguistic derivation from ancient Egyptian and Mesopotamian, such as the Egyptian terms " Mami " or " Mama," meaning "truth," "Uati," or "Uat-Ur" for "ocean water."

Either way, mermaids are celebrated all over the world, but the African water spirits are where her dominance is evident. Mami's power is great since water is needed by every living thing to survive. Mami has remained respected and celebrated from before the Europeans made contact with the African nations. There is some suggestion she was confused with the African manatee. Although African manatees live in both coastal areas and a few isolated inland waters, Mami is definitely a separate entity in much bigger waters.

Mami is often described as fair-skinned with a woman's upper body, usually nude, and the hindquarters of a fish or serpent. She spends a lot of time combing her long hair and looking into a golden mirror. The existence and spiritual importance of Mami is deeply rooted in the ancient tradition and mythology of the coastal southeastern Nigerians. Mami keeps expensive baubles such as combs, mirrors, and jewelry. Additionally, she often has a giant snake, the symbol of divinity, wrapped around her and laying its head between her breasts. She has the power to appear wholly human and has been known to wander markets or patronize bars. (Sounds like an excellent excuse when he gets home late).

Also known to manifest in many other forms, Mami has been witnessed as a man, too. This offers women an excuse for being out late.

The Mami Wata traditions continued to merge various tribal water deities, and she is not mistaken for a Manatee. Since the ancient age, Mami has been venerated in West, Central, Southern Africa, and the Americas as the enslaved people were imported across the ocean.

One of the most powerful deities in the African religion of Voudun (not associated with Voodoo), Mami is celebrated, loved, and feared to this day.

Like many mermaid deities, she is an immortal spirit that personifies polar opposites, such as beauty/danger, wealth/destruction, health/disease, and good/evil. Mami is incredibly powerful, dangerous, pleasant, sexual, and destructive able to destroy anything in her path.

Stories of the encounters with the Mami are widespread across Africa, as well as in ancient sagas.

In the Odessey, Captain O's return trip from Troy, their temptation and danger are reflected as the Sirens. Often Mami stalks the ocean's shores, and if she thinks someone is worthy, she may abduct them while swimming or traveling in a boat. Mami usually returns them safely to the beach, dry and with a new attitude toward their spirituality and religion. That change has made some rich, attractive and famous. Other encounters tell of her leaving her comb and mirror in the presence of sailors. If they take the items, she will haunt their dreams, requesting the return of her belongings in exchange for eternal sexual favors.

Her devotees wear her traditional colors of red, symbolizing blood, violence, danger, and white for spiritual beauty. They are known to present some items of wealth and expensive foods to celebrate her in the rituals of dancing and music. A trance-like state often accompanies the music. Mami Wata can possess the dancers and speak to them, wishing them a successful, healthy, fertile life, not just dancing and a late-night dip.

However, like all water-based deities, she is blamed for many of the misfortunes that happen in the sea but denies involvement with the Titanic. That was the telegraph operator's fault.

Inanna
aka
Ishtar

Time of before   *After*
    Mesopotamia/Greece

Inanna is known by many names (Ishtar, Isis, Neith, Metis, Astarte, Cybele, Brigit, etc.). However, some of her other names have less power and are not as complex. She embodies the divine – feminine and even more than a mother. She combines earth and sky, matter and spirit, vessel and light, earthly bounty, and heavenly guidance. Inanna was an ancient Mesopotamian goddess associated with love, beauty, sex, war, justice, and political power. She was crowned the "Queen of Heaven" and served as the patron goddess of the Eanna temple in the city of Uruk.

    Inanna was associated with the planet Venus and her most prominent symbols included the lion and the eight-pointed star. She was wed to the god Dumuzid (later called Tammuz), an ancient Mesopotamian god associated with shepherds; his main job was as the consort to Inanna. In the Sumerian King List, Dumuzid is an antediluvian king of Bad-tibira and Uruk. We add in Inanna's personal attendant, Ninshubur, the deity of vegetation and the underworld, and this team developed into the deities of early Greece.

Inanna, as Queen of Heaven and Earth. She symbolized wholeness, combining earth and sky, matter and spirit, earthly bounty, and heavenly guidance. Add a dessert cart, and there is nothing else to ask for. In her side gig as the Goddess of Grain, she provided the food of life and emotional nurturing. Grains and legumes were said to pour forth from her womb. (Every day or monthly?)

As Goddess of Heaven, Inanna brought gentle rains, terrible storms, cloudy skies, and floods. Her radiant, erratic morning and evening star had the power to awaken life, set it to rest, and usher in and out the sun and the moon. She symbolized consciousness of transitions and borders, flexibility, play, and unceasing change. Her energies were never contained or were secure. She represented life as a changing process, which also describes life in modern times.

As Goddess of War, she was more passionate than Athena, possessed of the wild instinct of an Artemis. She could be "all-devouring in power," with an "awesome face" and an "angry heart," yet singing with abandoned delight at her glory and prowess. Seven lions pull her chariot.

Then her representation of sexual love was equally passionate, singing joyous songs of desire, self-adornment and celebrating the delights of lovemaking. She craved and took, desired and destroyed, grieved, and composed songs of grief. Inanna wasn't shy about asserting her needs and celebrating her body. Then there was her Descent into the Underworld. In this tale, Innana goes far beyond the typical day-to-day and undergoes the ultimate spiritual initiation, a Descent into Hades. In her transformation, she lets go of all possessions and characteristics which feed the ego.

Hades wasn't respectful, and she ends up hanging on a nail as a rotting corpse in the bowels of the underworld. After acknowledging her shadow side, she returns to the living. From this time on, she is the complete, fully-formed goddess that she was always meant to be and more subservient.

In the Sumerian poem *Inanna Prefers the Farmer*, Dumuzid competes with Enkimdu, the farmer, for Inanna's hand in marriage. In *Inanna's Descent into the Underworld*, Dumuzid fails to mourn Inanna's death. When she returns, as goddesses are known to do, she allows the Galla demons to drag him down to take her previous position down under. Not much later, she has second thoughts, and this is when she decrees that Dumuzid will spend half the year in the Underworld, but for the other half of the year, he will be with her. His sister Geshtinanna, goddess of agriculture, fertility, and dream interpretation, will stay in the Underworld in his place, which produces the cycle of the seasons.

As Lady of Myriad Offices and Queen, Inanna was a healer, life-giver, and composer of songs. She created and gave birth. The behavior of emotions was in her keeping and not limited to love. She also had control of jealousy, grief, joy, and shyness.

Always two sides to each emotion. Eternally youthful and fierce, the harlot/virgin stayed independent. In another run-on list, Inanna was the embodied, playful, passionate, erotic, many-sided feminine.

It is believed that the "myths" of Inanna were created sometime between 1900 B.C. and 3500 B.C. It could have been much earlier in the pre-patriarchal time. Inanna's stories began to lose power as the patriarchal influences grew. Despite her power over everything, her position eroded, and Inanna became a wanderer.

There is no end date for Inanna, as she was adept at transforming into other religions and deities.

Neith

*from 6000 B.C.E.
Egypt*

The Egyptian goddess **Neith** is said to have emerged from the primeval floodwaters. Her name means, "I have come from myself." Her saga definitely springs from Innana. She is one of the oldest deities of ancient Egypt and never showed her age. She was worshipped early in the Pre-Dynastic Period around. 6000-3150 B.C.E. Neith's veneration continued through the Ptolemaic Dynasty 323-30 B.C.E., the last pharaohs to rule Egypt before Rome conquered it.

Initially, Neith was associated with water. In time, she promoted herself to the goddess of war, creation, the mother goddess who invented birth, and a funeral goddess who cared for and helped to dress the souls of the dead. Apparently, she didn't take weekends off. Neith was primarily worshiped in Lower Egypt and maintained status, and many of her attributes were transferred to Isis and Hathor. Neith was continually honored as the patron goddess throughout Egypt's history. Neith was considered a great protector of the people of the land and served as a mediator between humanity and the gods.

Celebrated as the creator of the world, or at the very least, Neith was present when it occurred. Her story said she gave birth to Atum (Ra), the sun god. Then he took over to complete the acts of creation. She has been honored for her great wisdom. In *The Contendings of Horus and Set*, Neith settled on who should rule Egypt and the world.

Once other deities appeared, they joined Neith. She remained celebrated as one of the prominent four goddesses, Isis, Nephthys, and Serket. The four appear on the jars in the tomb of Tutankhamun. Additionally, she stands to watch over Duamutef, One of the Four Sons of Horus, who guard the tombs. Also, Neith serves as one of the judges of the dead with Osiris, Anubis, and Thoth.

Her symbols are the bow and arrows, with a sword and shield, which illustrates her as the goddess of war. With her funerary tasks, she also has a weaving shuttle. When depicted as the goddess of creation, she wears the Red Crown of Lower Egypt.

Neith is frequently presented sitting on her throne, holding either a scepter or a bow and two arrows.

The inscription of her temple at Sais reads, *"I am all that has been, that will be, and no mortal has yet been able to lift the veil that covers me."*

Triple Goddess: Maiden/Mother/Crone

Yesterday and Tomorrow

The **Triple Goddess** is revered in many early religions and spiritual practices. A trinity of three distinct aspects or figures united as one. They are the life stages of women as well as the moon, and they were the rulers of heaven, earth, and the underworld.

Now the breakdown:

The **Maiden** represents enchantment, inception, expansion, the promise of new beginnings, birth, youth, and youthful enthusiasm, represented by the waxing moon, which doesn't mean you have to wax.

The **Mother** represents ripeness, fertility, sexuality, fulfillment, stability, power, and life represented by the full moon.

The **Crone** represents wisdom, repose, death, and endings represented by the waning moon. Testify Nana.

The Three have inspired the subject of study, poetry, and myth. Robert Graves, who wrote *The White Goddess and The Greek Myths*, said, "She is the continuing muse of all true poetry."

We cannot ignore the myth of the Three Graces, Aglaia (Brightness), Euphrosyne (Joyfulness), and

Thalia (Bloom). In time they brought in some friends, and it expanded to the nine muses in Greek Mythology. They are a famous band of inspiration. Notice that they grew by three times three. They were all the daughters of Zeus and Mnemosyne, goddess of memory.

1. **Clio**: The Muse Clio discovered history and guitar. Clio was represented with a clarion in the right arm and a book in the left hand.
2. **Euterpe** discovered several musical instruments, courses, and dialectics – the method of examining and discussing opposing ideas to find the truth. She was always depicted holding a flute, with other instruments around her.
3. **Thalia** was the protector of comedy; she discovered comedy, probably from mocking her father behind his back, architectural science, and agriculture. One of a series of goddesses of fertility. Thalia was always depicted holding a theatrical – comedy mask and sometimes a shepherd's staff.
4. **Melpomene** was Thalia's opposite. Melpomene was initially the muse of the chorus and became the protector of Tragedy. She is credited with the invention of tragedy, rhetoric speech, and Melos, an island paradise for musicians. She was depicted holding a tragedy mask and often the bat of Hercules.
5. **Terpsichore** was the protector of dance; she was the beginning of dance, the harp, and education. "Terpo" in Greek refers to being amused. She was

shown wearing laurels on her head, holding a harp, and dancing.

6. **Erato** was the protector of Love and Love Poetry and weddings. Her name comes from the Greek word "Eros," which refers to the feeling of falling in love, which has expanded in modern times, and her name is still in use. Erato's depiction is holding a lyre and love arrows and bows, and no, she was not shown dancing on a pole.

7. **Polymnia** was the protector of the divine hymns and mimicked art. She invented geometry, grammar, and lip-syncing. She was illustrated as looking to the Sky, holding a lyre.

8. **Ourania** was the protector of the celestial objects and stars; she invented astronomy. She is remembered bearing stars (not actual size), a celestial sphere, and a bow compass.

9. Not really last, **Calliope** was the superior Muse. Her task was to accompany kings and princes in order to secure justice and serenity. She was the protector of heroic poems and rhetoric art. According to the myth, Homer asked Calliope to inspire him. He then wrote the Iliad and Odyssey. Calliope holds laurels in one hand and the two Homeric poems in the other, which is even better than a review on Amazon.

Cihuacōātl – La Llorona – Weeping Woman

from 1502 *Present*
Central America

The Aztecs envisioned women who died in childbirth as roaming the world weeping. The **Cihuateteo** ("goddess women") were also called **Ciuapipiltin** ("honored women") because the deaths in childbirth were equal to any heroic death in war. The women were known to haunt crossroads, where they sometimes captured children.

They are said to appear every fifty-two days. In case you need to know, it is possible to distinguish them from living women by golden eyebrows and stark white complexions. Sometimes they are more frightening, with claws and a skull instead of a head. Temples were erected at crossroads, and cakes were offered to keep them from stealing children.

In contemporary folklore, La Llorona carries a dead child through the streets. This "weeping woman" is a grieving mother, sometimes called a seducer of men who died violently. She is a kidnapper of children in her spare time, which helps keep kids close to home. New Mexican legend claims she was never heard weeping until Cortés invaded Mexico.

After that event, she drowned her children and roamed moonlit nights.

La Llorona has been identified as Cortés's interpreter, La Malinche, described as a traitor for collaborating with the invader and cursed to wander after death. There are many stories of La Llorona (the wailing lady). The first mention was in 1502 when the goddess Cihuacōātl went into the streets dressed in white and crying and keening about the death of the Maya. There is a belief that this was the first warning of the coming of the Conquistadors. In Aztec mythology, Cihuacōātl, "snake woman," was one of several motherhood and fertility goddesses and was associated with midwives and healers. She is often paired with Quilaztli and is considered a protector of the Chalmeca people and patroness of the city of Culhuacan. She helped Quetzalcoatl create the current race of humanity by grinding up bones from the previous ages and mixing them with his blood. She is also the mother of Mixcoatl, whom she abandoned at a crossroads. Tradition says that she often returns there to weep for her lost son, only to find a sacrificial knife.

On the political side, Cihuacōātl held symbolism representing victory for the Mexican state and the ruling class. Occasionally depicted as a young woman, but more often known as a fierce skull-faced old woman carrying the spears and shield of a warrior. A meaner Central American specter was similar to but without the good intentions of the Irish Banshee.

In another story, in the town of San Pedro on Ambergris Caye, Belize, there was a beautiful young woman. She has long, straight black hair, and so alluring that she attracted the attention of many men. On the downside, she is selfish and vowed she would only marry a wealthy, handsome man. The legend goes that she did meet that man, and she played him by ignoring him and refusing his gifts. Well, Darling, she is just a "Rules" kinda girl, and she won her man. Oblivious to the fact, he also had some negative tendencies. It seemed to be a good marriage, and she became pregnant with their child.

Here is the twist: one legend says he left her for another woman. The second story says that he rejected her, maybe for getting older or fat, and only then did his mother make her life miserable and drove La Llorona to the forest. She felt there were minimal options, either a support group at the women's center and some community college classes or the route less traveled. Misses La Llorona picked the second option and drowned her newborn child in the river. Then she killed herself in anger, pain, and humiliation.

As a result, La Llorona was cursed to search for her lost baby eternally. From then on, she is seen or heard by the rivers, keening for compassion. La Llorona haunts areas where children play and swim. As time passed, she became even more bitter and is known to lure children to the forest, never to return. She specializes in capturing boys, but a few sassy girls have disappeared on a rare occasion.

A village usually knows when La Llorona is around by her loud wailing. Often, she is spotted in the trees on moonlit nights. If she appears to you, she will stop crying and become sweet and gentle. La Llorona opens her arms and welcomes men or troublesome boys to her caress. Only then are they trapped and taken to their demise. Struggling doesn't help; often, the victim will strangle in her long black hair.

La Llorona is known to take the form of a mother, auntie, or whatever it takes to lure a man to his death. She is also known to transform into a snake that wraps around the victim for the kill. A few children have escaped but are often mute for the rest of their lives.

There are three ways to protect against La Llorona. The surest one is to be home when you promised. Second, if possible, the victim should immediately pray, and she will move away. The third is to shine a light; our girl doesn't like direct lighting. So, if you are a man stumbling – er – wandering through the forest near a river late at night, sincerely try to find your way home. If you should meet a lovely lady waiting and crying, remember you have a slim chance of escaping. It is best to run to a clearing and shine that flashlight; hopefully, she will not follow. If you choose her open arms, there is a price to be paid. It may be even more expensive than the toll for staggering home so late in the night.

Much of her story seems similar to Ixchel, the ancient Mayan goddess of childbirth and war. Often depicted with jaguar claws or ears, she wears a serpent as her headdress and is also associated with the moon and the traditional Mayan sweat bath. She was so sacred to Maya women that they founded an island sanctuary, still called the Isla de Mujeres, dedicated to worshiping Ixchel off the coast of contemporary Cancun, Mexico.

Educators

"Let us remember: one book, one pen, one child, and one teacher can change the world."
— Malala Yousafzai

Without them, we couldn't read, write, cure, or do Algebra.

Aspasia

b: 470 B.C.   d: 400 B.C.

Greece

Aspasia was born in the Ionian Greek city of Miletus, which is now in Turkey. Her name means "the desired one" was probably not the name she was given at birth. Her father was Axiochus, and little more is known about her family. As some sources claim, she was born a free woman and not a Carian prisoner-of-war turned enslaved person. She probably belonged to a wealthy and cultured family because it took cash to consider education over hunting and gathering.

No one seems to know what caused her to travel to Athens. Most of her story is speculation, and another expert or university disputes every version. There has been a discovery of a 4th century grave inscription that mentions the names of Axiochus and Aspasius. Historians have tried to reconstruct history, but it is still speculation. Alcibiades II of Scambonidae was ostracized from Athens in 460 B.C. and may have relocated to Miletus, Aspasia's hometown. While in Miletus, he married a daughter of Axiochus, then sometime later, he returned to Athens with his wife. Was she our Aspasia?

Another angle is that she was a brothel keeper. She may have been a hetaera, a high-class Greek courtesan who could live free from many of the restrictions applied to Greek women. As a hetaera, she would have been free to participate in public life instead of confined to the home and kitchen.

Aspasia is mentioned in philosopher Plato's writings, Aristophanes, and no real mention of that possible husband. Some argue that Plato was so impressed by her intelligence and wit that his character Diotima in the *Symposium* was based on her. She is thought to have exercised considerable influence on Pericles, both politically and philosophically. Plato suggested that she helped compose Pericles' famous *Funeral Oratory* and trained Pericles and Socrates in oratory.

Pericles was a Greek statesman and general during the Golden Age of Athens. He was prominent and influential in Athenian politics, particularly between the Greco-Persian Wars and the Peloponnesian War. Thucydides, a contemporary historian, was acclaimed as "the first citizen of Athens." Around 461 to 429 B.C. is sometimes known as the "Age of Pericles," As well as the time of Aspasia's main squeeze era. Pericles had a son, Pericles the Younger. There is no mention of the mother; I'm betting on Aspasia. Younger had been elected general and executed after a naval disaster at the Battle of Arginusae.

In Plato's *Menexenus*, he satirizes Aspasia's relationship with Pericles. He quotes Socrates as claiming that she was a trainer of many orators and that since Aspasia educated Pericles, he would be superior in rhetoric to others. He also attributes authorship of the *Funeral Oration* to Aspasia and attacks his contemporaries' veneration of Pericles.

Aspasia's name is closely connected with Pericles' success and fame. Plutarch accepts her as a significant political and intellectual figure and expresses his admiration for a woman who "managed as she pleased the foremost men of the state, and afforded the philosophers occasion to discuss her in exalted terms and at great length."

Aspasia seems to have been the only woman in classical Greece to have distinguished herself in the public sphere and influenced Pericles and a bunch of philosophers. Some scholars believe Aspasia opened an academy for young women of good families and invented the Socratic method.

In modern times she has inspired authors and storytellers. It is virtually impossible to find the true history of Aspasia. We must use our imagination, but she indeed moved the potential of women forward as a philosopher, genius, and teachers. The world always needs an Aspasia.

Fatima Al-Fihri

b: 800   d: 878

Fez, Tunisia

Fatima was born around 800 C.E. in the town of Kairouan, in present-day Tunisia. She is of Arab Qurayshi descent. Her family was part of a large migration to Fez from Kairouan during the reign of Idris II. Although her family did not start wealthy, Mohammed al-Fihri's father was a successful merchant. Little is known about her personal life, except for what was recorded by 14th century historian Ibn Abi-Zar' over five hundred years or so later. Not sure if he had access to the Al-Qarawiyyin's archives which suffered a large fire in 1323 C.E.

Fatima was married, but her husband and father died shortly after the wedding. Her father left everything to Fatima and her sister, Maryam, his only children. Both girls had been well educated and studied the Islamic jurisprudence *Fiqh and the Hadith*, or the records of Prophet Muhammed.

They concluded that the money should be used to leave their legacy and not shopping. Both founded mosques in Fez, Fatima founded Al-Qarawiyyin referenced above, and Maryam founded Al-Andalus. They were inspired by Muslims fleeing to Fez as her family had done a few years earlier. Many of the immigrants were devout worshippers of Islam, and true to their faith, they were dedicated to learning. Fez urgently needed a mosque large enough to fit an ever-growing number of believers.

During her lifetime, Fatima was called the "mother of boys." According to historian Mohammed Yasser Hilali, this possibly stems from her charity and that she often took in students.

After buying land from a man of the "Hawaara" tribe, Fatima started her building project at the beginning of the Ramadan month of year 859 A.D. The Al-Qarawiyyin Mosque was named for the immigrants in her city. The mosque took eighteen years to construct, and when finished, Fatima went inside and prayed to Allah, extending thanks and gratitude.

Maryam built the Andalusian Mosque, named for the immigrants from Andalusia, which is present-day southern Spain. Although they started as mosques or religious gathering places for Muslims, Fatima's community outgrew their mosque. She purchased another mosque built around 845 C.E. Fatima supervised the rebuilding and expansion, and then she also bought the surrounding land, making it possible to double the size.

From the 10th century, the famous mosque of al-Qarawiyyin became the first religious institute and the most significant Arab university in North Africa, and it still stands today. Symposiums and debates were regularly organized there. According to the available documents, teaching chairs were established at the university and in other annexes throughout Fez. These records mention the existence of a great library.

The accuracy of this story has been questioned by some historians who see the symmetry of two sisters founding the two most famous mosques of Fez as unlikely and originated from legend. You know how history goes, questioning the ability of women. An inscription was discovered during renovations in the 20th century, buried beneath centuries of plaster. This inscription was carved onto cedar wood panels and written in a Kufic script, similar to foundation inscriptions during the 9th century in Tunisia. The inscription, recorded and deciphered by Gaston Deverdun, proclaims the foundation of the mosque was Dawud ibn Idris (a son of Idris II, who governed this region of Morocco at the time). The inscription might have come from the original mosque that Fatima had purchased. A building was also moved to the site in the 15th or 16th century, and the Idrisids held such religious significance to be reused in this way. The original foundation inscription of the Qarawiyyin Mosque itself might have been covered in the 12th century, just before the arrival of the Almohads in the city. With all of the suppositions, it is still stated that Fatima al-Fihri could have been a legendary figure rather than a historical one.

The university continues, and Fatima's life holds many secrets for historians. We can see over the centuries how women's history is often obscured. Another mystery surrounds the date of her death, which may have been around 878 A.D., but in reality, she lives on with every graduate.

NOTE: Sultans bestowed gifts upon the university, enabling the creation of a vast library. It is the world's oldest working library. Its contents consist of four thousand manuscripts, including a 9th century Quran and an original copy of Ibn Khaldun's influential 14th century critical examination of history using political and economic viewpoints.

In 2012, the Canadian-Moroccan architect Aziz Chaouni was awarded to renovate the library. A four-year plan was established, and when she first entered the library, it was in disarray. The floors were damaged, and there was even a fallen chandelier. Of course, the most significant concern was for the manuscripts. Chaouni created a humidity and temperature control room and added a new gutter system to prevent further water damage and air conditioning and solar panels. The library reopened in 2016.

Nana Asma'u

b: 1794   d: 1863

Nigeria

Asma'u bint Shehu Usman dan Fodio, known as **Nana Asma'u**, was an Islamic scholar, poet, and educational leader in what is now Northern Nigeria. Born the daughter of a powerful ruler, Nana Asma'u was taught that Allah wanted all women to learn from a young age. Her father, Shehu (the same as a sheik) Usman dan Fodio, the founder of the Sokoto Caliphate, was an Islamic leader respected for piety and learning. Her father believed that sharing knowledge was every Muslim's duty. As a highly respected family member, Nana's education started early. Most girls in northern Nigeria were/are married between the ages of eleven and fourteen, and their education ends unless they have a supportive husband, father, or older brother.

Nana's teachers were the Fulani women of their family. Her father saw that Nana also studied Arabic, Latin, and Greek classics. By the time her education was nearing completion, she could recite the entire Koran and was fluent in four languages.

Nana continued forward, becoming a teacher. She worked with not only children but also men and women. She established the Yan-Taru (the associates or disciples), a school for women. The women of the school would travel to rural areas to instruct the Hausa women throughout the country. Nana transformed the tradition of women, stressing that they had been the first teachers of Islamic religious knowledge and they should continue.

When not teaching, Nana corresponded with scholars and leaders all over the region. She wrote poetry about battles, politics, and divine truth. When her brother, Muhammed Bello, inherited the throne, she was drafted to be his advisor. Nana used her writings to help break the syncretistic practice of Islam in Hausaland. She converted many people to Islam and helped the newly reformed community of Muslims maintain their orthodox religious tradition.

Nana's teachings have spread worldwide, and her writings continue to be read, memorized, and recited. The concept of the Yan-Taru (translates to – those who have come together or the collective) continues to make education accessible, especially to women in the 21st century.

Nana could have settled for being respected for her learning and poetry, but she dedicated her life to education. The jajis (teachers) wore a malfa, balloon-shaped hat, which marked them as leaders. Even today, almost two centuries later, the modern-day jajis continue to educate women, men, and children in Nana Asma'u's name. They teach on, even if the hat does not.

Her poetry addressed divine truth, Sufi women saints, and jihad battles. She also wrote eulogies that today serve as historical documents providing insight into the turbulent political atmosphere at the time. Much of her poetry placed a strong emphasis on women leaders and the rights of women within the community ideals of the Sunnah and Islamic law.

She is held as an example of women's education, strength, and independence being possible under Islam. Often, she is referred to as a precursor to modern feminism in Africa. When the British sent Jean Boyd to educate Nigerians, she reported, "there is literacy here, there is God, so let me go back and try to learn from the very people I was supposed to educate."

Mary Lucinda Bonney Rambault

b: June 8, 1816   d: July 24, 1900
Hamilton, New York, USA

Born in Hamilton, New York, **Mary Lucinda Bonney** is remembered as a 19th century American educator. She was also an advocate for Native American rights and was considered one of the most influential in the Native American movement. Mary was the fourth child of six in her family of devout Baptists. Her parents were Benjamin and Lucinda (Wilder) Bonney. She was the granddaughter of Benjamin Bonney and Abel Wilder, both of Chesterfield, Massachusetts, and both served in the American Revolutionary War.

    Mary started her education at Ladies Academy in Hamilton, New York, then transferred to the Emma Willard School in Troy, New York. This was where she scored a classical curriculum nearly identical to that provided in men's colleges. After two years, Mary graduated in 1835 and began her teaching career. Mary taught in a variety of cities and states, ranging from New Jersey, New York, South Carolina, Rhode Island, and Philadelphia, among others. Once she moved to New York City, Mary became the academy's principal in De Ruyter.

In 1842 she moved to the South to work at a girls' school in Beaufort, South Carolina. After six years, she moved back north. This was when Mary started teaching in Providence, Rhode Island. After only a year, she moved to Philadelphia for another teaching position. Mary was outspoken and became part of an early movement for girls' education. She certainly spread her message all along the east.

In 1850, Mary's mother was widowed, and she wanted to provide a home for her. So, Mary returned to Philidelphia. Soon after the move, Mary co-founded the Chestnut Street Female Seminary with Harriette A. Dillaye. They had taught together at the Troy Female Seminary (Emma Willard School). The school began to grow. To accommodate the expansion, Mary leased the Ogontz Estate, the former home of banker Jay Cooke. This enabled Cooke to recover from some financial setbacks.

The school was renamed Ogontz School for Young Ladies after the estate. The school educated girls from the age of thirteen through eighteen, and they provided a liberal arts education, which included science, humanities, and physical education.

The school was successful and was donated to Pennsylvania State University decades later. The campus was developed as Penn State Abington, and in 1997 it was named one of several colleges in the commonwealth system.

Not one to stay still, Mary joined Amelia Stone Quinton, and they started the Women's National Indian Association. Initially, the intent was to defend Native American land rights against settler encroachment. Congress in 1878 proposed to take land that had been protected by treaty. Tribes had been removed from their original lands to "Indian Territory." Outraged, Mary started a petition drive in opposition. She turned to her previous associations and her missionary circle. Together the campaign collected about thirteen thousand signatures. She presented the petition to President Rutherford B. Hayes and Congress. In 1881 a second petition, with fifty thousand signatures, was presented to the Senate through Senator Henry L. Dawes (R-Massachusetts), sponsor of the act that bears his name.

Mary believed strongly in the assimilation of Native Americans into the majority culture; she supported the Dawes Act of 1887. This Act proposed allotment of lands in Indian Territory to individual native households, the end of tribal governments. Supporters of the act believed that by becoming citizens, Indigenous people would exchange their "uncivilized" rebellious ideologies for those that would help them become economically self-supporting citizens. They would be freed of the need for government supervision. Now that we can look back, history shows that the Dawes Act did not serve as intended.

Instrumental in the Indian Treaty-Keeping and Protective Association, Mary served as president. In 1882 they presented the government with a third petition, with nearly a hundred thousand signatures. This Association intended to grant tribal lands to the Native Americans.

In 1883, under Mary's leadership, the organization devoted itself to missionary work among the Native Americans, offering classes in English, religion, and domestic skills. She retired from the presidency in 1884 but remained active in Native American reform. Resigning from the presidency in November 1884, she supported the causes financially.

In 1888, at the age of seventy-two, Mary was a representative in the World's Missionary Convention in London, England. Reverend Thomas Rambaut, D.D., LL.D also attended. They had a forty-year friendship since they worked together in Robertville, South Carolina. They had maintained a devoted friendship, and Reverend Tom was also a prominent educator. While in London, they decided to marry. Apparently, this friendship had been more than pen pals.

When they returned to the USA, they settled in Mary's hometown of Hamilton, New York. The marriage was much shorter than the courtship; Reverend Tom died on October 15, 1890.

Now a widow, Mary moved in with her brother, who also lived in Hamilton, New York. She died in 1900 at the age of eighty-four. Her body is interred at Woodlawn Cemetery, Hamilton, Madison County, New York, USA.

Anne Sullivan

b: *April 14, 1866*
Feeding Hills, MA, USA

d: *October 20, 1936*
Forest Hills, NY, USA

Johanna Mansfield Sullivan was born in Feeding Hills, Massachusetts. Her parents, Thomas and Alice Sullivan, immigrated to the United States from Ireland during the Great Famine of the 1840s. Life was still difficult for the Sullivans after the move. The couple had five children, two died in infancy, and Anne was the eldest, born April 14, 1866.

Anne grew up in impoverished conditions and struggled with health problems. Anne contracted an eye disease called trachoma at the age of five, which severely damaged her sight. Trachoma usually begins in childhood and causes repeated, painful infections, making the eyes red and swollen. Over time the recurring irritation and scarring of the cornea cause severe vision loss. From this early infection, Anne was left partially blind. Her father, Thomas, was left to raise all three children after her mother's death. Thomas was often abusive, and Anne was strong-willed. In time Thomas gave up and abandoned his family.

Anne's sister was sent to live with relatives, but Anne and her infirm younger brother, Jimmie, were sent to live at the Tewksbury Almshouse, a home for the poor. Conditions at the Tewksbury Almshouse were deplorable. Underfunded, overcrowded, and in disrepair, the Almshouse housed an average of 940 men, women, and children during the years that Anne and Jimmy were there. Needless to say, the mortality rate at Tewksbury was very high, and within three months of their arrival, Jimmie Sullivan died, leaving Anne broken and alone.

Upon hearing about a commission coming to investigate the conditions at Tewksbury Almshouse, Anne took action. On their visit, Anne followed them around, waiting for an opportunity. Just as the tour concluded, she gathered her courage and approached a member of the team of inspectors. Knowing her only hope for an escape from poverty and the poor house would be an education. She told them that she wanted to go to school, and she was heard. That moment changed her life.

On October 7, 1880, Anne entered the Perkins Institution at fourteen. Anne had never owned a nightgown or hairbrush and couldn't even thread a needle. While Anne had never attended school, she was wise in the world's ways, having learned a great deal about life, politics, and tragedy at Tewksbury, a side of society unknown even to her teachers. Most of the girls at Perkins were the daughters of wealth. Some of Anne's fellow students ridiculed her because of her ignorance and rough manners. Some of her teachers were particularly unsympathetic and impatient with her. Anne had no previous formal education, and she couldn't write or spell her name. She was humiliated by her ignorance, and with her quick temper and tendency to challenge rules, she was often in trouble. However, Anne was extremely intelligent and was fast to learn.

While at Perkins, Anne underwent surgery to help improve her limited vision, which helped her settle into school life. Now with better vision, she quickly excelled in her studies. Sophia Hopkins, the house mother of her cottage, was warm and understanding with Anne. Anne never felt like she fit in, but Mrs. Hopkins treated her like a daughter and took Anne to her Cape Cod home during school vacations.

Anne had yet another surgery on her eyes, and this time, it dramatically improved her vision. At last, she could see well enough to read print. Anne also befriended Laura Bridgman, another remarkable Perkins resident. Fifty years before, Bridgman had been the first person who was deaf-blind to learn to speak. Anne spent a lot of time with her and learned the manual alphabet. They frequently chatted, and Anne would read the newspaper to the much older woman. Bridgman could be difficult, but Anne had more patience with her than the other students.

Her achievements continued, and in June 1886, not only did Anne graduate, she gave the Valedictory Address: *"Fellow graduates – duty bids us go forth into active life. Let us go cheerfully, hopefully, and earnestly, and set ourselves to find our especial part. When we have found it, willingly and faithfully perform it; for every obstacle we overcome, every success we achieve tends to bring man closer to God."*

The realization that she had no family to return to, and no qualifications for employment, was overwhelming. Anne feared that she would have to return to Tewksbury, and her fears tempered her joy at graduating. During the summer of 1886, Captain Keller of Alabama wrote to Perkins Director Michael Anagnos. The Captain asked for a recommendation for a teacher. His young daughter Helen had fallen ill when she was less than two years old and had lost her sight and hearing. It turns out that Helen's mother had read about Laura Bridgman's education at Perkins in Charles Dickens' *American Notes* and hoped that her daughter could be reached. The Kellers search for help ultimately led to educator Alexander Graham Bell, who recommended contacting Director Anagnos at Perkins School for the Blind.

The director admired Anne's intelligence and indomitable determination. He recommended Anne as the best candidate to teach the now seven-year-old girl.

Intimidated by the challenge, Anne knew this was the opportunity she needed. She spent the next few months studying the reports of Laura Bridgman's education by Howe and her other teachers. In March of 1887, she left for Tuscumbia, Alabama, to begin a new chapter in her life.

Due to the movie The Miracle Worker, many of us are aware of the challenge of entering Helen's world. Much has been written and reenacted about the day Helen Keller and Anne Sullivan first met and how the teacher finally broke through to Helen's dark and silent world. The methods Anne used when she began teaching Helen were very much like those Dr. Samuel Gridley Howe had used with her friend Laura Bridgman. They followed a strict schedule, introducing new vocabulary words in a formal lesson. Soon it was clear that the rigid routine did not suit her young pupil. Never one to be limited by rules, Anne abandoned the prescribed schedule and shifted the focus.

At this time, Anne noticed Helen's infant cousin learned language by being spoken to. This was when Anne entered Helen's world by following her interests and adding vocabulary to those activities. So, she talked to the girl constantly by fingerspelling into her hand. In her letters to Mrs. Hopkins, she discussed the reasons for her change in approach:

"I am convinced that the time spent by the teacher in digging out of the child what she has put into him, for the sake of satisfying herself that it has taken root, is so much time thrown away. It's much better, I think, to assume the child is doing his part and that the seed you have sown will bear fruit in due time. It's only fair to the child, anyhow, and it saves you unnecessary trouble."

Once Helen understood what was being given to her, the thirst for information seemed unquenchable. Remarkably, within six months, she learned 575 words, "multiplication tables as high as five, and the Braille system." Although Anne was a brilliant and intuitive teacher, she was ingenious to move beyond the earlier rigid prescriptive teaching methods. She continued to seek and receive support and advice from the director, Michael Anagnos, and others at Perkins.

Homeschooling had created a foundation for Helen's education, but Anne felt the isolation and limited materials in Tuscumbia held them back. She decided it would be best for Helen to enter the educationally rich environment of Perkins School for the Blind.

Perkins' role in the education of Helen Keller has been controversial. Before they arrived in Boston. Helen had become a central subject of Perkins' Annual Report by Director Michael Anagnos. He had drawn from Anne's letters on her prodigy's progress. He then embellished them, adding his own florid prose. Anne hated the exaggeration and worried that it might create unrealistic expectations of Helen that could harm her.

After Helen and Anne arrived on campus, the tensions continued. The Perkins resources were generous, but Anne disliked her loss of independence, and her relationship with Director Anagnos and Perkins was alternately warm and strained for years. Anne and Helen would live at the school and then take long breaks back in Alabama.

In 1891, Helen was accused of plagiarizing a story she wrote for Anagnos' birthday. This led to an investigation that deeply wounded the student and her teacher. The strained relationship with Perkins was finally severed when Helen wrote an autobiographical magazine article for Youth's Companion that pointedly failed even to mention the school.

Although they maintained some friendships from Perkins, they did not have any official interactions for many years. Even though Anne never returned to the Perkins campus, her influence at the school and her skills as a teacher are still profoundly respected.

There was no more significant influence on the education of deaf-blind children than Anne and her work with Helen Keller. No school in the United States has educated more children who are deaf-blind than Perkins. The use of Anne's child-centered methods is the centerpiece of the educational philosophy of the Perkins Deaf-blind Program to this day.

Anne continued her student education when Helen attended the Wight-Humason School in New York City. This is where Helen learned to speak. When the Keller family couldn't afford to continue paying Anne or manage Helen's school costs, several wealthy benefactors – including millionaire Andrew Carnegie – stepped in to help them with the costs. Despite the physical strain on her own limited sight, Anne was there to help Helen. They continued to Radcliffe College, and in 1900, Anne spelled the contents of class lectures into Helen's hand and spent hours conveying information from textbooks to her. As a result, Helen Keller became the first deaf-blind person to graduate from college. I hope that Anne got at the very least a certificate.

While working with Helen on her autobiography, Anne met John A. Macy, a Harvard University instructor. Macy helped edit the manuscript, and he fell in love with Anne. After refusing several marriage proposals from him, she finally accepted. The two were wed in 1905.

Anne didn't let her marriage interfere with her work with Helen. The newlyweds lived with Keller in a Massachusetts farmhouse. The two women remained inseparable. Anne continued to travel on Helen's lecture tours. When they were on stage, she helped relay Helen's words to the audience, as Helen's speech still wasn't clear enough to be widely understood.

It was near 1913 or 1914 that the marriage broke up. Macy went to Europe, and Anne stayed with Helen. They never divorced.

Anne's health began to fail, and Polly Thomson became Helen's secretary. The three women eventually took up residence in Forest Hills, New York. The trio struggled to make ends meet. In 1919, Anne played herself in the first film version of her life, *Deliverance*. The film proved to be a box office failure. So, as many do, Helen and Anne ended up touring on the vaudeville theater circuit. They shared their story of triumph with fascinated audiences for years.

By the late 1920s, Anne had lost most of her vision and had chronic pain in her right eye. She had it removed to improve her health.

On October 20, 1936, Anne died at her home in Forest Hills, New York. Her ashes were placed at the National Cathedral in Washington, D.C. – a distinct honor. At her funeral, Bishop James E. Freeman said, "Among the great teachers of all time, she occupies a commanding and conspicuous place.... The touch of her hand did more than illuminate the pathway of a clouded mind; it literally emancipated a soul."

Anna "Annie" Julia Haywood Cooper

b: 1858
Raleigh, NC

d: February 27, 1964
Washington D.C. USA

Anna Julia Haywood was born enslaved in Raleigh, North Carolina, in 1858. Her mother, Hannah Stanley Haywood, was held in bondage by George Washington Haywood, one of the sons of North Carolina's longest-serving state Treasurer John Haywood. He helped found the University of North Carolina. Her mother would not identify Annie's father, but George, who held her mother in bondage, carries a high possibility. The second choice is George's brother, Dr. Fabius Haywood, who held her brother Andrew.

Annie worked as a servant in the Haywood home until the end of the Civil War in 1865. Education had been limited, but in 1868, when Annie was nine years old, she received a scholarship from Reverend J. Brinton and entered the newly opened Saint Augustine's Normal School and Collegiate Institute in Raleigh. The local Episcopal diocese had founded the school to train teachers to educate the newly freed slaves and their families.

During her fourteen years at St. Augustine's, Annie distinguished herself as bright and ambitious.

She demonstrated great promise in all levels and disciplines. She learned Latin, French, Greek, English literature, math, and science.

St. Augustine's emphasis was to train men for the ministry or other universities during this period. The "Ladies Courses" were special classes for women students. She was discouraged from pursuing the higher classes, but Annie fought for the right. With her intellect and drive, she prevailed.

George A. C. Cooper, a teacher of Greek studies while at St. Augustine, was also an ordained Episcopal Minister. On June 1877, he married Annie; George was thirty at the nuptials, and she eighteen.

The marriage was short-lived as George died two years later, on September 28, 1879. After her husband's death, Annie entered Oberlin College in Ohio. With her academic qualifications, she was admitted as a sophomore. She continued to study courses designated for men, and Annie would never remarry. She graduated in 1884. At Oberlin, Annie was part of the "LLS," "one of the two literary societies for women. This group offered regular programs featuring lectures by distinguished speakers as well as singers and orchestras.

Annie gained work as a tutor, which also helped her pay for her educational expenses. Upon completing her studies, she taught briefly at Wilberforce College and then returned to St. Augustine. This time Annie was an instructor. Initially, she taught classics, modern history, higher English, and vocal and instrumental music. Her husband's early death may have contributed to her ability to continue teaching. If she had stayed married, she probably would have been encouraged or required to withdraw from the university to become a housewife.

She returned to Oberlin and earned an M.A. in Mathematics in 1888, along with Mary Church Terrell; they were the first women of color to accomplish this feat. Both received their Masters in 1890–91.

Annie published an essay on *Higher Education of Women*, which argued for the benefits of black women being trained in classical literature. She demonstrated an interest in access to education which would form much of her later career. Her essay preceded W. E. B. DuBois' similar arguments in his paper, *Of the Training of Black Men* (*Souls of Black Folk* 1903), by nearly a decade.

Annie moved to Washington, DC, in 1892, where she joined Helen Appo Cook, Ida B. Wells, Charlotte Forten Grimké, Mary Jane Peterson, Mary Church Terrell, and Evelyn Shaw to form the Colored Women's League in Washington, D.C. The goals of this service-oriented club were to promote unity and social progress for the African-American community. Helen Cook was elected president.

It was 1900 when Annie made her first trip to Europe. She was to participate in the First Pan-African Conference in London. Not limited to just the conference, Annie then went on to visit Scotland and England, followed by an excursion to Paris for the World Exposition. After a week at the Exposition, she went to Oberammergau to see the Passion Play, followed by traveling in Germany. She finished up the trip with a tour of Italy

Annie began teaching Latin at M Street High School in Washington D.C. and was soon named principal in 1901. Soon she was entangled in a controversy involving the differing attitudes about black education. Annie advocated for a model of classical education espoused in her paper. She, along with W. E. B. Du Bois promoted higher education and leadership for all eligible students rather than the vocational program that Booker T. Washington endorsed. As a result of this dispute, she left the school. She returned to the M Street school and fit her work around her doctoral thesis.

It was her later years when Annie was deeply involved with Frelinghuysen University, of which she was the president. The university provided continuing education to working African Americans at hours that did not interfere with their employment. After the University had funding difficulty, Annie moved to her own home. Never one to rest, she drove on.

On February 27, 1964, Annie died in Washington, D.C., at the age of 105. Her memorial was held in a chapel on Saint Augustine's College campus in Raleigh, North Carolina. She was buried alongside her husband at the City Cemetery in Raleigh.

Eve Ball

b: March 14, 1890
Kentucky, USA

d: December 24, 1984
New Mexico, USA

Katherine Evelyn Daly was born March 14, 1890, on her grandfather's plantation in Kentucky. She was born to Samuel Richard and Gazelle (Gibbs) Daly. Eve spent her early years in Clarksville, Tennessee, and later her family moved to a cattle ranch in Kansas. Her mother was the first female doctor in Kansas. Her father died when she was five years old, and her mother remarried when Eve was twelve. She had three full siblings and two half-brothers.

Eve enjoyed learning from a young age. Her grandmother taught her to read when she was only four years old. Eve's mother, not only a doctor but a teacher, instilled a love of education and a spirit of independence. These qualities were used to describe Eve for her entire life. Eve was sixteen when she started teaching school. She taught students of many ages, and some were adults. There are records of her coaching a junior high school boys basketball team at the same time. In 1918, Eve received her Bachelor of Science degree in education from Kansas State Teachers College. In 1934 she received her Master's in education at the University of Kansas.

She married a Captain in the Kansas National Guard, Joseph P. Ball. It was a short marriage as he died in World War I.

Following the end of the war, Eve spent the next few years teaching both elementary and secondary school in Kansas and then moved to Oklahoma to support herself. Eve also worked as a chemist at an oil refinery in Hobbs, New Mexico. This wasn't enough, so Eve opened a jewelry shop in Hobbs and ran a tourist shop at Casa Hermosa in Phoenix. Her efforts made it possible for Eve to purchase the Hermosa Inn, then called La Casa Hermosa, from artist Lon Megargee; the intent was to operate a dude ranch. Eve had to give up on that plan due to the massive amount of work, which took away her writing time. Next, Eve returned to Kansas City and taught history and literature at Kansas City Junior College and the College of Artesia. Her resume demonstrates the pay status of teachers and women.

In 1942 Eve officially moved to Ruidoso, New Mexico. Six years later, she bought an entire block of property near the Ruidoso Downs racing tracks and built an adobe home. Through the diversity of her life, Eve developed a great passion for documenting the history of the diverse peoples of New Mexico and the Southwest. She became deeply involved in collecting the oral histories of various peoples, a venture many historians of the time did not respect. Eve, however, felt strongly about preserving history from the mouths of those who experienced it. She also had a remarkable talent for gaining the trust and respect of those she wrote about. Many historical figures gave Eve their personal papers and photographs.

Eve is best known for her work with the Apache tribe. Her home in Ruidoso was near the Mescalero Reservation. She developed friendships and trust with the tribe. She provided a safe place to rest for the women on their long trek to town. As the years passed, Eve interviewed some of the critical Apache tribal figures, including Jaspar Kanseah (nephew of Geronimo), James Kaywaykla (nephew of Victorio and grandson of Nana), and Asa Daklugie (son of Juh). Eve became an expert on the Apache as she learned about their beliefs, history, problems, and internal politics. Well ahead of her time, Eve accomplished this before historians fully accepted oral tradition as a source. She was documenting the accounts of elders who had survived the army's campaigns against them in the last century. These oral histories offer new versions – from Warm Springs, Chiricahua, Mescalero, and Lipan Apache – of events previously known only through descriptions left by non-Indians.

Eve collected material for over twenty years before trying to publish it. She wrote dozens of stories for True West and Frontier Times. Eve dedicated a great deal of time to the families involved in the Lincoln County War, especially the Coe family. She also made connections to William Bonney, Billy the Kid. From these opportunities, Eve developed an interest in cowboys and early settlers. She published *Bob Crosby, World Champion Cowboy* in 1966, *Ma'am Jones of the Pecos* in 1969, *In the Days of Victorio* in 1970, *My Girlhood Among Outlaws* in 1972, and *Indeh: An Apache Odyssey* in 1980.

Eve also penned numerous short stories and drafts for various books that were not published. She has been honored for her contribution to Western American history, including an honorary doctorate from Artesia College, the Western Writers of America Golden Spur Award for the best short story, and the Western Writers of America Saddleman Award. In 1984 the United States Senate passed a joint resolution honoring Eve for her life's work and contributions to history.

Eve continued to write to her death. She had lost her eyesight but never her passion. Her books have been used as textbooks at colleges and many top universities.

Katherine Evelyn Daly Ball died December 24, 1984, at the age of ninety-four. She was cremated, and her ashes were scattered. Twenty-five years after her death, she was honored with a historical marker commemorating her life's achievements by the New Mexico Historic Women. It is located near Carrizozo, New Mexico. It states:

Eve Ball (1890-1984)
Author and Preservationist
A pioneer in the preservation of the history of people in Southeastern New Mexico, Eve wrote over 150 articles and numerous books chronicling Mescalero and Chiricahua Apaches, Anglo and Hispanic settlers. Her honesty, patience, and determination to learn from them won the confidence of Apache elders, saving oral histories certain to be lost without her. "Ahee-ih-yeh, Ms. Ball."

Emperors

*no *esses* required

A woman who is a sovereign ruler of great power and rank, especially one ruling an empire.

Synonyms:
ruler · sovereign · monarch · potentate · tsarina · imperatrix · autarch · queen · ethnarch · regina · matriarch · power behind the throne · et cetera *profanities included.*

Queen Pu-abi

b: *circa 2600 B.C.E.*   d. *circa 2340, B.C.E.*
Ur, Mesopotamia (Iraq)

A remarkable, intact tomb was discovered by Leonard Woolley during his excavations at the "Royal Cemetery of Ur" between 1922 and 1934. It was the tomb of a mysterious lady named "**Pu-abi**." Her name translates as Word of my father, and the title was discovered on one of three cylindrical seals. The two cuneiform signs that composed her name were initially read as "Shub-ad" in Sumerian. As the researchers kept digging, they reread this word in Akkadian as "Pu-abi" Her title is "nin" or "eresh," which means queen or priestess. Since Puabi's seal does not place her in relation to any king or husband supports a theory that she ruled on her own. Another suggestion is that she was the second wife of king Meskalamdug. The fact that Puabi, herself a Semitic Akkadian, was an essential figure among Sumerians indicates a high degree of power and influence among the ancient Sumerians and their Semitic neighbors.

During the Sumerian Early Dynastic III Period, c. 2550 B.C., burials of kings, queens, and princes were lavish. They often included human sacrifice meant to provide a royal retinue to accompany them into the afterlife. I am extending gratitude that practice has gone out of style. Queen Pu-abi's tomb was one of the most elaborate discovered royal graves. Not just a grave, she had an underground complex with a sloping passage that led into a large pit. This is where the vaulted stone burial chamber was located. Pu-abi was dressed for the occasion, she wore a golden headdress, and her wig was wrapped and adorned with golden leaves, flowers, rings, plates, and a golden lyre.

The number of grave goods that Woolley uncovered in Pu-abi's tomb was staggering. The reports list surgical tools needed for medical treatment in the afterlife. There was also a lapis lazuli-encrusted bull's head, golden tableware, and multiple gemstones, including carnelian, silver, lapis lazuli. Some were made into beads for extravagant jewelry and other fashion needs. We must not forget the rings and bracelets and a spare headdress, just in case. There was also a chariot adorned with lionesses' heads in silver to be ready if the other world's transportation was inadequate.

Pu-abi didn't go to the afterlife alone; there were a number of "death pits" also found near her chamber. The largest and most well-known death pit held seventy-four attendants, six men and sixty-eight women, adorned with gold, silver, and lapis decorations. One female figure appeared to be more elaborately adorned than the others. To this, they added fifty-two attendants: servants, guards, a horse, some lions, another chariot, and several other bodies, possibly retainers who the archeologist

Woolley suspected were poisoned so they could serve their mistress in the next world.

In Pu-abi's chamber, the remains of three other people were found, and these personal servants had minor adornments of their own. The pit located above Pu-abi's room contained twenty-one attendants, an elaborate harp/lyre, a chariot, and what was left of a large chest of personal grooming items. Due to the location of the pits and the general lack of evidence, it is largely unclear whether the death pits can be directly linked to Pu-abi. We don't know how long she ruled, but when Pu-abi died, the population dropped.

Evidence derived from CAT scans through the University of Pennsylvania Museum suggests that some of the sacrifices were probably violent and caused by blunt force trauma. A pointed, weighted tool could explain the shatter patterns on the skulls that resulted in death. The size and weight of the device fit the damage sustained by the two bodies examined by Aubrey Baadsgaard, a Ph.D. candidate at the University of Pennsylvania. Cinnabar, or mercury vapor residue, was observed as well. It would have been used to prevent or slow the decomposition of the bodies until the completion of the necessary funerary rites that appear elaborate and time/life-consuming.

As her burial plot was disturbed, Puabi's physical remains, including her badly damaged skull, are kept in London's Natural History Museum. The excavated finds from Woolley's expedition were divided among the British Museum in London, the University of Pennsylvania Museum in Philadelphia, Pennsylvania, and the National Museum in Baghdad.

Several pieces of the treasure were looted from the National Museum in the aftermath of the Second Gulf War in 2003. I have not found any notice of returning her to her original country.

Kandake
aka
Candace (S)

800 B.C.   *circa 1250 C.E.*
Kush (Ethiopia)

Candace (pronounced KAN'-dis) was not simply the name of some queen in the Bible. The "Candace" (or "Kandake") was the title given for a period of no less than a thousand years to those who would be the queens over the Ethiopian people in the country of Kush.

These queens were not just figureheads either; they were fully functioning heads of state. They were the warrior queens, which meant the commander-in-chief over the Kush armies. There are historical accounts of several wars where these Kandakes proved to be formidable forces in their leadership of these armies. The independently ruling Kandakes that we know of were: Shanakdakhete, Amanirenas, Amanishakheto, Amanitore, Amantitere, Amanikhatashan, Maleqorobar, and Lahideamani. It's generally agreed that during the rule of the Kandakes, Kush blossomed and became wealthier and more powerful than ever before.

The Biblical Queen of Sheba was based on the Gospels of Matthew (12:42) and Luke (11:31). The "queen of the South" is claimed to be a queen of Ethiopia, and research suggests her name was Queen Makeda. There is some suggestion that it is a misinterpretation of Kandake/Candace. She ruled the Ethiopian kingdom for more than fifty years. Her story has been told, retold, edited, and romanticized for a few thousand years.

In the 330s, when Alexander the Great was conquering the world in his famous World Tour, he stopped when he finally approached the door of one of the greatest generals of the ancient world. This leader also happened to be the Candace of Ethiopia. This intimidating Queen Candace was exalted as a master tactician and military field commander. In classical writings, Alexander visited Candace and found that she would not even consider admitting him into Ethiopia. The proud, strong black race leader warned him not to underestimate them. Her words to him were reported to be, "We are whiter and brighter in our souls than the whitest of you."

At this, Alexander the Great dared not destroy his reputation with a defeat at the hands of a woman. He stopped his soldiers at the border of Ethiopia and avoided the African armies led by this powerful woman. He didn't want to lose to a woman and have to change his name to "Alexander the Usually Effective," or "Alexander the Late," or "Alexander the Whipped."

There isn't a great deal of history written about the many Kandakes, but we know that for 1250 years (ending in 350 C.E.), they ruled the African version of the Egyptian-like kingdom of Kush and Sheba as a unique civilization. The Kandakes are heroic leaders in strength, pride, and reputation. But as with any dangerous force, there are two points of view. Roman sources describe her as a strong and brave warrior queen who fought ferociously alongside her soldiers. One Roman even called her 'man-like' and said her spirit 'was beyond her gender' – the highest compliment those misogynists could give. They have also been romanticized because we know who has been writing the history in those times.

The Candace is a hero, but they are villains for traditional white male authority figures, like Alex the G.

You go, GALS!

Sigrid the Haughty

b. 967	d. 1014

Scandinavia

Sigrid Storråda is described as the beautiful but vengeful daughter of Skogul-Tosti, a powerful Swedish nobleman. She is a queen appearing in Norse sagas as the wife of Eric the Victorious of Sweden. Sigrid appears mainly in late Icelandic sagas and Nordic stories. Many scholars lean toward the belief that she is a compilation of stories collected into one person. This practice is common in folklore and religious narratives that pass down to create lessons of guidance and faith. As we learned, this is also a common practice as many women's stories are lost or "edited." The reports of Sigrid all point to a person who was very proud of herself and spent years looking for Mr. Right.

The validity of all her stories is questioned, but she insists we tell her tale this way. Sigrid the Haughty was a rebellious girl who wanted to be popular and not waste her time on people beneath her. She was like that bitchy high school cheerleader (no names will be shared) whose Daddy bought her a Beamer for her sixteenth birthday. Attractive to look at but consistently reported to not be on the sweet side.

After the death of her husband, the prementioned Eric, there is the first story of mayhem. My favorite part of her legend is when two powerful suitors wished to wed this comely widow at the same time. One day, Harold the Greenlander and a Russian Prince came courting. Sigrid couldn't imagine marrying either a Greenlander OR a lowly Prince.

She arranged to meet them at an isolated cabin and set to learn more. Unlike your typical meet and greet, Sigrid served a fine grog and then drank them "under the table." Her next step in this dating plan was to lock them in and light it on fire. Harold died in the blaze, and the Prince escaped, but his eyebrows never grew back.

Eventually, the class of suitors rose to the King level. But even being a King wasn't enough to win Sigrid's heart. The first King didn't make it but didn't die. The King of Norway asked for her hand in marriage, but he was a Christian who thought his was the only religion, so he told her she had to convert. Sigrid said no, and he slapped her. Sigrid got haughty and responded, "That may well have been the death of you." One story says he was so afraid of what she'd do if she got her hands on him that he drowned himself in the sea to avoid capture. I like story two better. Sweyn Forkbeard, King of Denmark, eventually came to a calling, and he was able to prove himself a worthy catch. According to the sagas, Sigrid pushed Sweyn into war with King Olaf, the slapper. She only then married Sweyn, and the stories spin with his legend.

So, the moral of this story is that if you want to find your handsome-perfect prince, sometimes you have to toast a few groggy frogs.

Wu Zetian

b. 624 d. 705

China

Empress **Wu Zetian** was the only woman to rule as "Emperor" of China. Other women ruled before, But Wu's reign during the Tang Dynasty (618-907 C.E.) was reported as one of China's most influential and controversial monarchs.

Wu Zetian, also called Wu Zhao, and Wu-hou became a junior concubine of Emperor Taizong in 636 or 638 C.E. at the age of fourteen. Taizong is considered one of the most remarkable emperors in China's history. Wu was from a wealthy family and was the daughter of Wu Shihuo, a chancellor of the Tang Dynasty. Her father encouraged her to read, write, and develop her mind. Education was usually reserved for men throughout multiple cultures. Wu was another exception, and she also learned to play music, write poetry, and speak well in public.

Once Wu was moved to Taizong's palace, she was assigned to the laundry. One day she dared to speak to the Emperor as he passed by on the topic of Chinese History. From this initial conversation, they began to talk regularly. Taizong was surprised that his latest concubine could read, write, and have an intelligent conversation. He became fascinated by her beauty and wit in their discussions. Taizong was so impressed he took her out of the laundry and made her his secretary. In this new position, she was constantly involved in affairs of state at the highest level, and Wu must have performed her duties well because she became a favorite.

Wu attracted the attention of many of the men in court, and one of these was Prince Li Zhi, the ninth son of Taizong, who would become the next emperor. They began an affair, which was risky business since he was married and she was bound to his father as a concubine. Li Zhi was deeply in love with Wu but could not do anything because of his father and wife's situations.

When Taizong died, Wu and the other concubines had their heads shaved and sent to become nuns at Ganye Temple. As was the custom with the emperor's death, all concubines could not be passed on to be "used" by others and forced to end their time at court to start a new life of chastity and religion.

Well, Li Zhi stepped into the position as the new emperor and took the name Gaozong. One of his first decisions was to send for Wu and have her transferred back to court as his First concubine. He ignored the fact that he already had other concubines and that wife person. Wu was given the privileged position of first concubine, and Gaozong's wife, Lady Wang, and his former first concubine, Xiao Shufei, were jealous of each other but even more envious of the attention Gaozong paid to Wu. According to Wu's account, they conspired against her, but Wu started and finished her problems with them, according to historians. I like to imagine the details, but indeed it is a case of what the Emperor wants, he gets.

Lady Wang had no children, and Lady Xiao had a son and two daughters. In 652 C.E., Wu gave birth to a son, Li Hong, and the following year, another son, Li Xian. Neither of these boys was a threat to Lady Wang or Lady Xiao because Gaozong had already chosen a successor; his chancellor Liu Shi was Lady Wang's uncle. He proceeded to name Liu Shi's son, Li Zhong, as heir. This didn't suggest the women had worked out their differences, even though Wu had given birth to two sons in a row.

In 654 C.E., Wu had a daughter who died soon after birth. Reportedly the baby was strangled in her crib. Wu accused Lady Wang of killing her due to her jealousy. To add to it, Wang was the last person seen in the room and had no alibi. Wu then added an accusation of witchcraft and implicated Lady Xiao. Lady Wang and all the implicated others were found guilty of all the charges. Gaozong's following action was to divorce his wife, bar her mother from the palace, and exile Lady Xiao. Lady Wang's uncle, the named chancellor, was removed from his post, and his son was cut off as heir.

Wu was now promoted to the first wife of Gaozong and empress of China. She was also assured that her sons would rule the country after the death of her husband. Wu played the role of the shy, respectable emperor's wife like a public champion, but behind the scenes, she was the real power. Carefully Wu eliminated any potential enemies from the court. She had Lady Wang and Lady Xiao killed after they had entered exile. Although Wu's account claims that Lady Wang murdered her daughter, later Chinese historians all agree that Wu was the murderer and killed her child to frame Lady Wang.

The story of her daughter and the framing of Lady Wang to gain power is the most often repeated incident of her life. As some historians report, there is no way of knowing if it happened. At the murder/death, it was Lady Wu's word against Lady Wang's. Most who have written on Lady Wu have followed the story set down by the later Chinese historians without question. They often had a plan which did not include praising a woman who dared to rule like a man. The historians always portray Wu as ruthless, conniving, scheming, and bloodthirsty, and she may have been all of these things, and maybe not. We must consider the sources and politics over time.

Beginning in 660, Wu was effectively the emperor of China. She did not hold that title, but she was the power behind the office and took care of imperial business even when pregnant with her daughter Taiping. In 666 C.E., Wu led a group of women to Mount Tai (an ancient ceremonial center and they conducted rituals that traditionally were performed only by men. Having been raised by her father to believe she was equal to men, Wu saw no reason why women could not carry out the same practices and hold the same positions as men could. Wu didn't ask for permission and simply led the women to Mount

Tai. She also organized military campaigns against Korea in 668 C.E., which effectively reduced Korea to a vassal state.

Emperor Gaozong had nothing to do with either of these events, although his name would be attached to the campaign against Korea. Gaozong had a disease that affected his eyes and needed reports read to him. Wu probably read the information and edited where she saw fit. In 674 C, E, Gaozong took the title Tian Huang, Emperor of Heaven, and Wu changed her own to Tian Hou, Empress of Heaven. They ruled as divine monarchs until Gaozong died in 683 C. E.

Shortly after his death, Wu took the throne. There was an earthquake which was interpreted as a bad omen. A mountain appeared soon after, and she claimed it was a sign of divine approval. Wu placed her first son on the throne, who took the royal title Zhongzong. He refused to cooperate with his mother. Then his wife, Lady Wei, assumed too much power. Wei had her father appointed Chief Minister to her husband and tried to push through other measures favoring her family. It wasn't long for Wu to stop tolerating their disrespect. She had her first son charged with treason and banished with his wife.

Well, the second son, Zhongzong, was placed as Emperor Ruizong. She kept Ruizong under a kind of house arrest, confining him to the Inner Palace. Not easy to please, Ruizong was also a disappointment even in time out. Wu forced him to abdicate in 690 C.E. and finally proclaimed herself Emperor Zeitan, ruler of China, the first and only woman to sit on the

Dragon Throne and reign in her name and by her own authority.

Her last name, "Wu," is associated with the words 'weapon' and 'military force' and she chose the name 'Zeitan' which means 'Ruler of the Heavens.' She wanted to clarify that a new kind of ruler had taken the throne of China, and a new order had arrived. The first thing she did was change the state's name from Tang to Zhou (actually Tianzhou or Tiansou). It was customary, when a dynasty changed, to re-set history. To make it clear that she was the beginning of an entirely new era by calling her reign Tianzhou, granted by heaven. To ensure the security of her new authority, she had any members of the Tang Dynasty royal family imprisoned and proclaimed herself an incarnation of the Maitreya Buddha, calling herself Empress Shengsen, which means 'Holy Spirit.'

As early as 660 CE, Wu had organized a secret police force and spies in court and throughout the country. This system warned her of any plots in the making and enabled her to take care of threats to her reign. Emperor Wu used the intelligence she gathered to pressure some high-ranking officials who were not performing to her specifications to resign; others were banished or executed.

She reformed the structure of the government and got rid of anyone she felt was not carrying out their duties, so she reduced government spending and increased efficiency. She appointed intellectuals and talented bureaucrats in their place without regard to family status or connections.

No area of Chinese life was untouched by Emperor Wu, and her reforms were widespread because she took suggestions directly from the people. Under the older regimes, everything had to go through a number of different offices before it ever reached those in power. Wu eliminated all the bureaucracy by establishing a direct line of communication between herself and the people.

Wu improved the education system and organized teams to survey the land and build irrigation ditches. She also redistributed the land so that everyone had an equal share. Agricultural production under Wu's reign increased to an all-time high. Wu also reformed the military by mandating military exams for commanders to show competency, similar to her imperial exams given to civil service workers. The military exams were intended to measure intelligence and decision-making and followed with personal interviews of the candidates, instead of just being appointed because of family connections or their family's name.

In 697 C.E., Wu's hold on power began to slip as she became paranoid and spent time with her young lovers. Two brothers, known as the Zhang Brothers, were her favorites, and she spent time in closed quarters with them. This was considered scandalous (still is) because of her age and how young the Zhang brothers were. This practice was common for male rulers with young women as concubines, but it was shocking for an empress to do the same. Did she add together their ages for approval?

Due to her ongoing paranoia, she purged her administration. Anyone she suspected of disloyalty was banished or executed. The efficiency of her court dropped as she increased her time with the brothers Zhang. It was whispered around that she became addicted to aphrodisiacs. In 704 C.E., court officials could no longer tolerate Wu's behavior and had the Zhang brothers murdered. Wu was forced to abdicate for her exiled son Zhongzong and Wei's wife. She was in very poor health and died a year later.

The woman who had the audacity to believe she was as capable as any man to lead continues to be vilified. Now writers often qualify their criticisms, but there is no arguing that, under Wu Zetian, China experienced affluence and stability it had never known before. Her reforms and policies laid the foundation for the success of Xuanzong, the next emperor under whose reign China became the most prosperous country in the world.

Empress Wu was buried in Qian County, Shanxi Province, alongside Gaozong. A stele was erected outside the tomb, which later historians were supposed to inscribe with Empress Wu's great deeds. To this day, it remains blank. Despite all of her reforms and the prosperity she brought to the country, Wu is remembered mainly for her crimes against friends and family members – especially the murder of her daughter – and people did not think she was worthy of an inscription.

Philippa of Hainault (Queen Philippa)

b. June 24, 1310 *d. August 15, 1357*
Valenciennes, France *Windsor Castle, England*

Philippa was of Black Moorish ancestry, born in Valenciennes in the County of Hainaut in the Low Countries of northern France, June 24, 1310. Her parents were William I, Count of Hainaut, and Joan of Valois, Countess of Hainaut, the granddaughter of Philip III of France. Philippa was one of eight children and the second of five daughters, and her eldest sister Margaret married the German King Louis IV in 1324.

King Edward II decided that an alliance with Flanders would benefit England and sent Bishop Stapledon of Exeter as an ambassador. On his journey, he crossed into the county of Hainaut to inspect the daughters of Count William of Hainaut. He determined which daughter would be the most suitable as an eventual bride for young Prince Edward. His description was translated in The Register of Walter de Stapledon, Bishop of Exeter, 1307–1326:

The lady whom we saw has not uncomely hair, betwixt blue-black and brown... Her face narrows between the eyes and its lower part is more narrow than her forehead. Her eyes are blackish-brown and deep. Her nose is fairly smooth and even, save that it is somewhat broad at the tip and flattened, and yet it is no snub-nose... Her lips are full, especially the lower lip... Her lower teeth project a little beyond the upper; yet this is but little seen... All her body is well set and unmaimed; and nought is amiss so far as a man may see. Moreover, she is brown of skin all over, much like her father. And she will be of the age of nine years on St. John's day next to come, as her mother said. She is neither too tall nor too short for such an age; she is of fair carriage. The damsel is well taught in all that becometh her rank and highly esteemed and well beloved by her parents and of all her meinie, in so far as we could inquire and learn the truth. In all things, she is pleasant enough, as it seems to us

Growing up in the Low Countries, which was becoming a trading center, Philippa was well versed in finances and diplomacy. Her older sister Margaret succeeded their brother William II, Count of Hainaut, upon his death in battle.

Four years later, in the summer of 1326, Isabella of France, the Queen of England (also known as the She-wolf of France), arrived at the court of Hainaut seeking assistance to depose her husband, Edward II, from the throne. Prince Edward accompanied his mother to Hainaut, where she arranged the betrothal to thirteen-year-old Philippa in exchange for the help she was looking for. Since the Prince and

Philippa were second cousins, a Papal dispensation was necessary and approved by Pope John XXII on September 1327. Philippa arrived in England in December, escorted by her uncle John of Hainaut. They reached London on December 23, where she was greatly received.

Philippa and Edward wed at York Minster on January 24, 1328, eleven months after his accession to the English throne. Unlike many of her predecessors, Philippa did not alienate the English people by bringing foreigners into the court. Her formal coronation was postponed for two years as Isabella did not wish to relinquish her position as queen. On March 4, 1330, Philippa was crowned queen at Westminster Abbey, becoming the first Queen of color. At the time, Philippa was almost six months pregnant, and she gave birth to her first son, Edward, the following June.

It was October 1330. King Edward commenced his rule starting with a coup. He ordered the arrest of the de facto rulers, also known as his mother, Queen Mother Isabella, and her greedy lover, Roger Mortimer, 1st Earl of March. They had acted as his regents. Mortimer was executed for treason, and Queen Dowager Isabella was sent to Castle Rising in Norfolk, where she spent several years under house arrest. She still had privileges, and Isabella's freedom was restored after a few years. Surprisingly this isn't a show on Netflix.

Philippa proved to be the model of a queen. When she didn't have children, she worked tirelessly for the crown. She helped maintain a balance between royal and familial duties. Philippa was much admired in those difficult times. She was widely loved and respected as queen and had a successful marriage with Edward. As the financial demands of the recent Hundred Years' War were enormous, Philippa wisely advised the King to take an interest in the nation's commercial expansion as a different method of covering the expenses. She established the textile industry at Norwich by encouraging Flemish weavers to settle there and promoted the coal industry at Tynedale.

Over time, Phillipa and Edward had twelve children, five daughters and seven sons, of whom only six outlived her, and only four outlived the King. Two of her sons and one of her daughters died in infancy, and three of her children died of the Black Death in 1348. One daughter, Isabella of Woodstock, countess of Bedford and Soissons, lived into adulthood and had children. Their eldest was Edward, known as the Black Prince, who became a renowned military leader.

Philippa traveled with Edward to Scotland and the European continent in his early campaigns of the Hundred Years War. She was celebrated for her gentle nature and compassion, and she served as regent of England during Edward's absence in the War.

It was 1346. Philippa faced a potential Scottish invasion. She gathered the English army and met the Scots in a victorious battle near Neville's Cross. She rallied the English soldiers on horseback before the battle. Her appearance and words helped result in an English victory and the Scottish king being taken prisoner.

She is best remembered for persuading Edward to spare the lives of the Burghers of Calais, whom he had planned to execute as an example to the townspeople. This action helped maintain peace in England throughout Edward's long reign.

Philippa died of an illness on August 15, 1369, in Windsor Castle. Her body was interred at Westminster Abbey with an alabaster effigy by sculptor Jean de Liège. Eight years later, Edward III died and was buried next to her. In her honor, the Queen's College, Oxford was founded by her chaplain Robert de Eglesfield.

Enslaved

Many rose beyond what was "allowed," no matter what they were or were not taught. Many geniuses lost, but a few were able to stand for many.

Doña Marina / La Malinche

b. *circa 1500*   d. *circa 1551/2*
Central America

In the early 1500s, the Spaniards brought Christianity to South America and found it in their hearts to convert the Aztecs. Language barriers were making diplomatic communications between these two nations pretty much impossible. There was also an established society not taking to the conversion well. Captain Hernán Cortés began to find this Christian conversion to be quite tricky.

Doña Marina is the Spanish name given to one of Cortés' new slave girls. She was born in about 1500 to an Aztec Chief who died while she was still a child. Her mother remarried and had a son, which meant that the girl was to be promptly sold to the next group of traders that passed by. She began to enter history in 1522 after eventually becoming slave property of the military chief of the Mexican State of Tabasco. This was when she learned to speak Mayan as a second language, and soon after that, she was given as a valuable gift to Cortés, the leader of the Spanish Conquest.

Because she was both native-born Aztec and property of the Spanish Captain Cortés, she became entrenched in the middle of history. She has two historical names, "Doña Marina," which was given to her by the Spaniards, and "La Malinche" (the Captain's Woman) by the Aztecs. Both names are used today to reference her.

The story goes a little like an unfunny comedy skit; Cortés had an interpreter named Aguilar who spoke Spanish and Mayan. Still, when he went to the outlying Indians that spoke Aztec, he could no longer communicate. But in his possession, Cortés now had Doña Marina, the new girl who spoke Mayan and Aztec, so he started an "interpreter daisy chain." Cortés spoke Spanish to Aguilar, who spoke Mayan to Doña Marina, who relayed in Aztec to the Indians. Then visa versa back to Cortés. We've seen this four-way interpretation chain displayed on *I Love Lucy* episodes, but we are sure it wasn't funny in 1522.

She was a remarkable young woman who quickly learned to speak Spanish as a third language, leaving no need to invite Aguilar to parties. Eventually, her role as mediator between the Spanish and the Aztecs took a more profound meaning when she and Cortés became a family and began having children together. When he first received Malinche from the lord of Pontonchan after defeating them in battle, Cortés gave her to one of his captains, Alonso Hernandez Portocarrero. Later, Cortés took her back when he realized how valuable she was. When he went on an expedition to Honduras In 1524, he convinced her to marry another of his captains, Juan Jaramillo.

It is widely accepted that the children she bore were officially the first Aztec/Spanish-born children on the planet, and the DNA is the beginning of the Mexican race.

The controversy that lives today in the historical accounts of Doña Marina / La Malinche is whether or not she was a villainess, victim, hero, or whore. Dismissing the choices made for her, historical reports paint her as a strong, honorable, kind person who was not a volunteer but an unwilling recruit to her position as mediator. When gold was discovered in the Aztecs' possession, you can be sure that if Cortés couldn't get it from them using negotiations and trade, he would find another way to get it. And if not him, then the next civilized Christian group who heard about the gold would send their military to spread God's love and gather the wealth.

After a disastrous Honduras expedition with Cortés and still married to Juan Jaramillo, Doña Marina faded into obscurity. Almost nothing is known from this time on. Although her earlier fame wasn't something, she sought. Other than her son with Cortes, she had children with Jaramillo. She died fairly young, passing away in her fifties sometime in 1551 or early 1552. Modern historians only know approximately when she died because Martin Cortés mentioned her as alive in a 1551 letter, and a son-in-law referred to her as dead in 1552.

History was going to happen whether the Aztecs wanted it to or not, so bad or good. We leave her reputation up to you. Of this, though, we are sure; that Doña Marina / La Malinche has earned her place in this book.

Tituba

b. *circa* 1665
South America

d. Unknown
Salem, MA, USA

Tituba was originally from an Arawak village in or near the West Indies, although different reports move her birth around South America and the Caribbean. She was captured as a child, taken to Barbados, and sold into slavery. A merchant, Samuel Parris, purchased her when she was between twelve and seventeen years old. Parris was an unmarried merchant, and there is speculation that she may have been his concubine. As often reported, she was not an enslaved African but still a slave.

In 1680 Reverend Parris moved his household to Boston, Massachusetts; this included another enslaved person called Indian John. While in Boston, Parris became a minister, married Elizabeth, and started a family. In 1689 Tituba and John were married, and the families moved to Salem. It is believed that Tituba had only one child, Violet.

Puritan Salem was not the place to be different or an enslaved person, and Tituba was both. She would have been a person of suspicion in this repressed community, no matter what the scare would have been. Elizabeth Parris, the Pastor's wife, had a lot of responsibility but was often ill. Tituba stepped in and ran the house and pretty well raised the three children, Thomas, Betty, and Susannah.

In the evening, Tituba would entertain Betty and her cousin Abigail Williams with fortune-telling games and stories of magic from the Caribbean. These activities were strictly forbidden by Puritan code, and word spread through the neighborhood girls. Soon, several "circle girls" came over for the banned storytelling.

In the winter of 1692, Betty, Abigail, and Ann Putnam began exhibiting odd behavior with twitching, fits, and babbling. Tituba baked a "witch cake" with rye and Betty's urine and fed it to the dog. The dog was believed to be a "familiar" or witch's helper, and by eating the cake would break the spell and reveal the witches. When the girls were pressed to identify their tormenters, they denounced three social outcasts: Sarah Good, a homeless beggar; Sarah Osborne, an elderly woman; and Tituba. Tituba initially denied practicing witchcraft, but Reverend Parris beat her and demanded that she confess. He promised her freedom if she cooperated.

She was examined for three days by the local magistrate, John Hawthorne. Tituba finally confessed to practicing witchcraft and named other witches in the village, which may have saved her life. She was imprisoned but was not put on trial.

From here, the hysteria takes off like a rumor through a high school. Between 1692 and 1693, more than two hundred people were accused, and twenty were hanged. Giles Corey, an eighty-year-old farmer who refused to stand trial after being accused of wizardry, was denied the quicker execution of hanging and was "pressed" to death by stones piled on him one at a time. Five others died in jail, including Dorcus Good, four years old, chained to the prison wall for months. Four dogs were "bad boys" and found guilty. The mania only stopped when the county Magistrate and the respected Reverend Increase Mather intervened and stopped the trials and demanded the release of the prisoners. The trouble was that the prisoners had to pay their incarceration expenses before being released.

Parris did not keep his promises to Tituba and refused to pay the fees to release her. She was confined for thirteen months and was only released when some unknown person paid her fees and then bought her. Tituba moved from Salem. This person may have also bought John because Puritans were not likely to split a married couple.

We lose track of her from this point on. Her daughter Violet stayed with the Parris household until the Reverend died in 1720. The released accused were forever affected by poor health because of the prison condition and questionable reputations. The witch cake never became popularized.

Many theories have been discussed, including PTSD from the recent King Phillip's War, teen angst, and rebellion, except older folks, made accusations too. Mass hysteria does come to the forefront. My favorite is the speculation by Linda Caporeal, a theory about hallucinogenic fungi. It might sound far-fetched, but the fungus ergot can be found in rye and wheat under the right conditions. Hence that kind of witch cake would cause convulsions, hallucinations, and pinching sensations. This fungus is sometimes used to create LSD, which has been known to cause "bewitched" behavior.

Only one girl admitted her behavior; Ann Putnam stood before the church in 1706 and asked for forgiveness.

Mum Bett
aka
Elizabeth Freeman

b. 1748
Claverack, NY, USA

d. December 28, 1829
Stockbridge, MA, USA

Mum Bett entered this world about 1748. She was born into slavery, owned by Peter Hogebooma, who lived in Claverack, New York. Mum was raised and served there until she was thirty-three years old. At this time, around 1781, the American Revolution was raging. Mum and her sister Lizzie were given to Hogebooma's daughter, Hannah, as a wedding gift when she married Colonel John Ashley. Ashley was a well-known judge and patriot. After the wedding, they relocated to Sheffield, Massachusetts.

While working for the Ashley's, Bett would serve at many of Colonel Ashley's political meetings. The local leaders were working on a new Sheffield Declaration, also known as the Sheffield Resolves. This document included a Bill of Rights that stated, "Mankind in a state of nature are equal, free, and independent of each other, and have a right to the undisturbed enjoyment of their lives, their liberty and property." Mum overheard much of the discussion and was moved by the principles of the equalities of man. Later the Sheffield Declaration would be a basis for the new United States Constitution.

As the story goes, Mrs. Ashley became quite angry one day with Mum's sister Lizzie and attacked her with a fiery, hot kitchen shovel. In an effort to save her sister, Mum stepped in front of Lizzie and weathered the blow herself. The attack left a permanent scar on Mum's arm.

Sometime after this occurred, Mum went into town one day and stopped by the office of Theodore Sedgwick, an abolitionist, attorney, and future U.S. Senator. She knew the young lawyer as he was a participant at the political meetings held at the Ashley residence.

This was when Mum asked Sedgwick to sue for her freedom. Even though Mum could not read nor write, she had learned much. Sedgwick asked her why she believed she should be free. In a determined voice, Mum spoke, "By keepin' still and mindin' things." She further went on to explain that she had heard their discussions that all people were born equal, and after thinking long and hard, Mum concluded that she should try "whether she did not come in among them."

Although Sedgwick and Ashley were friends, even though Sedgwick had argued cases before Ashley, he took Mum Bett's case.

In the lawsuit, Sedgwick based the case on two arguments. The first was that there was no law in Massachusetts that established slavery, and secondly,

Toni Kief

even if such a law existed, it would be annulled by the new Constitution. Having asked for and received a trial by jury, they found in her favor after a short deliberation. Mum Bett had won her freedom.

Colonel Ashley appealed the case, but before it could be heard, he dropped the action when the Massachusetts Supreme Court ruled in another case that slavery was unconstitutional in that state.

Now free, Bett changed her name to "Elizabeth Freeman," and continued to work as a domestic and was paid for her labor. She worked for the Sedgwick household for the remainder of her life. In 1785, the family moved to Stockbridge, Massachusetts.

The initiator to overthrow slavery in Massachusetts Elizabeth Freeman died on December 28, 1829. She is buried in the Stockbridge cemetery at the central ring of the plot reserved for the Sedgewick family. Elizabeth is also the only black person to have been buried in the Stockbridge cemetery.

Sojourner Truth

b. 1797
New York, USA

d. November 26, 1883
Michigan, USA

Sojourner Truth was born into slavery as Isabella Baumfree in Swartekill, Ulster County, New York. She was one of the ten or twelve children born to James and Elizabeth Baumfree. Her parents were Africans captured from the Gold Coast in modern-day Ghana. Isabella was sold several times in her youth and married Thomas, arranged by her slaveholder John Dumont of Ulster County, New York. Together they had five children. Her first, Diana (1815), was fathered by Robert, her love from a nearby farm. His master, a Mr. Catlin, forbade the relationship. Her children with Thomas were Thomas, who died shortly after birth, Peter (1821), Elizabeth (1825), and Sophia (1826).

In 1799, New York first began with some abolition legislation. Complete emancipation was finalized on July 4, 1827. Isabella's master, Dumont, promised to grant freedom on July 4, 1826. However, on that date, he changed his mind. Isabella stayed long enough to spin a hundred pounds of wool which she believed satisfied her obligation. She then escaped with her infant daughter, Sophia, leaving behind her other children. The New York emancipation had some fine print, and to gain freedom, the enslaved persons had to serve to their twenties. Isabella later explained: "I did not run off, for I thought that wicked, but I walked off, believing that to be all right."

Isabella was taken in by Isaac and Maria Van Wagener, who settled her remaining one-year service requirement with Dumont for twenty dollars. A year later, New York passed the law to emancipate all enslaved people, but Dumont had already sold her five-year-old son Peter into slavery in Alabama. With the help of the Van Wageners, Isabella sued in court to recover her son. After several months of litigation, she became the first black woman to win such a case against a white man.

Isabella became a devout Christian during her stay with the Van Wageners. In 1829, she accepted a housekeeper's job working for Elijah Pierson, a Christian Evangelist, and moved to New York with her son Peter. She remained with Pierson until 1832 when she accepted a job with "Prophet" Robert Matthews, another preacher.

Shortly after her move, Elijah Pierson died, and Isabella, along with Matthews, was accused of theft and poisoning her former employer. They were acquitted, and Robert Matthews moved west, leaving Isabella in New York. Isabella continued to work as a housekeeper.

Believing that she received instructions from the Holy Spirit, Isabella took the name "Sojourner Truth." Sojourner became a Methodist and traveled as a preacher in honor of her new calling. She joined the Northampton Association of Education and Industry, which supported women's rights and religious tolerance.

In 1849, she came forward and spoke out on abolition and women's suffrage. The same year she started working on her memoir with Olive Gilbert. The following year William Lloyd Garrison privately published her book, *The Narrative of Sojourner Truth: a Northern Slave*. With the income from her speaking engagements and the book, she could purchase a home.

Sojourner spoke at the first National Women's Rights Convention in Worchester, Massachusetts. The organizers invited her back for the Ohio Women's Rights Convention in 1851. This is where Sojourner gave her most celebrated "*Ain't I a Woman*" speech.

The Civil war began on April 12, 1861, and Sojourner Truth helped recruit black troops while raising food and clothing contributions for Union Negro regiments. Near the end of the war, on October 29, 1864, she met with Abraham Lincoln at the White House. Not someone to let discrimination pass unnoted, while in Washington, she challenged the discrimination of the segregated streetcars by riding them to and from work at Freedman's Hospital.

Sojourner died on November 26, 1883, at her home in Battle Creek, Michigan, at the age of eighty-six.

– Ain't I A Woman –

1851

Well, children, where there is so much racket, there must be something out of kilter. I think that 'twixt the negroes of the South and the women at the North, all talking about rights, the white men will be in a fix pretty soon. But what's all this here talking about?

That man over there says that women need to be helped into carriages, and lifted over ditches, and to have the best place everywhere. Nobody ever helps me into carriages, or over mud-puddles, or gives me any best place! And ain't I a woman? Look at me! Look at my arm! I have ploughed and planted, and gathered into barns, and no man could head me! And ain't I a woman? I could work as much and eat as much as a man – when I could get it – and bear the lash as well! And ain't I a woman? I have borne thirteen children, and seen most all sold off to slavery, and when I cried out with my mother's grief, none but Jesus heard me! And ain't I a woman?

Then they talk about this thing in the head; what's this they call it? *[member of audience whispers, "intellect"]* That's it, honey. What's that got to do with women's rights or negroes' rights? If my cup won't hold but a pint, and yours holds a quart, wouldn't you be mean not to let me have my little half measure full?

Then that little man in black there, he says women can't have as much rights as men, 'cause Christ wasn't a woman! Where did your Christ come from? Where did your Christ come from? From God and a woman! Man had nothing to do with Him.

If the first woman God ever made was strong enough to turn the world upside down all alone, these women together ought to be able to turn it back , and get it right side up again! And now they is asking to do it, the men better let them.

Obliged to you for hearing me, and now old Sojourner ain't got nothing more to say.

Harriet Ann Jacobs

b. *February 11, 1813*
Edenton, NC, USA

d. *March 7, 1897*
Washington D.C., USA

Harriet, at one time, was one of the most famous women born into slavery. We have a wealth of her comments about her life in her book, *Incidents in the Life of a Slave Girl*. **Harriet Ann Knox** was born in 1813 in Edenton, North Carolina, to her father, Elijah Knox, owned by Andrew Knox, and Delilah Horniblow, owned by John Horniblow. We actually have a quote from Harriet, "I was born a slave, but I never knew till six years of happy childhood had passed away."

Her father was a skilled carpenter, and he earned enough to allow Harriet and her brother, John, to live with their parents in a comfortable home. Her grandmother, Molly Horniblow, was influential in Harriet's life; she was a confidant who doled out encouraging advice and bits of crackers and sweets for her grandchildren.

At the age of six, Harriet's mother died, and she was sent to live with her mother's owner and mistress, Margaret Horniblow. The family welcomed Harriet and taught her to read, write and sew. Harriet was relatively happy there until Mrs. Horniblow died in 1825. Harriet hoped for emancipation, but instead, she was given to Mrs. Hornblower's three-year-old niece, Mary Matilda, daughter of Dr. James Norcom.

"*...though we were all slaves,*" Harriet wrote, "*I was so fondly shielded that I never dreamed I was a piece of merchandise, trusted to them for safekeeping, and liable to be demanded of them at any moment.*"

Harriet was eleven, and her brother John, who Dr. Norcom had purchased, moved into the physician's household. It was a different welcoming, in Harriet's own words, "*When we entered our new home, we encountered cold looks, cold words, and cold treatment,*" Harriet recalled. "*The degradation, the wrongs, the vices that grow out of slavery are more than I can describe.*"

After Harriet's father's death, the Norcom's residence "*seemed even more dreary than ever.*" Over the years, Dr. Norcom's unwanted sexual advances and his wife's vindictive jealousy made life a torment. "*The secrets of slavery are concealed like those of the Inquisition,*" she wrote. "*My master was, to my knowledge, the father of eleven slaves. But did the mothers dare to tell who was the father of their children? Did the other slaves dare to allude to it, except in whispers among themselves? No indeed? They knew too well the terrible consequences.*"

Dr. Norcom forbade Harriet from marrying a free black carpenter. Later, Harriet entered a liaison with Samuel Tredwell Sawyer, an unmarried white lawyer and future U.S. Congressman. Before the birth of her first child, Harriet moved to her grandmother's home, where Dr. Norcom continued to pursue her throughout the years. Harriet repeatedly refused to become his mistress, so he banished her to his son's plantation.

Her union with Samuel Tredwell Sawyer produced two children, Joseph in 1829 and Louisa Matilda in 1833. Once she learned that her children would join her as plantation slaves. No matter her partner's position, he did her no favors. This was when Harriet plotted her escape. She was convinced that if she left, the children would remain with her grandmother, avoiding the brutalities of slavery. *"Whatever slavery might do to me,"* she wrote, *"it could not shackle my children. If I fell a sacrifice, my little ones were saved."*

Harriet went into hiding, first with friends and later at her grandmother's. She stayed in a small space above a storeroom. It measured about nine feet long and seven feet wide, and the highest point was just three feet. As she hid from her captors, she wrote, *"At times, I was stupefied and listless; at other times I became very impatient to know when these dark years would end, and I should again be allowed to feel the sunshine, and breathe the pure air."*

Her children were unaware of her presence, but Harriet could hear and occasionally observe Joseph and Louisa Matilda as they grew. *"Season after season, year after year, I peeped at my children's faces and heard their sweet voices, with a heart yearning all the while to say, 'Your mother is here.'"*

In her personal " prison, "she remained hidden for nearly seven years, with no room to stand or move."

Finally, there was an opportunity to escape. Her partner, and the children's father, Samuel Tredwell Sawyer, stepped up. He purchased the children and Harriet's brother John, and he promised they would be freed. When Louisa Matilda was seven years old, he made arrangements for her to move north and stay with a family in New York City.

"For the last time, I went up to my nook. Its desolate appearance no longer chilled me, for the light of hope had risen in my soul." In 1842, with the help of a friend, Harriet boarded a boat in Edenton harbor bound for Philadelphia. Once there, she caught a train, moved to New York, and reunited with her daughter and brother. A year later, her son, Joseph, joined the family now in Boston.

Harriet traveled between New York and Boston to connect with her family. She had a job as a nursemaid for the family of Nathanial Parker Willis. Even though Harriet was miles away from Edenton, Dr. Norcom didn't give up and continued in his efforts to re-enslave her. Harriet's employer Mrs. Cornelia Willis was an anti-slavery sympathizer. Mrs. Willis arranged to purchase Harriet and free her.

"My heart was exceedingly full," wrote Harriet. *"I remembered how my poor father had tried to buy me when I was a small child and how he had been disappointed. I hoped his spirit was rejoicing over me now. I remembered how my good old grandmother had laid up her earnings to purchase me in later years and how often her plans had been frustrated."*

For a while, Harriet and her brother worked in Rochester, N.Y., in the Anti-Slavery Office and Reading Room, where they became acquainted with Frederick Douglass, Amy Post, and other abolitionists. *"It is painful for me, in many ways, to recall the dreary years I passed in bondage. I would gladly forget them if I could."* With Amy's encouragement, Harriet began writing about her experiences in 1853.

Failing in her attempts to have the book published, she had it "printed for the author" in 1861. *Incidents in the Life of a Slave Girl* was published in 1861 under the pseudonym Linda Brent. The British edition, *The Deeper Wrong*, was published the following year. During most of the 1860s, Harriet performed relief work, first nursing black troops and teaching, and later, she teamed with Louisa Matilda, aiding freedmen in Washington, D.C., Savannah, Ga., and Edenton. Harriet then opened a boarding house in Cambridge, Massachusetts.

In some following years, Harriet and her daughter moved to Washington, D.C., where Louisa Matilda organized the National Association of Colored Women meetings.

On March 7, 1897, Harriet died in Washington and was buried next to her brother in Mount Auburn Cemetery, Cambridge, Massachusetts.

Mary Fields

b. 1832
West Virginia, USA

d. December 5, 1914
Montana, USA

African American women were active on the American Frontier, but little is written to study them. **Mary Fields** was born into slavery in 1832 or 1833; her exact birthday is unknown. Mary's birthplace and other details about her early childhood are also missing. What is known is that she worked for the Warner family in West Virginia in the years leading up to the Civil War.

Mary was emancipated in 1863 or shortly after the Emancipation Proclamation was signed. She wasted little time and left West Virginia and the Warner's, and she headed north by way of the Mississippi River. In her travels, Mary obtained several jobs on some of the steamboats. It appears she disembarked at Toledo, Ohio. This is where Mary gained employment at the Ursuline Convent of the Sacred Heart. Mary was assigned to the laundry and soon bought supplies, managed the kitchen, and maintained the gardens and grounds.

Mary was known to lose her temper and was quick to yell at anyone who stepped on the grass after she had cut it. It would appear that Mary's gruff nature didn't fit into the serene calm that was the convent.

It is unclear why Mary left Toledo, other than ticking off nuns. There is some suggestion that she moved to take care of Mother Amadeus Dunne, Mother Superior, in Toledo. Some records take their friendship back to the Warner family in West Virginia, though this claim is not substantiated.

We find her next at Saint Peter's Mission near Cascade, Montana, where Mother Amadeus Dunne was serving. She again took on many tasks for this new convent. Mary was dismissed from the mission due to crass behavior, unruly temper, and penchant for drinking and smoking in saloons with men. The final straw appears to be when Mary and the mission janitor got into an argument that progressed to them both drawing guns. While neither ever fired, this incident was enough to make the area's Bishop demand the nuns relieve Mary of her duties. I'm curious why either one of them would be packing heat to work in a religious mission.

She moved into town and tried to open a couple of eateries and a laundry service, but they failed. In 1895, Mary was in her early sixties, and she obtained a contract from the United States Post Office Department to be a Star Route Carrier. She became an independent contractor who used a stagecoach to deliver the mail. Mary was the first African American woman and the second woman to receive a Star Route contract from the Post Office. This contract was secured with the help of the Ursuline nuns.

Mary's reputation of being no-nonsense and fearless was a perfect fit for a mail carrier. She earned her name "Stagecoach Mary" due to her mode of postal transportation. Mary needed to protect the mail and the stagecoach passengers simultaneously. The threats weren't limited to bandits but also wild animals and the extreme weather of Montana. During this time, she was known to carry both a rifle and a revolver.

Mary spent eight years delivering the mail as a Star Route Carrier. During this time, Mary gained the respect and affection of the locals of the Cascade, Montana community. They honored her fearlessness and generosity and topped it off with a salute for her sincere kindness to children. Mary retired from being a Star Route Carrier in the early 20th century. After her retirement, Mary settled into life in Cascade, Montana. With no pension and social security was nonexistent, Mary opened a laundry and babysat local children.

Mary drank and wore men's clothing at times, smoked, and carried guns. Yet, in death, she has become this powerhouse woman. Mary Fields died on December 5, 1914. After her death, the townspeople raised money to have her buried in a cemetery on the road she frequently drove that linked Cascade to the mission. Mary's funeral was said to be one of the largest in town.

Johana July

b. 1857
Mexico

d. January 8, 1942
Texas, USA

Johana July, a black Seminole Native American, was born around 1857 in Nacimiento de Los Negros, the settlement established in northern Mexico following the emigration of Indian and black Seminoles from the Indian Territory in 1849.

The Spanish strategy for their claim to Florida initially forced the local indigenous tribes into a mission system. The Natives in this plan were to serve as a militia to protect the colony from the neighboring British in South Carolina. However, the biggest enemy was a combination of raids by the South Carolinians and bingo – the European diseases. Florida's native population was quickly decimated. The Spanish authorities then encouraged the indigenous tribes and runaway slaves to move into their Floridian territory.

As early as 1689, enslaved Africans fled from the South Carolina Lowcountry to Spanish Florida, seeking freedom. These were people who gradually formed what has become known as the Gullah culture of the coastal Southeast. King Charles II of Spain, in 1693, offered the fugitives liberty in exchange for defending the Spanish settlers at St. Augustine.

Around 1870, the U.S. Army was desperate for translators and scouts familiar with the border with Mexico. They chose some of the black Seminoles. The July family took this opportunity and settled near Eagle Pass, Texas, in 1871.

Johanna was a spunky girl remembered as tall and barefoot. She wore bright homespun dresses, with her hair in thick braids and long gold earrings. Her horsemanship was her pride. After her father died and her brother took off, it was one of the only ways she could earn a living. Her daring nature led her to become a horse breaker. Johanna rejected the saddle and rode bareback sideways with no bridle. She simply draped a rope around the horse's neck and looped it over their nose.

As a girl, Johanna wasn't required to do a woman's work about the home. Her mother always had the meals ready for her, and her clothes were washed. Her job was to work the livestock and train horses. She was able to take over her father's duties for the U.S. Army and area ranchers.

Being practically forced into the job, Johana tamed the horses for soldiers from the nearby Fort Duncan by riding. Her system was to ride the wild horses and mules into the Rio Grande River. As the horse tired from swimming, she would grab the mane and gently mount. The horses, nervous at being in the water, were worn out and finally grateful to be ridden to dry land again. They tended to obey Johana after that.

Near the age of eighteen, Johanna married a Seminole scout named Lesley. She knew nothing of housekeeping, sewing, or cooking; you know, woman's work. Her life had been outside in the barn and fields. She could judge a horse's age, endurance, and speed, she knew where the eagles nested and the coyote kept her whelps. She could find the dark pools where the yellow cat fed in the Rio Grande, but that wasn't what Lesley expected when they moved to Fort Clark away from the Rio Grande and her horses.

However, as hard as she tried to be a dutiful wife, there were days when she attempted to sew and the thread knotted, the material was cut wrong, and the whole garment wouldn't fit. She scorched the beans and rice, got the stew too dry, and forgot to put the corn to soak. Her husband came in with harsh words and a brutal fist. It was contrary to the kindness and sharing she had known. Johanna became more of a prisoner, utterly contrary to the life she knew.

The encounters with her husband continued to escalate. Johanna wasn't one to endure the unendurable, and one night, she quietly slipped away from the house. She crept to a neighbor's field where a workhorse was kept. Since there was no rope, she cut strips into strings, and she wove a rope as she rode away. Once at her mother's home, Johanna stayed. She never returned to Leslie, even though he came after her several times. He even shot at her and tried to lasso and tie her. Guess he didn't mind the lousy cooking as much as he claimed.

Life changed little for Johanna as she aged. After the death of Leslie, she married two more times, and the last time was on February 16, 1909. That marriage was with Charles Lasley, and they ran a successful business raising cattle, breaking horses, and selling hides. Charles died in 1925.

In 1928 Johanna filed for a U. S. military pension as Lesley's widow. They had never really divorced, and the pension record listed her as "Jhonar Lasley." Johana explained that she received a little money from his military pension, which may explain why she gave her name as Johana July to the WPA interviewer. However, a WPA photograph lists her name as "Johanna Lesley, ex-slave, Brackettville."

Johana lived the rest of her days on Rufford Street in Brackettville, Texas, next to her granddaughter. So, there must have been a child or two, and I hope they brought her food with that cooking thing. Family members recall her as that old lady who rode side-saddle and went barefoot around the house. On January 18, 1942, Johanna died and was laid to rest in the Seminole Cemetery, now called the Seminole Indian Scouts Cemetery, the burial location for a large portion of the Black Seminole Scouts, their families, and descendants in Brackettville, Texas.

Explorers

Some escaped the kitchen and society's expectations to wander the world, and in some cases – more than the world.

Aud Ketilsdatter
or
Unnur Ketilsdóttir
aka
Aud the Deep-Minded

b. 834   *d. 900*
Møre og Romsdal, Norway   *Dala, Iceland*

Aud (Unn) Ketilsdatter also known as "Deep-Minded Queen Of Dublin," "Unn Deep-Minded," "The Deep-Minded." Aud was born to a military family of Møre og Romsdal, Norway. She was the second daughter of Ketill Flatnose Bjornsson and Ingveldur Ketilsdóttir. Her father was a great military leader and sometimes referred to as a king. There is almost nothing I could find about her childhood besides having five brothers and sisters. This Norwegian family fled a tyrannical King and moved to the Scottish Hebrides. Soon after, they were part of a raid on Ireland.

    Near this time, Aud was married off to Ólafur "Hvíti (The White)" Ingjaldsson, the King of Dublin. Together they had a son, Thorstein the Red. Olafur died due to questionable circumstances and maybe some disloyalty. Aud wasn't accused.

Rather than marry again, she took her son, Thorstein, to the Hebrides and was instrumental in building him into a leadership position in Scotland. Thorstein married and had six daughters and one son while becoming a great warrior king. He conquered large parts of northern Scotland before dying in battle due to betrayal by his people.

After learning of her son's death, Aud wasn't someone to sit and mourn; she commissioned the construction of a knarr – a Viking-era ship often used for ocean travel. For unknown reasons, the vessel was built secretly in the forest, but since her husband's and son's deaths had betrayal elements, probably a good choice. After its completion, she gathered family, a large crew and added some previous captives. One of the many sagas reported Aud announcing, "I mark the tide, we sail away at night unseen from Gills Bay. No matter what the old laws say, I am the Captain." Apparently, everyone agreed as they set sail for Orkney.

Once they landed, Aud arranged the marriage of one of her granddaughters, Groa, the daughter of Thorstein the Red. Then they pulled up anchor and sailed again to the area of Breiðafjörður in Iceland. She still had a crew of twenty Vikings. Once they landed, she had gained respect proving herself capable, independent, and strong-willed.

Twenty men were under her command – crew and prisoners from Viking raids near and around the British Isles. Per her promise, Aud gave these men their freedom once they were in Iceland. Aud dismissed the usual class divisions between enslaved and free. She announced that each had all the rights of a freeborn man. She also issued land to farm so they could survive.

When Aud arrived in the western region of Iceland, she claimed all the land in Dalasýsla between the rivers Dagverdara and Skraumuhlaupsa for her family. No mention was found if anyone had claimed the land before. As a single woman, Aud was unlike other early Icelandic settlers, and she settled in what became known as Hvamm, Breidafjord, Iceland. Her reasons for making the voyage are not known today; we can imagine what we wish. Conflicting theories have emerged over the centuries, but none can be proven. The stories came from folktales and sagas that evolved through the centuries. In an age dominated by men, Aud ruled as a clan chief, settling disputes, granting favors, and throwing celebrated feasts.

In later poetry and sagas, it was stated or sung that Aud was a baptized Christian and credited with bringing Christianity to Iceland. She was reported to have erected crosses where she could pray on a prominent hill within her lands, now known as Krossholar (Krosshólaborg).

Near 900 CE, there was a great three-day wedding festival. The story from the *Landnamabok* (The Book of Secrets) says she declared the celebration should continue for three more days, "This will be my funeral feast." She died that night, sitting up against pillows.

Aud, the Deep-Minded, was given a full Viking Ship funeral, the only recorded woman ever to be honored in this way. She was one of the first great Viking matriarchs and the 9th century settler prominent in the history of the settlement of Iceland.

Due to the history being borne from songs and folk tales and not records available, there is a suggestion. Aud was the mother of one or five children, and in one report, she bore one more child sixty-six years after her Viking funeral. Aud died in Hvammi, Dala, Iceland, 900 C.E.

Jeanne Baret

b. *July 27, 1740*
Autun, France

d. *August 5, 1807*
Saint-Aulaye, France

Jeanne Baret was the first woman to circumnavigate the globe. Jeanne was born to a farming family on July 27, 1740. Her parents were Jean and Jeanne Baret. So, everyone in the house would come running when Jean was called out. Her father was probably a day laborer who helped with farming and harvesting. It is probable his work and the nature around her were what sparked her interest in plants.

She was relatively young when she became an herbalist, and she certainly gained training from other women in the close-knit community. Despite no formal education, Jeanne developed a strong knowledge of botany. She was recognized as an "herb woman" and healer due to her intelligence and depth of knowledge on the healing properties of local flora. She would have also dispensed medical advice to the local villagers as an herb woman, which was common in those years. It is proposed that Jeanne taught scientists about plants in the area. Step one to building the pharmacy industry.

Some years later, Jeanne gained employment as a housekeeper to Philibert Commerson. He was educated in medicine, natural history, and botany.

Commerson had moved close to Jeanne's hometown to collect and study plants. Due to their shared knowledge and interests, they became close friends.

When Commerson's wife died in 1762, their relationship changed. They began to live together and had a child out of wedlock in 1764. This was when they moved to Paris and gave up the baby for adoption. Jeanne continued as a housekeeper and eventually a nurse for Commerson.

In 1765, Louis-Antoine de Bougainville, a French admiral and explorer, was tasked to discover new territories for France. Bougainville invited Commerson to join him as his botanist. Commerson insisted that his assistant, Jeanne, accompany them, but the French Navy did not allow women onboard ships.

In order to accompany them, Jeanne dressed as a boy and adopted the name "Jean" Baret. She/he was hired to work as Commerson's assistant. Two ships, the Boudeuse and the Etoile, pulled anchor in 1766 for the journey, and Jeanne was aboard the Étoile.

Their goal was to sail around the world. Stop one in this massive journey was in Montevideo, Uruguay. Commerson and Jeanne collected plant samples and observed the surrounding environment. At this part of the trip, Commerson became sick, and Jean took over most of the work. After Montevideo, they sailed on to Rio de Janeiro, Brazil. The team was to perform the same exploration and study of the local flora. It is stated that Jeanne discovered a strange new flowering vine adorned with bright pink and purple flowers. Jeanne named the new plant Bougainvillea after the leader of the expedition.

They sailed around the Strait of Magellan at the tip of South America. The Etoile reached Tahiti nearly a year later, in 1767. They were awed by the beauty of the island (travelers still are) and the inhabitants. Jeanne successfully hid her true identity by staying very private and defensive until arriving in Tahiti. Historians don't know the actual story of how this occurred. One account reports that the Tahitian natives quickly noticed her gender when she went ashore, so when she returned to the Étoile, she confessed.

Jean/Jeanne continued on the ship from Tahiti to New Ireland, now Papua, New Guinea. She recognized that staying aboard was sometimes dangerous because some of the crew members wanted their own proof of her sex. Jeanne went ashore and was attacked while studying shells. After this, Jeanne rarely went ashore.

In 1768, the ship stopped in Mauritius, an island in the Indian Ocean, to restock supplies. When the Etoile and Boudeuse were ready to turn home to France, Jeanne and Commerson decided to remain on Mauritius.

Jeanne and Commerson stayed on Mauritius as guests of Pierre Poivre, the governor of the island. Jeanne continued to serve as Commerson's housekeeper and nurse until he died in 1773. At some point, she met a French soldier named Jean Dubernat; they double Jeaned and married in May 1774.

They were able to catch a ship late in 1774 and returned to France. When she stepped ashore in France, Jeanne completed her circumnavigation around the world. They moved to Saint-Aulaye, Dubernat's hometown, where she remained until her death, August 5, 1807, at the age of sixty-seven.

Jeanne Baret is seldom recognized for her achievement as the first woman to circumnavigate the world. We must acknowledge her work and collections of exotic plants that are still valued today. Jeanne didn't record her experiences during the voyage, but several crew members kept logs. Due to their record-keeping, we learned what she dealt with, especially when she revealed her true identity. Bougainville and Commerson detailed much of what she accomplished. In one translation of Commerson's notes, he credits Jeanne as the first female to circle the world. He continued to say she should be honored for her accomplishments, knowledge of the plants, and other specimens she collected. With the money she had accumulated, she settled with Dubernat in his native village of Saint-Aulaye, Dordogne, where they bought property.

She married the French officer Jean Dubernat on May 17, 1774. In 1775 the couple returned to France, which finalized her circumnavigation eight years after it began. In 1785, Baret was granted a pension of two hundred livres a year by the Ministry of Marine. The document was granting her this pension makes clear she was honored for her accomplishments.

Jeanne Baret Duernat passed away at the age of sixty-seven in Saint-Aulaye, France, on August 5, 1807.

Many of the specimens she and Commerson gathered remain in the French National Herbarium at the Muséum National d'Histoire Naturelle. In 2012, a species of nightshade was named after Baret, the Solanium baretiae.

Mary Henrietta Kingsley

b. October 13. 1862　　　　d. June 3, 1900
Cambridge, England　Cape Town, South Africa

Mary Henrietta Kingsley was a British explorer who made pioneering trips to West and Central Africa. She was the first European to enter some remote parts of Gabon.

Mary Kingsley was born in Cambridge, England, on October 13, 1862. She was taught to read at home, but she never had a formal education. She stayed home and cared for her invalid mother until her mother and father died in 1892. At that time, Mary was thirty years old. After their passing, Mary decided to complete her father's studies on religious fetishes. This decision was when Mary's adventurous life began. Her first trip was to the Canary Islands.

Although a woman traveling alone was almost unheard of at this time in history, she did not let this deter her. Once she returned from the Canary Islands, she quickly scheduled a trip to Africa to continue her research on religion.

In August 1893, Mary left Britain on a cargo ship with a Captain Murray bound for West Africa. They sailed along the coast from Freetown, Sierra Leone, to Luanda, Angola. After several months, she turned inland from Guinea to what is now called Nigeria.

Mary collected insects and fresh-water fish specimens for the British Museum. Mary didn't hold back and continued to explore the lower Congo River.

It wasn't long after returning to England she booked another trip on the Batanga, also commanded by Captain Murray. She left Liverpool, England, on December 23, 1894. This cruise wasn't like the cruises we have now, but they first went to the Canary Islands and then Sierra Leone, where they changed course and traveled to Gabon in West Africa. Once there, she took a steamboat and then a canoe up the Ogowé (now the Ogooué) River.

Mary paid for her trip by trading British cloth for ivory and rubber. She was the first European to visit some of the remote parts of Gabon and the French Congo. Mary proceeded to go see the Fang tribe. The Fangs had a bad reputation for fierceness and cannibalism. Mary wasn't devoured, and on the next leg of the journey, she climbed the southeast face of Mt. Cameroon, the tallest mountain in West Africa.

After returning to England in 1895, Mary wrote *Travels in West Africa* (published in 1897). There was some dispute with her book, as Mary voiced her opposition to many of the European practices in Africa and her compassion for the African natives. Needless to say, this wasn't a selling point in England.

It was 1899 when Mary returned to Africa. The Boer War was raging between Great Britain and the Afrikaner Republic of South Africa. Mary started working as a journalist and a nurse in Simon's Town, South Africa. Her nursing duties were for the Boer prisoners of war. Her book West African Studies came from this visit and was published in 1899.

After contributing her nursing services for about two months, she developed symptoms of typhoid and died on 3 June 1900. She was thirty-eight years old.

An eyewitness reported: *"She rallied for a short time but realized she was going. She asked to be left to die alone, saying Mary did not wish anyone to see her in her weakness. Animals,"* she said, *"went away to die alone."*

Due to her wishes, Mary was buried at sea. She was accorded honor as a party of West Yorkshires collected her coffin from the hospital and placed it on a gun carriage transporting her to the pier. She was loaded onto Torpedo Boat No. 29 and put to sea as it rounded Cape Point. Once her coffin was dropped, it wouldn't sink, much like Mary herself. The casket was pulled aboard. weighted with an anchor and returned to the sea.

Gertrude Bell

b. July 14, 1868
Durham, England

d. July 12, 1926
Baghdad, Iraq

We could characterize **Gertrude Bell** as the female Laurence of Arabia ("Florence of Arabia," if you will). But that doesn't do her justice. Unlike T. E. Laurence, now better remembered looking like Peter O'Toole in movies and adventure stories. "Miss Bell" remains a well-remembered figure in the country she helped create: Iraq.

Gertrude Margaret Lowthian Bell was born on July 14, 1868, in Durham, England. Her grandfather, Sir Isaac Lowthian Bell, was a member of Parliament who worked alongside Prime Minister Benjamin Disraeli. She grew up in a wealthy family in Redcar, a Yorkshire town. Her father, Sir Thomas Hugh Bell, was a businessman and industrialist. Her mother, Mary, died while giving birth to her younger brother Maurice in 1871.

When her father remarried, she was still young, which expanded her family, adding a half-brother and two half-sisters. Gertrude went on to attend Oxford University, where she studied history. She was no slouch in her studies and graduated with the first first-class modern history degree the university had ever awarded to a woman. Gertrude proceeded to travel the world – twice.

Shortly after graduation, she traveled to Tehran, Iran, where her uncle, Sir Frank Lascelles, served as British minister. This trip sparked her interest in the Middle East, where she would focus much of her energy for the remainder of her life.

Gertrude returned home and taught herself archeology, French, German, Arabic, and Persian. In 1899, she returned to the Middle East and visited Palestine and Syria, touching off a period of sustained travel including Asia and Europe. She was a renowned mountaineer in her spare time. Her writings on her experiences across the globe informed British audiences about the distant parts of their empire.

Gertrude's works published during the two decades preceding World War I include *Safar Nameh* (1894), *Poems from the Divan of Hafiz* (1897), *The Desert and the Sown* (1907), *The Thousand and One Churches* (1909), and *Amurath to Amurath* (1911). She also maintained a vast correspondence during this period, eventually compiled and published in 1927. In her travels to the Middle East, she met with some of the most influential leaders.

During World War I, Gertrude initially worked with the Red Cross in France. Her connections and knowledge made her an invaluable recruit to British intelligence, and she joined the British intelligence unit in Cairo, Egypt, known as the Arab Bureau. She collaborated with the famous British traveler T.E. Lawrence and worked to forge alliances with Arab tribes.

After the British forces captured Baghdad in 1917, Gertrude became involved in the political reinvention of Mesopotamia. She helped colonial authorities install ruler Faisal I as monarch of Iraq. Due to her fluency in Arabic and Persian, Gertrude was key in assisting the British diplomats and local rulers in constructing a stable government. She was the only woman present at the 1921 Conference in Cairo, convened by Winston Churchill to determine the new state's boundaries. Gertrude mapped the borders of what would become Iraq.

Gertrude remained in Baghdad after Faisal's 1921 ascension. She worked to fund and construct an archaeological museum. She pioneered the idea of retaining antiquities in the country of origin rather than transporting them to European learning centers. The result of her work resulted in the National Museum of Iraq, which held one of the world's most significant collections of Mesopotamian antiquities. The museum collections were damaged in the aftermath of the 2003 invasion of Iraq by the United States.

Days before the government was inaugurated and her project was complete, Gertrude was found dead from an overdose of sleeping pills – whether accidental or intentional. She had suffered from pleurisy and repeated bouts of malaria. Her health was further undermined by stress and overwork as the prolific author of books, articles, political correspondence, and intelligence reports. She was never married. In the last months of her life, she was grieving the loss of her younger brother.

She died from an overdose of sleeping pills in her Baghdad home, just two days short of her fifty-eighth birthday. Known and respected as "Al Khatoun" by the Iraqis, her funeral and subsequent burial were widely attended. One of her Iraqi colleagues once told her that the people of Baghdad would talk of her for a hundred years, to which she responded: "I think they very likely will." By accounts, for better or worse, they have. Her body was interred at the British Cemetery of Baghdad, Baghdad, Iraq.

Osa Johnson

b. *March 14, 1894*
Chanute, KS, USA

d. *January 7, 1953*
New York, NY, USA

Osa Helen Leighty was born March 14, 1894, to Ruby (Holman) Leighty and William Leighty in Chanute, Kansas, USA. Not much on her early years besides attending Chanute High School. She eloped in 1910 at the age of sixteen with adventurer and photographer Martin Johnson, ten years her senior. It was stunning to make such an exciting match at that age. The couple spent the next three years traveling across Canada, the United States, and Europe playing the vaudeville circuit. Martin was the lecturer and exhibited photographs he had taken in the South Seas when he accompanied Jack London on his voyage of the Snark. Osa was a part of the show, dancing and singing Hawaiian songs.

By 1912 they had accumulated enough money so they could travel to the South Sea islands. Together they made a motion picture record of cannibal and head-hunting tribesmen, which set the stage for their life. They alternated lengthy photographic trips into the field with lecture and exhibition tours at home. They made motion picture records of wildlife for the American Museum of Natural History and gathered much valuable geographic and ethnological information.

In 1917, the honeymoon was over, and they traveled to the Solomon Islands. The first stop was the island of Malaita, and they spent a month visiting several villages. They filmed Solomon's ceremonies and customs on the island of Launguia in the Ontong Java Atoll.

The next stop was New Hebrides, where they visited Vao, Espiritu Santo, and Malekula. This was where they came in contact with the local tribe known as the Big Nambas and their chief, Nagapate. This meeting ended up being a problematic encounter not at all pleasant. Osa and Martin had to run for their lives, barely escaping as they ran through the miles of mountains and rainforest.

The film footage they captured was used to create the silent film *Among the Cannibal Isles of the South Pacific*, a sixteen minute documentary released in 1918. Not to settle down, in 1919, the Johnsons returned to the New Hebrides, this time with an armed escort. They started in Vao, then to Malekula, and filmed the Big Nambas again. They continued to Tomman and Espiritu Santo returning home with twenty-five thousand feet of film and a thousand photographs.

In February 1920, the Johnsons went to North Borneo and sailed up the Kinabatangan River. They captured film and photos of water buffalo, orangutans, elephants, and other wildlife. This collection was turned into the full-length feature *Jungle Adventures* in 1921.

They turned their attention to Africa later in the same year. They started in Kenya, where they worked to document wildlife and nature in areas where human interaction had not yet disturbed things. When they arrived home, they had produced a hundred thousand feet of film, which was produced into the motion picture *Trailing African Wild Animals*.

Martin Johnson was the principal photographer in the field and developed the blind, making it possible to record without being seen. Osa took to hunting and became a crack shot. Osa became the guard, hunter, and pilot. The Johnsons went on multiple African safaris and expeditions between 1923 and 1935, leading to magazine articles and films. On the fifth African trip, from 1933 to 1934, they flew the length of Africa while filming aerial scenes of large herds of elephants, giraffes, and other animals moving across the plains. At the suggestion of game warden Blaney Percival, the couple set off to explore an uncharted lake in the north. On their journey, they passed Mount Kenya, rising majestically out of the plains, and photographed their first rhinos and lions. Against all odds, the Johnsons found the lake. They observed a massive variety of animals at the water's edge. "It's paradise," Osa remarked while standing on a hilltop. And so the lake received its name. After pitching camp, they set to work. The Johnsons stayed at Lake Paradise for three months, during which they shot thousands of feet of film. When their financial resources were exhausted, the couple returned to Nairobi.

They were the first pilots to fly over and film Mount Kenya, and this footage was used in the 1935 feature film *Baboona*.

Osa was fond of living at Mount Marsabit in northern Kenya near Paradise Lake. She could translate the communication between the natives and the film crews, which gave her an advantage when producing films like Martin's *Safari* and *Simba: King of the Beasts*.

Things didn't always go perfectly, other than being chased by cannibals. Because of Osa's health, the Johnsons' stay in Africa was cut short, and they returned to America. After she left the hospital, the couple undertook a series of speaking engagements. Disaster struck on January 13, 1937. On a return flight from an engagement in Salt Lake City, Utah, the Western Air Express plane they were traveling on crashed near Los Angeles. Martin was killed, Osa suffered a back injury and a broken leg, and eleven others were also injured. Osa continued with his work and produced the film *Jungles Calling* in 1938 as a tribute to Martin.

She continued with her expeditions and signed a contract with Darryl Zanuck at Twentieth Century Fox in 1939. Osa led an expedition and filmed the safari scenes for the film *Stanley and Livingstone*. The *Los Angeles Times* described her as the first woman to take responsibility for an African Expedition. *I Married Adventure*, her autobiography, was the best-selling non-fiction book in 1940. (*Note:* I read it in 1965, and the only book I have ever read more than once and still think of it.)

She has already proved she wasn't one to sit still. It was 1952 when the TV series *The Big Game Hunt* began, the first wildlife Television series.

Their motion pictures, which were highly successful in commercial distribution, included *Jungle Adventures* (1921), *Head Hunters of the South Seas* (1922), *Trailing African Wild Animals* (1923), *Simba, the King of Beasts* (1928), *Across the World* (1930), *Wonders of the Congo* (1931), *Congorilla* (1932), *Baboona* (1935), and *Borneo* (1937), along with numerous short features. They also collaborated on several books: *Cannibal-Land* (1922), *Camera Trails in Africa* (1924), *Lion* (1929), *Congorilla* (1931), and *Over African Jungles* (1935). Osa Johnson wrote *Jungle Babies* (1930) and *Jungle Pets* (1932).

Osa took some crafting time and designed a line of accurately detailed animal toys for the National Wildlife Federation.

In 1953 Osa Leighty Johnson died in New York of a heart attack at the age of fifty-eight. The Martin and Osa Johnson Safari Museum, located in Kansas, opened in 1961 and is still in operation today. She inspired and collaborated on fourteen feature films, thirty-seven educational short films, eleven books, and many lectures with her husband, Martin. They are buried side by side at Elmwood Cemetery, Chanute, Neosho County, Kansas, USA.

Valentina Tereshkova

b. *March 6, 1937*
Bolshove Maslennikovo, Russia

Valentina Vladimirovna Tereshkova was born on March 6, 1937, in the Bolshoye Maslennikovo, a village on the Volga River northeast of Moscow. Her parents had migrated from Belarus. She was the second of three children born to Vladimir Tereshkova and Elena Fyodorovna Tereshkova. When she was two years old, her father was killed fighting in World War II.

After her father's death, her mother moved the family to Yaroslavl, seeking better employment opportunities, and gained employment at the Krasny Perekop cotton mill. Valentina began school when she was eight or ten years old. In her teens, Valentina scored a job in the same textile mill in 1954. She continued her education through correspondence courses and graduated from the Light Industry Technical School in 1960.

During the late 1950s and 1960s, the Space Race between the United States and the Soviet Union escalated for space travel supremacy. The competitiveness between the two nations for "one-upping" achievements was (still is) fierce, and the Soviets were determined to be the first to send a woman into space.

Valentina became interested in parachuting and trained in skydiving at the local Aeroclub, making her first jump at twenty-two. Still employed in the textile factory, she kept it a secret from her family as she trained as a competitive parachutist. At the same time, Valentina joined the local Komsomol (Communist Youth League) in Yaroslavl and served as the organization's secretary in 1960 and 1961. She became a member of the Communist Party in 1962.

After Yuri Gagarin became the first man in space in 1961, Tereshkova volunteered for the Soviet space program. Although she did not have any experience as a pilot, she was accepted into the program because of her 126 parachute jumps. At the time, cosmonauts had to parachute from their capsules seconds before they hit the ground.

Four women were chosen to become cosmonauts, but only Valentina was sent into space. On June 16, 1963, Vostok 6 was launched, with Valentina aboard. It is reported she called out as the craft took off, "Hey sky, take off your hat. I'm on my way!" (in Russian, it is Эй, небо, сними шляпу. Я иду). She made forty-eight trips around the earth in 70.8 hours – just under three days. (By comparison, Yuri Gagarin was the first earthling in space, and he orbited the earth once, and the four American astronauts who flew before Tereshkova orbited a total of thirty-six times.) While circling, Valentina spoke with Soviet leader Nikita Khrushchev, who said, "Valentina, I am very happy and proud that a girl from the Soviet Union is the first woman to fly into space and to operate such cutting-edge equipment."

At the same time, Valery F. Bykovsky had been launched two days earlier in Vostok 5; both landed on June 19. She parachuted from the craft to earth from twenty thousand feet when she returned from the voyage. According to the RT news channel, an error in the spacecraft's automatic navigation software caused the ship to move away from Earth. Valentina noticed this, and Soviet scientists quickly developed a new landing algorithm. She landed safely but received a bruise on her face.

Once on land in the Altay region near today's Kazakhstan-Mongolia-China border, villagers helped Tereshkova out of her spacesuit and asked her to join them for dinner. She accepted and was later reprimanded for violating the rules and not undergoing medical tests first. Valentina was awarded the title of Hero of the Soviet Union.

On November 3, 1963, Tereshkova married Andrian Nikolayev, a cosmonaut. On June 8, 1964, their daughter, Yelena Adrianovna Nikolayeva, was born and was a subject of medical interest because she was the first child born to parents who had both been exposed to space. Yelena later became a medical doctor and is still the only child that both parents had made that trip.

Valentina graduated with distinction from the Zhukovsky Military Air Academy in 1969. She became a prominent member of the Communist Party and represented the USSR at numerous international events, including the United Nations conference for the International Women's Year in 1975. She led the

Soviet Committee for Women from 1968 to 1987, was pictured on postage stamps, and had a crater on the moon named after her. Valentina and Nikolayev divorced in 1980.

In 2007, Vladimir Putin invited Valentina to celebrate her seventieth birthday. At the time, she said, "If I had money, I would enjoy flying to Mars." In 2015, her spacecraft, Vostov 6, was displayed as part of an exhibit at the Science Museum in London called "Cosmonauts: Birth of the Space Age." Valentina attended the opening and spoke lovingly about her spacecraft, calling it "my lovely one" and "my best and most beautiful friend – my best and most beautiful man."

Despite the success of her flight, it was nineteen years before another woman (Svetlana Savitskaya, also from the USSR) made the flight. The first American woman to go to space was Sally Ride in 1983.

Valentina has been in hot water since with Putin, as she spoke out against changing the constitution to allow him to remain in office.

"Once you've been in space, you appreciate how small and fragile the Earth is." – Valentina Tereshkova.

Innovators

NOTE: Women and Patents

On May 5, 1809, Mary Kies became the first woman to receive a patent in the United States for weaving straw with silk. Many innovations and inventions by women existed before this time, but the laws made it illegal for women to own property and obtain patents. This led some women to apply for patents in their husbands' names if they decided to apply at all. Eli Whitney assisted a couple with their application, and I question some of his claims.

As recently as 2016, only 10% of U.S. patent holders were women, even though women account for half of the doctoral degrees in science and engineering. This disparity is partly due to the U.S. Patent and Trademark Office being more stringent and often rejecting patents with women as sole applicants. Further, when patents sought by women are approved, they often have added parameters that make the description of the patents far more detailed. These revisions tend to lower the scope of the patent, making it weaker and less valuable. Even in the modern era, women are still pioneers in their fields. Though women's patent holders have increased fivefold from 1977 to 2016, there's still a long way to go before women are fairly represented in their fields.

Since women sometimes used their first and/or middle initials when signing documents, it is unknown how many women inventors there have been.

Lady Elizabeth Wilbraham

b. *February 14, 1632*   d. *July 27, 1705*
Weston-under-Lizard, England

Elizabeth Mytton was born on Valentine's Day, February 14, 1632, to Thomas Mytton and Cecilia (Skeffington) Mytton in Weston-under-Lizard, England. Elizabeth was born into a wealthy family, but little is known about her private life and youth. At the age of nineteen, she married Thomas Wilbraham, the heir to the Baronetcy of Wilbraham. The new couple went on an extended honeymoon and traveled throughout Europe. Besides the romance of marrying a Baron, she used this opportunity to study architecture.

While they visited the Netherlands, Lady Elizabeth met architect Pieter Post. He was the creator of the Dutch baroque style of architecture. Additionally, she studied the works of Palladio in Veneto, Italy, and the Stadtresidenz at Landshut, Germany. Her husband fully supported his new wife's zeal for architecture. Due to her social position in the aristocracy, along with being the wife and not the husband, meant that she could never openly lay claim to her designs. This has shrouded her proper place in history. Lady Elizabeth is reported to be one of the best architects in history.

After fifty years of research, historian John Millar dubbed her the United Kingdom's first female architect. A woman couldn't pursue a profession up to and during the 17th century. Millar stated she designed more than a dozen houses for her family, demonstrating her distinctive and unusual design details. Lady Elizabeth was a prominent designer of grand houses of the era, even though women weren't allowed to do so.

Although there is no written record, and her name isn't on any of the cornerstones, John Millar went on to say that Lady Elizabeth designed around four hundred buildings. Some of these are Belton House (Lincolnshire), Uppark House (Sussex), and Windsor Guildhall (Berkshire). One building she is credited to have built was her own Staffordshire family home. Weston Hall is another project that confirms her style, an estate with unusual architectural details. Cliveden House (Buckinghamshire) and Buckingham Palace also reflect her work.

It is suggested that Lady Elizabeth had worked as a tutor to a young Sir Christopher Wren and helped him design eighteen of the fifty-two London churches that he worked on following the 1666 Great Fire of London. It appears that he may be credited with several of Elizabeth's projects.

Women could not pursue any career in 17th century Britain other than housekeeper, prostitute, or tutor, so if Wilbraham had designed any of Britain's public buildings, she could not take credit for them. It is theorized that Lady Elizabeth would have appointed male architects to supervise the construction of her buildings. This makes it challenging to picture her architectural accomplishments and influence accurately. Lady Elizabeth wasn't allowed on the construction sites, so she would send men to carry out her designs. These men were often perceived as the architects and stayed silent about her participation.

Lady Elizabeth designed the layout of Mayfair, St James's and designed the grand houses, churches, and buildings where the newly fashionable tea salons were held. The early Bluestocking Salons were initially held in Mayfair by another of Mayfair's Restoration doyens, Margaret Cavendish – the Duchess of Newcastle in her Mayfair house in the 1660s.

One positive of not supervising the construction work is that Lady Elizabeth was incredibly productive, averaging eight projects a year. She and the Baron had three daughters, Elizabeth, Margaret, and Grace. In 2008 some private letters were discovered and passed to the Staffordshire Record Office. These showed that Lady Elizabeth was searching for suitable husbands for her daughters. According to the marketing executive of the Weston Park Foundation, "The letters explain the importance of a suitable match within the aristocracy of the day. She was certainly a powerful lady and knew what she wanted and how to get it."

Even though women were barred from serving as architects, the word had spread through the extremely important patrons of architecture throughout the

Early Modern period. Like Catherine and Marie de' Medici, Queens commissioned chateaux, chapels, and churches to represent their various roles and positions. Those who had the funds saw architecture as a way to memorialize their families and themselves in stone. Many of these structures, like the buildings overseen by Lady Elizabeth, still stand today. This sounds like a fantastic tour.

Lady Elizabeth Mytton-Wilbraham died July 27, 1705, at the age of seventy-three in Weston-under-Lizard, South Staffordshire Borough, Staffordshire, England. She is buried at St Andrew Church, Weston-under-Lizard, South Staffordshire Borough, Staffordshire, England.

Tabitha Babbitt

b. December 9, 1779   d. December 10, 1853
Massachusetts, USA

Sarah Tabitha Babbitt was born in Hardwick, Massachusetts, on December 9, 1779, the daughter of Seth and Elizabeth Babbitt. She was a weaver, and on August 12, 1793, she joined the Shakers at the Harvard Shaker community in Massachusetts.

Molly Edmonds' article in *How Stuff Works* explains that around 1810, Tabitha watched two men cutting wood with a two-handled pit saw. She believed that they were wasting too much energy on the achieved result. This observation set Tabitha to think, and she came up with a new type of saw. Her saw didn't need two men, nor did it waste so much energy. Tabitha attached a circular blade to her spinning wheel, and voila was the prototype for the first circular saw. The proposed round blade increased efficiency. Then she took it another step, and the circular saw was connected to a water-powered machine.

The first circular saw she allegedly made is in Albany, New York. In the summer of 1948, a version of Babbitt's saw, built to her specifications, was on display at a Shaker exhibit at Fenimore House in Cooperstown, NY, as a loan from the New York State Museum.

Saws of all kinds, particularly the circular saw, are used daily to cut wood on construction sites. It might seem strange that a woman had the wherewithal and means to develop it, but to the Shaker community, it wasn't strange at all. The Shakers, at the time, were led by a woman named Ann Lee, a blacksmith's daughter who sought a more personal religion than the Church of England. The Society was comprised of people who had left the original Quaker faith. They were known to embrace equality and not patent innovations so that all could use them.

At that time in history, women could not obtain patents, and they would have to turn to men to accomplish that task. Because Tabitha did not patent her circular saw, her invention's reference exists only in Shaker lore. There is controversy over whether she was the actual first inventor of the saw. She also improved the spinning wheel head used to make the yarn. Tabitha designed a doubleheader that allows women to spin twice as much yarn in a short time.

Additionally, Tabitha contributed to the invention of cutting multiple nails from a sheet of iron instead of forging each nail individually. Eventually, it is believed that she was amid her work of making false teeth at the time of her death. The Shakers have given credit to Eli Whitney for the nails, and it has been suggested that he obtained the patent for the Cotton Gin on behalf of Caroline Greene and two unnamed enslaved people for the cotton gin production.

Others claimed the invention. Two French men patented the circular saw in the United States after reading about Babbitt's saw in Shaker papers. According to her religious beliefs, Tabitha did not even try to patent any of her inventions.

She died on January 1, 1853; she was seventy-three years old. Tabitha Babbitt is buried at the Shaker Burying Ground, Harvard, Worcester County, Massachusetts, USA.

I believe in Tabitha.

Sarah E. Goode

b. 1855
Toledo, OH, USA

d. April 8, 1905
Chicago, IL USA

Sarah Elisabeth Jacobs was born in 1855 in Toledo, Ohio. She was the second of seven children of Oliver and Harriet Jacobs. Oliver Jacobs, a native of Indiana, was a carpenter. Sarah was enslaved from birth and received her freedom at the end of the Civil War. After the war, Sarah moved to Chicago, Illinois. Her husband, Archibald Goode, was a carpenter, and together they built a furniture store. Archibald described himself as a "stair builder" and an upholsterer. They had six children; only three would live to adulthood.

Sarah was the second African American woman to receive a U.S. patent. Patent #322,177 was issued on July 14, 1885. The first known African-American woman to receive a patent was Judy W. Reed on September 23, 1884, for her "Dough Kneader and Roller."

Many of the Goodes' customers were working-class and lived in small, limited apartments. Due to the cramped space, Sarah designed a foldable bed. So, her inspiration came from the needs of her community and challenging times.

Sarah designed a cabinet bed that helped people utilize their minimal space. It was an entirely usable desk with storage, and when unfolded, it became a full-size bed. Her innovation made it possible for people to have a bed for the night and still utilize the space as a roll-top desk, complete with compartments for stationery and other writing supplies during the day.

Sarah Goode died in Chicago in 1905 from an unknown cause; she was fifty. Sarah is buried in Graceland Cemetery, Chicago, Illinois.

In 2012, the Sarah E. Goode STEM Academy (formerly known as Southwest Area High School project), a science and math-focused high school, was opened in her honor on the south side of Chicago.

Mary Anderson

b. *February 19, 1866*
Birmingham, AL, USA

d. *June 27, 1953*
Monteagle, TN, USA

On February 19, 1866, **Mary Anderson** was born to John C. and Rebecca Anderson on Burton Hill Plantation in Greene County, Alabama. Her father died in 1870, and the young family was able to survive on the proceeds of John's estate. In 1889, Rebecca and her two daughters moved to Birmingham and built the Fairmont Apartments on Highland Avenue soon after their arrival.

In 1893, Mary left home to start a cattle ranch and vineyard in Fresno, California. She returned in 1898 to help care for an ailing aunt, and the two of them moved into the Fairmont Apartments with her mother, her sister Fannie, and her husband. Mary's aunt brought an enormous trunk with her, which contained a collection of gold and jewelry. When it was finally opened, the windfall allowed the family to live comfortably from that point forward.

In the thick of winter of 1903, Mary took some of the inheritance from her aunt and took a trip to New York City. While there, the weather was deep into winter, and Mary was having a difficult time sightseeing. She noticed the driver of the trolley car she was riding on was having a severe problem.

Mary noticed that drivers would reach through the side window every few minutes to wipe the snow and sleet off the windshield by hand. There were times when they would have to stick their heads out the window while driving, trying to see. Forgetting about the sights around her, Mary pondered how to resolve this issue. Then inspiration struck. Once she returned home, Mary drew what seemed to be a practical solution. She designed a blade to connect itself to the vehicle's interior, allowing the driver to operate the windshield wiper from inside. She applied for a patent on June 18, 1903.

On November 10, 1903, Mary Anderson was awarded U.S. Patent #743,801 for her "window cleaning device for electric cars and other vehicles to remove snow, ice, or sleet from the window." However, Mary was unable to get anyone to bite on her idea. All the corporations she approached turned her wiper down out of a perceived lack of demand. They all rejected her invention, and it took time for the men in charge to recognize the value of her vision. Initially, they stated it would be too much of a distraction.

Discouraged, Mary stopped pushing the product, and after the contracted seventeen years, her patent expired in 1920. Though mechanical windshield wipers were standard equipment in passenger cars around 1913, Mary never profited from the invention. By this time, the prevalence of automobiles (and, therefore, the demand for windshield wipers) had skyrocketed. Mary removed herself, allowing corporations and other business-people access to her original conception.

In the early 20th century, very few people outside of the major metropolitan areas owned cars, and they didn't go fast enough to need windshields, let alone wipers. Mary Anderson was ahead of her time, and her invention was forgotten until her patent lapsed and others could copy her idea.

Little is known about Mary after this. Mary, her sister Fannie, and their mother were again living in the Fairmont Apartments in Birmingham. She died at their summer home in Monteagle, Tennessee, on June 27, 1953. Mary Anderson was inducted into the National Inventors Hall of Fame in 2011.

The windshield wiper, May Anderson's legacy, was adapted for automotive use. In 1922, Cadillac began installing the wiper as a piece of standard equipment on its cars, just two years after her patent expired. By the 1940s and 1950s, when cars were much more common and affordable, windshield wipers were standard, and they're now a legal requirement. Heck, today, they even have a washer and multiple speeds.

I'm due for new blades and will announce at Jiffy Lube that they are being bought to honor Mary Anderson. Thank you, Mary.

Beulah Louise Henry

b. *September 28, 1887* d. *February 1, 1973*
Raleigh, NC, USA *New York, NY, USA*

Beulah Louise Henry was born in Raleigh, North Carolina, on September 28, 1887. She was the daughter of Walter R. and Beulah Henry. Additionally, Beulah was the granddaughter of former North Carolina Governor W. W. Holden and a direct descendant of President Benjamin Harrison and Patrick Henry. Beulah loved painting and music and was creative. She may have had mild Synesthesia, a condition where the mind will assign sensory attributes to other senses, for instance, associating colors with sounds. This is a condition that has been found in some artistic and creative people.

Young Beulah had a habit of pointing out things that she saw that were wrong and imagined improvements. One of her first ideas was a mechanical hat tipper that would automatically tip a man's hat when greeting someone. By the time she was nine years old, she was already drawing sketches of inventions.

From 1909 to 1912, she attended North Carolina Presbyterian College and Elizabeth College in Charlotte, North Carolina, where she submitted her first applications for patents for her inventions. At the age of twenty-five, in 1912, her first patent was granted for a vacuum ice cream freezer. This device made ice cream that didn't require constant cranking like earlier manual ice cream makers. Speeding up the making of ice cream is enough to put her on this list.

Beulah never married, and in 1924, she moved to New York City. She lived in New York hotels and joined a variety of scientific societies. One of her more prominent inventions was a "snap-on" parasol, which would allow women to change their parasol's pattern to match their outfits without needing to buy an entirely new umbrella. This innovation was highly successful, which was the beginning of the Henry Umbrella and Parasol Company. Later, she founded B.L. Henry Company, which financed her well enough she could carry on with her other innovations.

Beulah worked as an inventor for the Nicholas Machine Works from 1939 to 1955. Additionally, she served as a consultant for many companies that manufactured her inventions, including the Mergenthaler Linotype Company and the International Doll Company.

Beulah's creations did not always follow the same theme or category, unique from most inventors. One focus Beulah had in terms of innovations was improving women's lives. For instance, she invented a hair curler, vanity case, and a rubber sponge soap holder.

Beulah also delved into the market of children's toys, not limited to her inventing a new method for stuffing dolls. Beulah devised a way to inflate lifelike dolls and toys with rubber tubing, which immensely reduced the toys' weight as a substitute for traditional, heavy stuffing.

Her most famous invention is the "Double Chain Stitch Sewing Machine." She wanted to make a sewing machine that could eliminate the problem of tangled thread. Bobbins were used and had to be rewound and broke frequently; she saw this problem and put some thought into it. Her ideas moved to action, and Beulah's invention would double the existing sewing machines' speed and allow the user to use smaller thread. The resulting stitch was also just as strong as the previous method. This innovation permitted sewists and tailors to improve production by eliminating time spent fixing and untangling threads and messing with bobbins. Although it has been adapted for modern times, this invention is still used. It is primarily used in factories as it is faster than the typical sewing machine and breaks less often.

Another one of Beulah's inventions, patented in 1936, was the "Protograph." The device made four typewritten copies of documents at a time without carbon paper. She soon added the "continuously-attached envelopes" to aid in mass mailings.

Beulah didn't have an engineering education but had an incredibly creative mind. Beulah could not be restricted by what was then technically possible and could focus on what could be. She claimed that the design would often come to her fully formed in her head. Because Beulah didn't have engineering skills training, she sometimes used others to build her products. Beulah used things she could find around her home, such as soap, clips, and buttons, and went from there. If the engineers told her it couldn't be done, she would school them with available supplies.

A partial list of Beulah's inventions includes:
- Vacuum ice cream freezer (1912) US 1037762
- Umbrella with a variety of different colored snap-on cloth covers (1924)
- First bobbinless sewing machine (1940)
- "Protograph" – worked with a manual typewriter to make 4 copies of a document (1932)
- "Continuously-attached Envelopes" for mass mailings (1952)
- "Dolly Dips" soap-filled sponges for children (1929)
- "Miss Illusion" doll with eyes that could change color and close (1935)
- Hair Curler (1925)
- Parasol Bag (1925)
- Umbrella Runner Shield Attachment (1926)
- Water-Sport Apparatus (1927)
- Poodle-Dog Doll (1927)
- Ball Covering (1927)
- Foot Covering (1927)
- Sealing Device for Inflatable Doll Bodies (1929)
- Valve For Inflatable Articles (1929)

- Henry Closure Construction (1930)
- Henry Valve for Inflatable Articles (1931)
- Duplicating Device for Typewriting Machines (1932)
- Duplicating Attachment for Typewriters (1932)
- Writing Machine (1936)
- Multicopy Attachment for Typewriters (1936)
- Movable Eye Structure for figure Toys (1935)
- Double Chain Stitch Sewing Machine (1936)
- Feeding and Aligning Device (1940)
- Seam and Method of Forming Seams (1941)
- Sewing Apparatus (1941)
- Typewriting Machine (1941)
- Device for Producing Articulate Sounds (1941)
- Duplex Sound Producer (1944)
- Continuously Attached Envelopes (1952)
- Can Opener (1956)
- Direct and Return Mailing Envelope (1962)

Beulah Louise Henry was often called "Lady Edison." She remained active in the Audubon Society, the League for Animals, and the Museum of Natural History. She lived a busy life till the very end and died on February 1, 1973.

Beulah Louise Henry was inducted into the National Inventors Hall of Fame in 2006.

Dr. Patricia E. Bath

b. November 4, 1942
Harlem, NY, USA

d. May 30, 2019
San Francisco, CA, USA

Patricia E. Bath was born on November 4, 1942, in Harlem, New York. Her father, Rupert, was a Trinidadian immigrant and the first black motorman in the New York City subway system. Her mother, Gladys, was a descendant of enslaved Africans and Cherokee Native Americans; she worked as a domestic. Patricia attended Julia Ward Howe Junior High School and Charles Evans Hughes High School.

In 1959, this dynamo, Patricia, received a grant from the National Science Foundation to attend the Summer Institute in Biomedical Science at Yeshiva University in New York. She started working on a project studying the relationship between cancer, nutrition, and stress. Patricia graduated from Hunter College in New York City with a B.S. degree in chemistry. She moved on to Howard University Medical School, and Patricia graduated with an M.D. degree with honors. She earned the Edwin J. Watson Prize for Outstanding Student in Ophthalmology.

In 1970 Patricia was the first African American resident in ophthalmology at New York University's School of Medicine. How she had time to date, I don't know, but she married Beny Primm in 1972 and gave

234   * more than a footnote

birth to her daughter. In 1973, Patricia began as an assistant surgeon at Sydenham Hospital, Flower and Fifth Avenue Hospital, and Metropolitan Surgical Hospital.

In 1974, Patricia completed a fellowship in corneal and keratoprosthesis surgery. Next year, Patricia relocated to Los Angeles, California, and became the first African American woman surgeon at the University of California.

In her downtime, Patricia co-founded the American Institute for the Prevention of Blindness, claiming, "eyesight is a basic human right."

Her invention of the Laserphaco Probe instigated her trip to Berlin University in Germany. While there, Patricia expanded her innovative laser technology. As a result, she developed and tested a model for a laser instrument to be used in cataract treatment. By 1983, Patricia worked to create and chaired the Ophthalmology Residency Training program at UCLA-Drew.

To no one's surprise, Patricia received a patent for her invention on May 17, 1988, and became the first African American female doctor to receive a patent for a medical invention. She continued to work at UCLA and Drew University during the development of her laser cataract removal instrument, and, in 1983, she developed and chaired an ophthalmology residency training program. She wasn't finished with firsts for women, and Patricia continued with her work and firsts in education and training programs.

Patricia was inducted into the International Women in Medicine Hall of Fame in 2001. She now holds five patents in the United States. Three are related to the Laserphaco Probe. In 2000, she was granted a patent for the use of pulsed ultrasound to remove cataracts, and in 2003 she combined the laser and ultrasound technologies to remove cataracts for another patent.

Thanks to Patricia and her tireless education and research with the laserphaco probe, she has improved in using lasers to remove cataracts. Patricia continued to strengthen her discoveries and is responsible for restoring vision for many, some of whom had lost sight decades before.

On May 30, 2019, Dr. Patricia Bath died at a University of California, San Francisco medical center from cancer-related complications, aged seventy-six. As we age, most of us will owe her a salute of gratitude.

Dr. Shirley Ann Jackson

b. August 5, 1946
Washington DC, USA

Shirley Ann Jackson was born on August 5, 1946, in Washington, D.C., to George Hiter Jackson and Beatrice Cosby Jackson. When she was young, her mother would read aloud the biography of Benjamin Banneker, an African American scientist and mathematician who helped build Washington, D.C. It wasn't just her mom; her father encouraged her interest in science and helped with projects for school.

The Space Race of the late 1950s impacted Shirley as a child, spurring her interest in a scientific investigation. Shirley attended Roosevelt High School in Washington, D.C., where she took accelerated math and science classes. When Shirley graduated as valedictorian in 1964, the assistant principal for boys at the high school encouraged her to apply to the Massachusetts Institute of Technology (MIT). She became one of the first African American students to attend MIT, and she was one of the only two women there.

In 1973, Shirley graduated with a Ph.D. degree in theoretical elementary particle physics, the first woman to do so in MIT's history. Her thesis was entitled The Study of a Multiperipheral Model with Continued Cross-Channel Unitarit. She had worked

Toni Kief

with James Young, the first African American tenured full professor in the physics department at MIT. In 1975, her thesis was published in the Annals of Physics.

After graduation, Shirley was hired as a research associate in theoretical physics at Fermilab (Fermi National Accelerator Laboratory). While there, Shirley studied medium to large subatomic particles, and she focused on hadrons, a subatomic particle with a strong nuclear force.

In 1974, after two years with the Fermilab, Shirley became a visiting science associate at the European Organization for Nuclear Research in Switzerland. This was where she worked on theories of strongly interacting elementary particles. In 1975 upon her return to Fermilab, Shirley was elected to the MIT Corporation's Board of Trustees.

What next? In 1976, Shirley went to work on the technical staff for AT&T-Bell Telephone laboratories. She focused on the electronic properties of ceramic materials in hopes that they could act as superconductors of electric currents.

While at Bell, Shirley met the physicist Morris A. Washington. They both had impressive resumes, and as busy as they were, they both needed to work at Bell. They went on to marry and have one son, Alan, who is now a Dartmouth College alumnus, That same year, she was appointed professor of physics at Rutgers University. In 1980, Jackson became the president of the National Society of Black Physicists, and in 1985, she began serving as a member of the New Jersey Commission on Science and Technology.

Shirley continued to serve as a professor at Rutgers while working for AT&T Bell Laboratories in Murray Hill, New Jersey. In 1995, President Bill Clinton appointed Shirley to serve as Chairman of the US Nuclear Regulatory Commission (NRC), a double first, becoming the first woman and first African American to hold that position. She had "ultimate authority" for all NRC functions pertaining to an emergency involving licensees of the NRC. While serving on the commission, she established the International Nuclear Regulators Association, and Shirley served as the chair from 1997 to 1999. This association consisted of senior nuclear regulatory officials from Canada, France, Germany, and Spain.

On July 1, 1999, Shirley became the eighteenth president of Rensselaer Polytechnic Institute, another first for her sex and race. Since her appointment, she has helped raise over a billion dollars in donations for philanthropic causes. While there, Shirley oversaw a significant capital improvement campaign, including constructing an Experimental Media and Performing Arts Center and the East Campus Athletic Village.

In the 21st century, it was April 26, 2006, the faculty of RPI (including several retirees) voted 155 to 149 against a vote of no-confidence in Dr. Shirley. It was the fall of 2007 when the Rensselaer Board of Trustees suspended the faculty senate, thus prompting a strong reaction from the community that resulted in various protests, including a "teach-in."

In its 2009 review of the decade 1999–2009, McClatchy Newspapers reported Shirley as the highest-paid currently sitting college president in the US, with a 2008 salary of approximately 1.6 million dollars. Mom and Pop must be very proud.

On December 4-5, 2009, Shirley celebrated her tenth year at RPI with an extravagant "Celebration Weekend," which featured tribute concerts by Aretha Franklin and Joshua Bell, among other events.

In June 2010, it was announced that the Rensselaer Board of Trustees unanimously voted to extend Shirley to a ten year contract renewal, which she accepted.

A 2015 Time Magazine article cited her as the highest-paid college president, who "took home a base salary of $945,000 plus another $276,474 in bonuses, $31,874 in nontaxable benefits, and $5.8 million in deferred compensation…." In the fall of 2018, another contract extension was approved by the board of trustees through the end of June 2022.

According to the Times Union, published on June 25, 2021, "For years, she has drawn criticism from civil liberty groups who say her administration works overtime to quell dissent and free speech among students and faculty. In recent years, her administration moved to take control of the school's student-run student union and hired police officers to film students protesting in order to identify them for disciplinary action. The Foundation for Individual Rights in Education, a Philadelphia-based nonprofit group promoting civil liberties on college campuses, even included RPI on its list of ten worst campuses for freedom of expression".

On June 25, 2021, Jackson publicly announced she would be stepping down from her post as president on July 1, 2022. Apparently, her 401k was sufficiently funded.

In February 2020, Shirley joined the Nature Conservancy Global Board. She will be serving on this board till October 2029. Board Chair Tom Tierney says, "To successfully take on the most pressing environmental challenges facing us, TNC needs people with ambition and big ideas."

Dr. Shirley Jackson remains an advocate for women and minorities in the sciences and now nature. Despite her incredible achievements, there have also been difficulties. She brought needed attention to the "Quiet Crisis" of America's predicted inability to innovate in the face of a looming scientific workforce shortage. She remains a driving force in America and the world.

Maybe a Pope

Reduced to gossip.

Joanna Papissa
aka
Joannes Anglicus

b. *855*
Germany

d. *857*
Vatican City

Placed comfortably at the intersection of history, gossip, and myth, a woman exposed stood alone. A Millennium has passed, and her legend still burns with the extraordinary intelligence that drove her to infamy and an unplanned life path.

Born in Germany, **Agnes** was always different from the other girls, and she never seemed to fit within her gender. During the Y1K's, there was no opportunity for a girl's education. Her father supplied her earliest tutoring, and when he had no more to give, she dressed as a boy to continue with school. Agnes craved the company of books and academia.

Mastering Greek, Latin, and liberal arts in record time, she became the paramour of a most learned man from Athens. He encouraged her, and she amazed him in return. As they traveled, she would thrive with every new experience. In Europe, only the Catholic Church offered elite education, so the academic and his young student moved to Rome.

Centuries have passed, and there remains a story that she became a monk just to follow her teacher. Agnes was proficient with a wide diversity of knowledge and was unequaled in school. There was no shame in her charade; it was only a necessary inconvenience for a life of learning. Soon she was working with the Catholic hierarchy and was considered a most celebrated master teacher.

John Anglicus, aka John VIII, aka Pope Joan of Germany, was elected Pope for two years, seven months, and four days, and the last day was a wild ride. On Via Sacra, Rome, a pregnancy was exposed as she stopped a procession and delivered a son. Instead of declaring a miracle, stones were thrown figuratively and literally. Was she dragged through the street by the horse she rode on and then buried at the site? Does she rest at St. Peters? That legend was fueled for years as a marble bust of a female Pope was on display. Later it was recarved to look like Pope Zachary the Thrifty. I like to believe the forgiving church fathers sent her into seclusion to think about what she had done and raise her son. Much of Catholic history doesn't support that hopeful theory.

As soon as her sex was exposed, her hard work and accomplishments were relegated to the evil arts, so abhorrent the thought of a brilliant-successful woman. The papal community still denies her over a thousand years later.

Joan shook up the power structure of the most influential organized religion. On some level, the dung chair used by Popes in certain ceremonies for a private masculine confirmation affords some satisfaction. There are books, movies, and a musical in her name for a woman claimed to have never existed. With an ongoing fear of feminine power in the modern era, I can't help but wonder how many ladies have donned britches for life uncommon.

Medicine

Throughout history, women have always been healers. They discovered the healing herbs, cultivated them, and produced the medicines. They were not only healers but also pharmacists, midwives, and counselors traveling from village to village. They were at the battles, treating and bandaging wounds. Before any recorded history, they passed on their knowledge and compassion to others. The beginning of recorded history and the women practicing the science began around 3500 B.C.E., probably even earlier. When Queen Puabi of Ur's grave was investigated, surgical instruments were discovered with the ancient belief that she would be able to practice surgery in the afterlife. The priestesses of Isis in ancient Egypt were physician-healers.

Women's practice of medicine has been true since the very beginning, and modern times have often diminished their skills and practice, sometimes called wise women, other times witches. We must thank you for our survival. We will honor a very few of them now.

Dr. Agnodice

*4th century B.C.E.
Athens, Greece*

In my searches, **Agnodice** is listed as the first female physician to gain an official practice. Due to the healers, we survived to the point of recorded history. Since day two, we all know that women have been herbalists, midwives, and healers. She was the first gynecologist in the history of medicine that could set up an approved office and hire a receptionist.

Deep into the 4th century B.C. in Athens, Greece, Agnodice was appalled by the number of maternal and perinatal mortalities in the city. This was a time in Athens that women couldn't practice medicine, and the ones who did practice midwifery were called evil or witches by the boys in charge. So, Agnodice took action. She dressed in men's clothes, cut her hair, and set out for Alexandria and medical school. These were the pre-student loan days.

She studied medicine under Herophilus, a Greek physician. Once her studies were complete, Agnodice returned to Athens, hung up her diploma, and started to practice what she had learned. There was a day Agnodice met her first female patient who was already in labor. Dr. Agnodice offered to help with the delivery, and the woman declined. It was apparent that Agnodice appeared to be a man. (Which proves one of the big whys that midwives were established). Men physicians were not to touch women in certain areas. This was when Agnodice removed her clothing and revealed that she, too, was a woman. The woman immediately agreed.

Word spread, and this began her attending women regularly. Some other doctors became suspicious, as they knew very well that women seldom sought care during pregnancy and delivery from a doctor. There was an exception as they sought Agnodice, and the doctor community wasn't in on the secret.

So, whispers around the Parthenon spread that Agnodice was a seducer and corruptor of women. When the PMA (Parthenon Medical Association – I made that up) took action and sought legal assistance.

Our doctor was called to the hill where the highest governmental council was held and, later, a judicial court practiced Areopagus. Now the phrase "the hill you chose to die on" makes sense. She was to stand trial for their suspicions.

How would she prove her innocence?

Agnodice removed her clothing and showed the court that she was a woman. Her accusers, who had bought the charges, were outraged. She had broken the Athenian no-girls-allowed law by practicing medicine as a woman.

She was sentenced to death!

The women of Athens learned of this injustice and stormed into the court and defended Agnodice. It was recorded that they stated, "You are not husbands, but enemies because you condemn her who discovered safety for us."

The Athenians changed the law. From that time on, women were allowed to legally study and practice midwifery in Athens.

Historically there has been a dispute on the story of Agnodice. The first theory is that there were no midwives before Agnodice, which is impossible. The second proposes that earlier midwives were forbidden by law from legally practicing. It has been suggested that doctors were trying to take over the practice due to the potential income from offering herbs for birth control and abortions.

There is no date of birth or death known for Agnodice, so her story continues.

NOTE:
If we go way back, we have to look at Metrodora, a Greek physician, sometime around 200-400 CE, shortly after Agnodice's time. She was the author of the oldest medical book written by a woman, On the Diseases and Cures of Women. The book was referenced frequently by other medical writers during ancient Greek and Roman times and was used in Medieval Europe. Metrodora is known to be the first female medical writer and was influenced by the works of Hippocrates, a prominent Greek physician (460-370 B.C).

Susan La Flesche Picotte

b. June 17, 1865   d. September 17, 1915
Omaha Native Reservation, Nebraska USA

Susan La Flesche was born June 17, 1865, on Nebraska's Omaha reservation to Chief Iron Eye (Joseph La Flesche) and his wife, One Woman (Mary Gale). Her parents were culturally Omaha with European and Indigenous ancestry and had lived for a time beyond the reservation's borders. Susan was the youngest of four girls, including her sisters Susette (1854–1903), Rosalie (1861–1900), and Marguerite (1862–1945). Susan's older half-brother Francis La Flesche, born in 1857 to her father's second wife, became renowned as an ethnologist, anthropologist, and musicologist (or ethnomusicologist), who focused on the Omaha and Osage cultures.

After a trip to Washington D.C. in the 1830s, Chief Iron Eyes announced to his people, "There is a coming flood which will soon reach us, and I advise you to prepare for it." He believed his children's survival depended on education from this time on. He was not limited to the traditional and insisted on Euro-American education. As Susan grew, she learned the traditions of her heritage, but her parents believed some of the traditional rituals could be detrimental in the white world. As a result, Susan, the youngest daughter, was not given a traditional Omaha name, and they prevented traditional tattoos across her forehead. Susan spoke Omaha with her parents (especially her mother, who knew English and Spanish but refused to speak them). Her father and oldest sister Susette encouraged her to speak English with the sisters to improve her fluency in both languages.

When still young, Susan watched a Native woman suffering while waiting for the doctor. A call had been made multiple times, and he never arrived. The woman died the next day. Later Susan wrote of the experience, "I saw the need of my people for a good physician." The woman's death not only changed a girl but also the tribe.

Her early education was at the mission school on the reservation. It was run first by the Presbyterians and then by the Quakers. After President Ulysses S. Grant's "Peace Policy" in 1869, the school became a boarding school. The intent was to teach Native children the practices of European Americans and assimilate them into white society. The truth about many of the reservation schools is now coming out.

After several years at the mission school, Susan left the reservation for Elizabeth, New Jersey. She studied at the Elizabeth Institute for two and a half years before returning home in 1882. She began to teach at the agency school.

After a couple of years, Susan left to study at the Hampton Institute in Hampton, Virginia. Originally, Hampton Institute was established as a historically black college after the American Civil War. By 1884 it had become a destination for Native American students. Susan's sister Marguerite, her stepbrother Caryl, and ten other Omaha children attended at the same time. The girls were taught "housewifery" skills, and the boys were taught vocational skills. Susan pushed past the standard requirements and graduated on May 20, 1886. She was class salutatorian and awarded the Demorest prize, which is awarded to the graduating senior who receives the highest examination scores during the junior year.

Like the times, female graduates of the Hampton Institute were encouraged to teach or return to their reservations and become Christian wives and mothers. Susan chose another option and applied to medical school. It was common for women to be the healers in Omaha Indian society. Yet it was highly uncommon for any Victorian-era woman in the United States to go to medical school. Few medical schools accepted women, so Susan applied to the Woman's Medical College of Pennsylvania (WMCP). It was one of the limited number of medical schools to educate women.

Medical school was expensive and beyond Susan's ability to pay. She then turned to a family friend, Alice Fletcher, an ethnographer from Massachusetts. Susan had helped Fletcher in her recovery after a flare-up of inflammatory rheumatism. Luckily, Fletcher had connections and access to a broad network of contacts within women's reform organizations. She directed Susan to appeal to the Connecticut Indian Association, a local auxiliary of the Women's

National Indian Association. The WNIA intended to "civilize" the Aboriginal tribes by encouraging Victorian values of domesticity among the women. They also sponsored field matrons to teach Native women "cleanliness" and "godliness."

Susan utilized their motives when she wrote for help. She described her desire to enter the homes of the Omaha people as a physician and teach them hygiene to cure their ills. She utilized their Victorian virtues of domesticity, which followed the Association's goals. In return, the Association stepped up and financed Susan's medical school. In addition, they also covered housing, books, and other supplies. Our doctor-to-be is considered the first person to receive aid for professional education in the United States. In return, the Association requested she remain single during her time at medical school and for some years after her graduation. They described that this would allow her to focus and build her medical practice.

No matter the difficulty and barriers, Susan overcame it all. She became the first Native American woman in the United States to get a medical degree after graduating from Woman's Medical College of Pennsylvania in 1889. This was when women in America faced enormous backlash for attempting to obtain a medical degree, then add being of a minority race as well. Male doctors wrote that academic stress could make women infertile, and having smaller brains made them incapable of medical practice. Susan graduated a year early and was first in her class. The boys could not be reached for comment.

Susan returned home to the Omaha reservation and began to care for members of her tribe. As the only physician, Susan served more than 1200 people across over four hundred miles at the age of twenty-four. Once settled into a demanding medical service, Susan married Henry Picotte in 1894. They went on to have two sons, Caryl and Pierre. Even with a family, Susan was dedicated to her calling and continued to serve her people as their doctors. Often, she would take her children along on house calls.

Not limited to medical care, Susan also gave community members financial, legal, and spiritual guidance. While personally fighting a terminal illness, Susan lobbied for the prohibition of alcohol on the reservation and improved living conditions. She tirelessly campaigned for public health and the legal allotment of land to members of the Omaha tribe. Our gal continued to fight against alcohol for the rest of her life. In the early 1900s, when the peyote religion arrived on the Omaha reservation, she gradually accepted it to fight alcoholism. Many members of the peyote religion were able to reconnect with their spiritual traditions and reject alcohol.

In 1913, with help from her husband, community, and donations, she opened the first hospital on a not governmentally funded reservation. Never forgetting the absent doctor from her childhood, Susan helped anyone who needed assistance, regardless of race or ethnicity.

During her career, Susan left a legacy as she cared for thousands of Native and non-Native patients across Nebraska. Susan had suffered for most of her life from chronic illness. In medical school, she had been bothered by breathing issues, and after a few years working on the reservation, she was forced to take a break to recover her health in 1892. She had chronic pain in her neck, head, and ears. After a fall from her horse, she added significant internal injuries. Later in life, Susan lost her hearing.

As Susan aged, her ongoing health problems grew even more. By the time the new reservation hospital was built in Walthill in 1913, she was too frail to be its sole administrator. She died of bone cancer on September 18, 1915.

Services by both the Presbyterian Church as well as the Amethyst Chapter of the Order of the Eastern Star were performed. Near her husband and parents, Susan La Flesche Picotte is buried in Bancroft Cemetery, Bancroft, Nebraska. She worked her entire life to connect the two worlds, as her father had wisely recognized would be necessary. Great appreciation was evident at her funeral as three priests eulogized her. The final one to speak was a member of the Omaha tribe who delivered the last words in the Omaha language. Susan was born of the Omaha Tribe and maintained her affiliation, and built the community her entire life.

Dr. Alice Ball

b. July 24, 1892   d. December 31, 1916
Seattle, WA, USA

Alice Augusta Ball was born in Seattle, Washington, on July 24, 1892. She was the third of four children born to Laura Ball and James Ball Jr., a newspaper editor, lawyer, and photographer.

In 1903, Alice attended Central Grammar School in Oahu, Hawaii. She returned to Washington in 1905 and continued her education. Alice graduated from the University of Washington with degrees in Pharmacy and Pharmaceutical Chemistry. By then, she had begun to publish her research papers. In 1915, Alice became the first woman and first African American to graduate from the College of Hawaii with a Master's degree in science and chemistry.

Alice was interested in treating Hansen's Disease, also known as leprosy, that swept through Hawaii from the early 1800s to the late 1900s. Considering the potential impact of Hansen's on the native Hawaiian population, the Legislative Assembly passed the "Act to Prevent the Spread of Leprosy" in 1865. Persons with the illness or suspected of carrying it were quarantined to the designated Kalaupapa Peninsula in Molokai, a remote and relatively inaccessible area in Hawaii. The victims were expected to live off the land; many religious volunteers went and helped as best they could. The most famous was Father Damien, and several books have been written about him. He also died of Hansen's in 1889.

After graduation, Alice was offered a position in the School of Chemistry at the College of Hawaii, adding more firsts to her resume. Alice became obsessed with treatment for Hansen's disease during her time at the College. She successfully developed an injectable therapy for Hansens. She developed this from the medicinal oil from the Chaulmoogra Tree, used in traditional medicines in India and China. Alice didn't quit and developed a water-soluble, injectable form of chaulmoogra oil. This was used for years to treat Hansens.

While completing her master's thesis, The Chemical Constituents of Piper Methysticum, or The Chemical Constituents of the Active Principle of the Ava Root, she was approached by Dr. Hollmann. New patients with Hansen's disease were often sent to Kalihi Hospital, and Dr. Hollmann, the assistant director. He asked Alice for help in his hopes of isolating the active agents in chaulmoogra oil. For hundreds of years, doctors, scientists, healers, and pharmacologists have worked to find a cure. It didn't take Alice long to accomplish the challenge.

Alice Augusta Ball died suddenly at twenty-four on December 31, 1916. She had fallen ill during her research. Alice had returned to Seattle for treatment a few months before her death. The cause of her death is unknown. There was a suggestion that it may have been chlorine poisoning due to exposure in some of the intense laboratory classes she taught.

In 2000, the University of Hawaii honored Alice by mounting a bronze plaque in her honor on the only Chaulmoogra Tree on the UH-Manoa campus. Most of her multiple awards from Hawaii were recognized in the 2000s, and the Hawaii Board of Regents honored Alice with a Medal of Distinction. David Lassner, the president of the University of Hawaii, stated, "We are incredibly proud of Alice Ball and are grateful to the people, many within our institution, who worked so hard over these past decades to research and bring forward her remarkable history and accomplishments after so many years."

Florence Sabin

b. *November 9, 1871*
Central City, CO, USA

d. *October 3, 1953*
Denver, CO, USA

Florence Rena Sabin was born on November 9, 1871, in Central City, Colorado, the second daughter of George K. Sabin, a mining engineer, and Serena Miner Sabin, a schoolteacher. When she was seven, her mother died of puerperal fever. She and her older sister Mary then grew up in Denver and Chicago with the help of their uncle Albert Sabin and spent some time in Vermont with their paternal grandparents. Both girls attended Vermont Academy and were encouraged to go on to college.

Florence showed an early talent for math and science, but she hoped to become a pianist until high school. Another student's rude comment pointed out her musical talent was average on a good day, and Florence redirected her energies toward academia. She followed her sister to Smith College, bypassing the music dream and majoring in zoology. Florence received her Bachelor of Science in 1893, and due to the encouragement of the college physician, she planned to go on to medical school. Florence would follow his advice only after teaching high school for three years to earn the cost of her first year of study at John Hopkins University, which had become a coeducational medical school.

It was 1896 when she entered medical school as one of fourteen women in a class of forty-five. Not long after starting, Franklin P. Mall, one of Hopkins' outstanding scientists, noticed her. Mall became Florence's mentor, advocate, and intellectual role model. He encouraged her to pursue "pure" science and suggested two projects. His support was instrumental in establishing her reputation in research.

One of the projects was designing a three-dimensional model of a newborn baby's brainstem. This became the basis of a widely used textbook, An Atlas of the Medulla and Midbrain, published in 1901. The other project was an investigation of the embryological development of the lymphatic system. After only a year as an intern at John Hopkins Hospital, Florence won a research fellowship from the Baltimore Association for the Promotion of University Education for Women. From this opportunity, she published two more notable papers.

In 1902, Florence became the first woman faculty member at John Hopkins, teaching embryology and histology in the Department of Anatomy. She was promoted to associate professor in 1905 and to full professor in 1917, becoming the first woman to hold that rank at that prestigious university.

Florence stayed with John Hopkins until 1925 and was a distinguished researcher and teacher. Her work on the origins of the lymphatic system was demonstrated by injecting colored substances into the lymphatic channels that were formed from an embryo's veins rather than from other tissues.

This was contrary to the established belief. She also researched the origins of blood vessels, blood cells, and connective tissue. Florence also perfected a technique of supravital staining, which allowed the study of the living cells.

In 1924, she became the first woman president of the American Association of Anatomists. She was the first woman elected to membership in the National Academy of Sciences and received many other awards the following year. While accepting the Pictorial Review of achievement award in 1929, she said:

"I hope my studies may be an encouragement to other women, especially to young women, to devote their lives to the larger interests of the mind. It matters little whether men or women have the more brains; all we women need to do to exert our proper influence is just to use all the brains we have."

In 1938, Florence retired to Colorado. Soon after, Governor Vivian asked her to lead the State Health Committee. Colorado had one of the highest infant death rates in the country, the third-highest scarlet fever rates, and the fifth-highest diphtheria total. Dr. Florence reformed health care by writing eight health bills passed by the legislature.

In 1947 Mayor Quigg Newton declared Florence the new Denver Manager of Health and Charities. She soon began a city-wide x-ray and public education program that reduced the Denver tuberculosis rate by 50%.

Florence died of a heart attack at the age of eighty-one in Denver in 1953. To honor her great works, the

State sent a statue of her to represent Colorado in the Statuary Hall at the Capitol in Washington.

I genuinely hope she kept playing piano, she earned it every day.

Gertrude Elion

b. January 23, 1918
Manhattan, NY, USA

d. February 21, 1999
Chapel Hill, NC USA

Born to immigrant parents in New York City on January 23, 1918, **Gertrude Belle Elion** was soon known as Trudy to Robert Elion, a Lithuanian Jewish immigrant and a dentist, and Bertha Cohen, a Polish Jewish immigrant. For her first seven years, Trudy lived with her parents in a small apartment adjoining her father's dental office. When her brother was born, the family moved to more spacious quarters in the Bronx, where they prospered. While Gertrude's mother attended to the baby, Trudy spent more time with a grandfather who had newly arrived from Europe. She attended school and excelled with, in her words, an "insatiable thirst for knowledge."

Her family lost their wealth after the Wall Street Crash of 1929. Trudy's education continued. At the age of fifteen, she graduated high school. At the same time, Trudy gained more motivation from her grandfather's death from cancer. Trudy later stated, *"I had no specific bent toward science until my grandfather died of cancer. I decided nobody should suffer that much."* Trudy entered Hunter College in New York City at the age of nineteen. She graduated summa cum laude in chemistry.

It wasn't easy to find employment after graduation because most laboratories refused to hire women chemists, an age-old theme. So, Trudy worked part-time as a lab assistant and continued her education at New York University. She also worked as a substitute high school teacher for a few years while completing her Master's degree in 1941. Trudy never obtained a doctorate until later, when she was awarded an honorary Ph.D. from the Polytechnic University of New York and an honorary Doctor of Science degree from Harvard University.

In 1937, after completing her chemistry studies at Hunter College in New York, Trudy lost her fiancé to a bacterial infection. This loss magnified her passion for finding cures.

When World War II began, it created more opportunities for women in all aspects of the industry. Trudy was able to get work in quality control in food and consumer-product companies. It was in 1944 that she was hired at Burroughs-Wellcome (now GlaxoSmithKline). Trudy would stay with them for forty years, working in partnership with Dr. George H. Hitchings. He recognized her curiosity, drive, knowledge and permitted her to take more responsibility.

Together they began an unorthodox course of creating medicines by studying the chemical composition of diseased cells. At the time, the practice had been more of a good idea, trial-and-error methods. The team used the differences in biochemistry between normal human cells and pathogens (disease-causing agents) to design drugs that could block viral infections.

Trudy and her team designed drugs to combat leukemia, herpes, and AIDS. They discovered treatments to reduce the body's rejection in kidney transplants between unrelated donors.

In all, Trudy developed forty-five patents in medicine and was awarded twenty-three honorary degrees. Among the many drugs, she developed were the first chemotherapy for childhood leukemia, the immunosuppressant that made organ transplantation possible, the first effective anti-viral medication, and treatments for lupus, hepatitis, arthritis, gout, and other diseases. With her long-time research partner, Dr. Hitchings, they revolutionized the way drugs were developed, and her efforts have saved or improved the lives of countless individuals.

Trudy officially retired in 1983, but she remained active. She held the titles of scientist emeritus and consultant at her old company. Trudy also served as an adviser for the World Health Organization and the American Association for Cancer Research. Even though she never married and probably had no time for dating, she enjoyed photography and travel. Also, with a passion for opera, ballet, and theater, she filled her life. With no children of her own, she bragged about being the "favorite aunt" to her brother's children.

In 1988, Trudy was awarded the Nobel Prize in Medicine with George Hitchings and Sir James Black. Not held to one certificate on the wall, Trudy also received the National Medal of Science in 1991. That same year, Trudy became the first woman to be inducted into the National Inventors Hall of Fame and was inducted into the National Women's Hall of Fame. In 1997, she was granted the Lemelson-MIT Lifetime Achievement Award. One of her several passions, Trudy always encouraged other women to pursue a career in science.

 She maintained the partnership with Dr. Hitchings, and he died one year before she did. Gertrude Belle Elion passed away of a cerebral hemorrhage at a hospital in Chapel Hill, N.C., on February 21, 1999.

Simona Kossak

b. May 30, 1943
Krakow, Poland

d. March 15, 2007
Białystok, Poland

Simona Kossak was the daughter of Jerzy Kossak and was born into a renowned artistic family of painters who loved both Polish landscapes and history. Her sister, Gloria, was a painter and poet. Simona also had aunts Maria Pawlikowska-Jasnorzewska, a prolific Polish poet known as the Polish Sappho and "queen of lyrical poetry," and Magdalena Samozwaniec, a celebrated author. Simona was meant to be a son and the 4th Kossak – spattered in paint and deep in verse. Needless to say, there is a reason she is in this chapter.

Simona is remembered for her efforts to preserve the remnants of natural ecosystems in Poland. Her work primarily dealt with the behavioral ecology of mammals. She sometimes referred to herself as a "zoo-psychologist Polish biologist, ecologist, author, Ph.D. in forestry, and uncompromising conservation activist. Her partner was Lech Wilczek, a naturalist, photographer, and writer. They both dreamed of loneliness and silence, but it turned out that they found a common language and complemented each other. Simona would conduct scientific research, make broadcasts on the radio and write books, and Lech would take photographs and improve their home.

Simona spent more than thirty years in a wooden cabin in the Białowieża Forest. She lived without electricity or access to running water. She shared her bed with a lynx, Agata, and the rest of her home with the massive Zabka, a tamed boar. Kind of surprising she had a partner. Simona believed that one should live simply and close to nature. Only among animals did she find what she had never experienced from humans. Simona was like a mother to animals and built intimacy with many of the forest inhabitants

As a dedicated student and activist, Simona fought to protect Europe's oldest forest. With her work as a scientist and ecologist, Simona authored *The Białowieza Forest Saga* and *The National Park in the Białowieza Forest*. She also was part of several award-winning films.

Her close affiliation with the forest and creatures was unexplainable and considered a magical phenomenon. Often, she was called a witch because of her way of life and was often witnessed chatting with the animals. Most of us do this with our dogs and cats. Simona also had a terrorist crow, which didn't help; it was known to steal gold and attack bicycle riders.

Her photographer partner beautifully documented Simona's life. In 1980. The Scientific Council of the Forest Research Institute awarded Simona with a doctoral degree in Forest Sciences based on her dissertation, *"Research on the trophic situation of roe deer in the habitat of fresh mixed coniferous forest in the Białowieża Primeval Forest."* In 1991, she earned a postdoctoral degree in Forest Sciences based on her dissertation *"Environmental and intraspecific determinants of the feeding behavior of roe deer in the forest environment,"* which I doubt many of us have read. In 1997, she received the academic title of Professor of Forest Sciences.

Simona worked at the Mammal Research Institute of the Polish Academy of Sciences in Białowieża and the Forest Research Institute at the Department of Natural Forests as the director from January 2003 until her death. She was also one of the originators of the UOZ-1 repeller, a device that warns wild animals of passing trains. In October 2000, Simona was awarded the Golden Cross of Merit.

Simona died in 2007 at a hospital in Białystok, Poland, after a serious illness and is buried at Poryte Cemetery, Podlaskie, Poland. She never officially wed, nor had any two-legged children.

Political / Activists

"An activist is someone who cannot help but fight for something. That person is not usually motivated by a need for power or money or fame but in fact, is driven slightly mad by some injustice, some cruelty, some unfairness, so much so that he or she is compelled by some internal moral engine to act to make it better."
— Eve Ensler

Florence Kelley

b. September 12, 1859   d. February 17, 1932
Pennsylvania, USA

Florence Kelley was an American social and political reformer who fought for government regulation to protect working women and children. She was the first female factory inspector in the United States and helped found the NAACP.

Florence was born on September 12, 1859. Her father was William D. Kelley, an abolitionist, founder of the Republican Party, judge, and longtime U.S. Congressman, and Caroline Bartram Bonsall in Philadelphia. They were Quakers and deeply committed to abolishing slavery, universal suffrage, and women's education and literacy.

Influenced mainly by her father, Florence said, "*I owe him everything that I have ever been able to learn to do.*" Florence was often ill as a child and highly susceptible to infections, and her father would read to her. Even at ten, her father educated her on his activities with the issues of unfairness and child labor. Her mother, Caroline Bartram Bonsall, was not a lesser figure, and she worked with the famous Quaker botanist, John Bartram. Florence had five sisters, all dying young, and two brothers. When she missed school, she would be in her father's library, reading.

Unfortunately, Florence's parents died, and she was adopted by her grandparents, Isaac and Kay Pugh. Her great-aunt, Sarah Pugh, lived as a Quaker and strongly opposed slavery. Aunt Sarah's decision to deny the use of cotton and sugar because of the connection to slave labor made an impression on Florence. Aunt Sarah was an outspoken advocate for women and told many stories about oppression she suffered or witnessed in her life.

Florence was admitted to Cornell University at the age of sixteen, graduating in 1882. She wanted to study law at the University of Pennsylvania but was denied admission due to her sex. Florence continued her education in law and government at the University of Zurich, the first European university to grant degrees to women. Florence joined a group of students advocating socialism. This was where she joined the Intercollegiate Socialist Society and became a German Social Democratic party member. Not only a student but a dedicated activist for woman's suffrage and African-American civil rights.

While in Zurich, Florence married Lazare Wischnewetzky in 1884. They had three children, Nicholas (b. 1885), Margaret (1886–1905), and John Bartram (b. 1888). They were divorced in 1892, and Florence's husband tried to take custody of the children in the Chicago courts.

Florence earned a law degree at Northwestern University School of Law in 1894. In her spare time, she assisted with establishing the New Century Guild of Philadelphia, along with Gabrielle D. Clements and led by Eliza Sproat Turner. They offered classes and programs to help working women, and Florence taught the evening classes.

The New Century Guild intended to increase the quality of working and living conditions of the lower class in urban areas. They helped lead the battle for labor laws, protecting child laborers, minimum wage, and eight-hour working days. Florence organized the New York Working Women's Society Campaign in 1889 and 1890 to add women as officials in the office for factory inspection. By 1890, the New York legislature passed laws creating eight new positions for women as state factory inspectors.

From 1891 through 1899, Florence lived at Jane Addam's Hull House settlement in Chicago, a community of university women whose primary purpose was to provide social and educational opportunities for working-class people and immigrants in the surrounding neighborhood. The "residents" (volunteers at Hull House) held classes in literature, history, art, domestic activities, and many other subjects. Hull House also held free concerts for everyone, offered free lectures on current issues, and operated clubs for children and adults. In 1892, the Illinois Bureau of Labor Statistics hired her to investigate the "sweating" system in the garment industry, and the federal commissioner of labor asked her to survey Chicago's 19th ward. By 1893 she was appointed chief factory inspector, a newly created position, by Illinois Governor John Peter Altgeld.

From 1899 through 1926, she lived at the Henry Street settlement house in New York City. In 1899, she founded and served as the first general secretary of the National Consumers League (NCL), which she held for thirty years. Through her work at the NCL, she helped prepare the Brandeis Brief, a defense of ten-hour workday legislation for women that set the precedent of the Supreme Court's recognition of sociological evidence, used later in Brown v. Board of Education. She also helped launch a minimum-wage campaign that eventually led to the passage of fourteen state laws for women, and then she later helped extend the legislation to male workers.

It was 1902 when Florence founded the National Child Labor Committee. Not to rest on her laurels, in 1909, with her friend, author W.E.B Dubois, they organized the National Association for the Advancement of Colored People (NAACP). In 1919, she was a founding member of the Women's International League for Peace and Freedom. She also served as vice president of the National American Woman Suffrage Association for several years. She continued to advocate for working women and children until her death.

Florence Kelley died on February 17, 1932, in Philadelphia, Pennsylvania. She was named an Angel hero by The My Hero Project.

Victoria Claflin Woodhull

b. September 23, 1838 *d. June 9, 1927*
Homer, Ohio, USA *Bredon Norton, England*

Victoria California Claflin was born the seventh of ten children in Homer, Licking County, Ohio. Her mother, Roxanna "Roxy" Hummel Claflin, was born to unmarried and illiterate parents. She followed the Austrian mystic Franz Mesmer and the new spiritualist movement. Her father, Reuben "Buck" Buckman Claflin, Esq. was a lawyer known as con-man and, as a side gig, sold non-prescription medications, also known as snake oil.

In the research, there is a belief that her father was sexually abusive and with violent beatings. He also used starvation as punishment. Multiple biographers have disputed sexual abuse. There was a quote from Victoria "Buck made me a woman before my time." Victoria followed her mother's interest in spiritualism. She spoke that "Banquo's Ghost" from Shakespeare's *Macbeth* gave her hope for a better life.

When Victoria was eleven, she had only three years of formal education, but her intelligence was evident. She was forced to leave school and home when her father burned their heavily insured house. She and her family had to escape. His arson and fraud were discovered when he tried to collect the insurance, and then vigilantes chased him out of town. The town raised funds to pay for the rest of the family to leave Ohio.

At the age of fourteen, Victoria met twenty-eight-year-old Channing Woodhull, a doctor from a town near Rochester, New York. He had practiced medicine in Ohio when the state did not require medical education or licensing. The story goes that he abducted Victoria to marry. They wed on November 23, 1853, just after Victoria's fifteenth birthday.

The marriage didn't fare well, and it didn't take long to discover her husband was an alcoholic and a cheater. They had two children, Byron and Zula Maude Woodhull. Victoria often worked outside the home to support the family. Byron was born with an intellectual disability in 1854, which Victoria believed was caused by her husband's alcoholism. Another version recounted that her son's disability was caused by a fall from a window. After their children were born, Victoria divorced her husband and kept his surname.

Victoria remarried when she was twenty-eight to Colonel James Harvey Blood. He had served in the Union Army in Missouri during the American Civil War and was elected as city auditor of St. Louis, Missouri.

Victoria and her sister, Tennie Claflin, became spiritual advisers to seventy-six-year-old Cornelius Vanderbilt, the wealthy railroad magnate. The sisters served as mediums to help him contact the spirit of his dead wife, and he also used their talents to gain financial insights from the spirit world. Vanderbilt bankrolled Victoria and Tennie's ventures on Wall Street. Once they were making money in the stock market, they opened Woodhull, Claflin & Company, a brokerage firm. As they made a great deal of money, many men's magazines criticized and sexualized them. Victoria believed and worked under the belief that women's ability to earn money was better protection against the tyranny and brutality of men and was more important than the vote.

On May 14, 1870, Victoria and Tennie used the money they had made from their Wall Street ventures and began Woodhull & Claflin's Weekly, a newspaper. They addressed women's issues with unusual frankness supporting the concept that women could live as men's equals at work, in the political arena, and still maintain a family. They wrote in favor of sex education, free love, short skirts, spiritualism, vegetarianism, and licensed prostitution.

The newspaper quickly evolved into a radical political, economic and social forum that shaped Victoria's budding reform crusade. The sixteen page weekly published exposés on stock swindles, insurance frauds, and corrupt Congressional land deals, but that did not stop other well-known brokerage firms and banks from advertising on the front page. The paper promoted women's suffrage and announced Woodhull's candidacy for President of the United States.

In Victoria's "Steinway speech," delivered on Monday, November 20, 1871, in Steinway Hall, New York City, she said:

"To woman, by nature, belongs the right of sexual determination. When the instinct is aroused in her, then and then only should commerce follow. When woman rises from sexual slavery to sexual freedom, into the ownership and control of her sexual organs, and man is obliged to respect this freedom, then will this instinct become pure and holy; then will woman be raised from the iniquity and morbidness in which she now wallows for existence, and the intensity and glory of her creative functions be increased a hundred-fold . . ."

In this same speech, she added:

"Yes, I am a Free Lover. I have an inalienable, constitutional and natural right to love whom I may, to love as long or as short a period as I can; to change that love every day if I please, and with that right neither you nor any law you can frame have any right to interfere."

It was 1872 when Victoria went as far as to criticize well-known clergyman Henry Ward Beecher for adultery over his affair with his parishioner Elizabeth Tilton. Victoria was prosecuted on obscenity charges for sending accounts of the affair through the mail and was briefly jailed.

Victoria was nominated as a presidential candidate by the Equal Rights Party in 1872. The prosecution added to sensational coverage during her campaign for the presidency. Victoria was in jail on election day with her husband – Colonel Blood, and sister; they were charged for publishing an obscene newspaper.

The Party had nominated the formerly enslaved abolitionist, women's rights advocate, statesman, and author Frederick Douglass for Vice President. Douglass did not acknowledge his nomination, but Victoria actively campaigned for the office. This was forty-eight years before women received the right to vote after the 19th Amendment. Quite innovative, even in modern times, but especially in 1872, to have a woman and a black man on the ballot.

Six months later, Victoria, her husband, and her sister were acquitted on a technicality for publicizing Beecher's affair. However, they paid nearly $500,000 in bail and fines before being cleared of the charges. Victoria continued not on the morality of Beecher's affair but the hypocrisy that permitted powerful men to be sexually free but denied the freedom to women.

As a consequence of the story in Woodhull's newspaper, Elizabeth Tilton's husband sued Reverend Henry Beecher for "alienation of affection." Beecher stood trial in 1875 for adultery in a proceeding that proved to be one of the most sensational legal episodes of the era, holding the attention of hundreds of thousands of Americans. The trial ended with a hung jury.

1876 was the year of her divorce from Colonel Blood, and by 1877 she was broke but was able to find the cash for a move to England. She worked as a lecturer and toned down some of her presentations. A wealthy banker, John Biddulph Martin, was at one of her presentations, and they wed on October 31, 1883. She took his last name and was known as

Victoria Woodhull Martin. She started a magazine, The Humanitarian. From 1892 to 1901, she remained active in the British women's suffrage movement and various causes but did distance herself from her radical ideas on sex and love. After her husband died in 1901, Victoria gave up publishing and retired to the country at Bredon's Norton, Worcestershire, England.

Victoria died of heart failure at her home at Norton Park in Bredon's Norton, Worcestershire, England, at the age of eighty-eight on June 9, 1927. There is a cenotaph in the town of Tewkesbury's abbey in her memory. In 2001 she was posthumously inducted into the National Women's Hall of Fame. The abbey also offers locally-made mustard balls.

Mary Soutar-Brooksbank

b. December 15, 1897   d. March 16, 1978
Aberdeen, Scotland

Mary Soutar, a Scottish mill worker, songwriter, and socialist, was born December 15, 1897, in an Aberdeen slum. She was the oldest of either five or ten children (who had time to count in the constant pandemonium). The family moved to Dundee when Mary was eight or nine years old. She had lost a baby brother to diphtheria before the age of three. With the questionable number of children, she clearly had multiple losses at a young age.

Mary's father, Sandy Soutar, was from St. Vigeans, Arbroath, Scotland, and was an active trade unionist amongst the dockworkers, and he helped to found the Aberdeen Dockers' Union. Her mother, Rose Ann Gillan-Soutar, was a fisher lassie and domestic servant. The Soutar family was blacklisted in Dundee because of their trade union activities.

Raised in poverty, Mary went to work illegally in Dundee's jute mills with her mother. Mary was a bobbin shifter by the age of eleven. They worked long hours, and at times out of desperation, Mary worked some agricultural jobs. Mary had her first experience of trade unionism at the age of fourteen when she participated in her first strike for a pay increase. A young woman walked around the area mills blowing a whistle to call the workers out on strike. The girls at her mill successfully marched for and received a 15% pay raise.

At twenty-one, Mary rejected Roman Catholicism to become an atheist. She was encouraged by John McLean to join the Communist Party to fight for women's rights, equality, and the demise of capitalism. Mary was in the thick of things. Due to unemployment and the ongoing poverty, even with the 15% raise, she moved into domestic service in Glasgow. While in Glasgow, she attended John MacLean's last meetings at the Scottish Labour College.

It was in 1924 that Mary wed Ernest Brooksbank, a journeyman tailor. Mary maintained her activity with the Communist Party. As a consequence of her actions, she spent three stints in prison; the longest sentence was three months, all for her labor rights actions.

While incarcerated in the Perth Prison, she was supported by the Railway Women's Guild of Perth, who brought her food. The authorities at Perth placed her under psychiatric observation but concluded that she was sane. The prison governor lent Mary a book on women in politics, which inspired her to write her first poem – Cycling Days.

A key to her political activity in the 1930s was the Means Test. This test supposedly determined if a person or household is eligible to receive some sort of benefit or payment. During a demonstration and rally organized by the National Unemployed Workers' Movement in 1931, the police attacked the crowd and the platform. Mary was amongst those arrested and charged with rioting. After her release, she helped form the Working Women's Guild and continued her activism. Mary twice ran for office as a Communist party candidate.

Expelled from the Communist Party in 1933, Mary spoke out critically of Joseph Stalin, which moved her politics towards a sympathetic stance on Scottish nationalism.

She led a campaign for better housing and pensioners' rights. Mary later got involved in opposition to World War I and founded the Working Women Guild to fight for better health and social services. With a membership of over three hundred. she led the National Unemployed Workers Movement to march to Forfar. They lobbied the County Council for assistance and rights. Mary remained instrumental in the labor movement contingents throughout Scotland.

Throughout her life, Mary kept a book of poetry and songs. Mary's songs were mostly about working-class life, and perhaps her most famous work, The Jute Mill, includes the lines:

Oh dear me, the world is ill-divided,
Them that works the hardest are the least provided.
I maun work the harder, dark days or fine,
Tae feed and cled my bairnies affen ten and nine.

You can hear the song sung by Mary and other folksingers at the Scots Language Centre: Scotslanguage.com – Work Songs. The archives hold her original notebook of songs and poems at the University of Dundee, and Ewan MacColl recorded some of her songs.

Mary died at Ninewells Hospital in Dundee on March 16, 1978, at the age of eighty-two. The library in Dundee was named in her honor, and the Brooksbank Centre on Pitairlie Road was named for her when the library was closed.

A verse from her Jute Mill Song is inscribed in Iona marble on the Scottish Parliament Building's Canongate Wall, displaying quotations from Scottish writers and poets.

Eunice Hunton-Carter

b. July 16, 1899
Atlanta, GA, USA

d. January 25, 1970
Harlem, NY, USA

Eunice Hunton was born in 1899 in Atlanta, Georgia. Her parents were social activists and college-educated. Her father, William Alphaeus Hunton Sr., was the founder of the black division of the Y.M.C.A. Her mother, Addie Waites Hunton, was a social worker and active with the N.A.A.C.P. and the Y.M.C.A. She was selected with another woman to travel to France during World War I to report on the condition of United States black servicemen.

The social action didn't start with her parents. Eunice's paternal grandfather Stanton Hunton purchased his freedom from slavery before the American Civil War. Her brother, W. Alphaeus Hunton Jr., was an author, academic, and activist noted for his involvement with the Council on African Affairs and promoting Pan-African identity. Eunice's parents' awareness instilled a sense of duty to serve, and their children stepped up.

Eunice graduated from Smith College in Northampton, Massachusetts, with a Bachelor's and a Master's degree. In the 1920s, Eunice began as a social worker in New York and New Jersey while attending Fordham Law School. She became the first black woman to receive a law degree from Fordham. She passed the New York bar exam and married Lisle Carter Sr., one of the first African-American dentists in New York. They settled in Harlem, Manhattan. They had one child, Lisle Carter Jr., who continued the family tradition as a lawyer and was a political appointee in the John F. Kennedy and Lyndon B. Johnson administrations.

Now back to Eunice and her accomplishments. She drew the attention of Mayor Fiorello LaGuardia and the New York state special prosecutor Thomas Dewey in 1935. La Guardia and Dewey gathered a team to fight organized crime, and they selected Eunice. She was assigned to work in Harlem, which was predominantly black at the time. She was the first female African-American assistant District Attorney in the state. Continuing on her firsts, Eunice was one of the first prosecutors of color in the United States. She also worked with the Pan-African Congress and in United Nations committees to advance the status of women.

She was prime to handle the massive prostitution racketeering investigation. As a prosecutor, Eunice noticed that multiple defendants used the same bondsman and lawyer and similar stories for their defense. Eunice put it all together and speculated that the consistency suggested that New York's prostitution was a racket. Eunice met with Dewey to explain her case, and for this reason, Dewey appointed her to his now-famous "Twenty Against the Underworld" squad. She worked on the investigation that confirmed her suspicions. It was discovered that racketeers were deeply involved in illegal prostitution and collected 50% of earnings.

Previously, Thomas Dewey, as the chief assistant U.S. attorney, had won a conviction against New York bootlegger Waxey Gordon and prosecuted the mobster Dutch Schultz. Once Dewey had Eunice's information, he ordered a raid on local brothels. Over a hundred sex workers were arrested, and several agreed to testify about the Mob's ties.

Little did Eunice know she would become involved with the biggest leader of the Cosa Nostra (later known as the Mafia), Charles "Lucky" Luciano. Luciano started his criminal career in the Five Points gang and was instrumental in developing the National Crime Syndicate. He is considered the father of modern organized crime in the United States, and it was in 1931 that he abolished the boss of bosses title held by Salvatore Maranzano. He was also the first official boss of the modern Genovese crime family.

Based on Eunice's investigation, Luciano was charged with pandering on a large scale. His defense stated that he was not directly linked to the brothels and was railroaded by the prosecution. In a dramatic cross-examination of Luciano, Dewey asked how the wealthy mobster could afford an extravagant lifestyle on the $22,500 reported on his tax returns. The sensational trial ended in a guilty verdict and a sentence of thirty to forty years. He was paroled in 1946 and deported to Italy. Luciano's conviction was the foundation of U.S. history's most successful court action against organized crime.

The case generated national fame for Dewey, which he rode to become the governor of New York. Additionally, he had two unsuccessful runs for the White House. He benefited greatly from Eunice's prosecutor skills and had genuine respect for her. They maintained a connection, and she often advised him.

Eunice also served on the Executive Committee of the International Council of Women through the UN, an organization with representatives from thirty-seven countries. In 1947, Eunice was one of fifteen American women invited to attend the first International Assembly on Women in Paris, to discuss "human and educational problems affecting peace and freedom." While there, Eunice met with Madame Simone Sohier-Brunard of Belgium, the Union of Colonial Women president. They worked on comparing conditions in African colonies with the status of African Americans in the United States. Additionally, she served on the board of the Y.W.C.A.

This short biography reads like a resume. Eunice Roberta Hunton Carter passed away in 1970, at the age of seventy. in New York City. Her grandson Stephen L. Carter, a professor at Yale Law School, wrote Invisible: *The Forgotten Story of the Black Woman Lawyer Who Took Down America's Most Powerful Mobster* and participated with his daughter Leah Aird Carter in our 2020 webinar *Invisible No More: The Eunice Carter Story*.

Eunice Hunton Carter excelled when her sex and race held little opportunity and blazed a path for all women.

Felisa Rincón de Gautier

b. *January 9, 1897*   d. *September 16, 1994*
San Juan, Puerto Rico

Felisa "Doña Fela" Rincón Marrero, later known as Doña Fela, was born on January 9, 1897, in Ceiba, Puerto Rico, southeast of San Juan. She was born to an upper class family, her father, Enrique Rincón Plumey, was a lawyer, and her mother, Rita Marrero Rivera, was a schoolteacher. She was the eldest of nine children, and Doña Fela's mother died while they were all relatively young. The family moved to San Juan when Doña Fela was ten years old. When she wasn't caring for her siblings, she was often sent to live with relatives.

However, her father was determined to give her the best education possible. Although she did not graduate from high school, she went to Fajardo, Humacao, and Santurce. Doña Fela left school to help care for her siblings. In the summers, she visited her uncle in San Lorenzo, where she learned how to prepare medications and became a pharmacist.

In her teens, Doña Fela became a very accomplished seamstress, making it possible for her to move to New York City to study fashion. Upon returning to San Juan, she opened a successful business, "Felisa's Style Shop." For the entirety of her life, Doña Fela was known for her style. There was never a time that Doña Fela appeared in public without her bright red lipstick, elaborate "up-do," and nail polish.

Doña Fela's political stance was reflective of her father, and she joined the Liberal Party, with which her father was well-connected. She became outspoken in the campaign for women's suffrage in Puerto Rico. At that time, Puerto Rican women had to pass literacy tests, and she was the fifth Puerto Rican woman to register and vote in the election of 1932. It wasn't long before she became a representative of the Liberal Party, dedicating time to travel door to door registering women to vote. Moved by the poverty, she witnessed while canvassing the slums of San Juan inspired her to continue in the battle.

Following the Liberal Party's defeat in the 1936 election party division, Doña Fela helped Luis Muñoz Marín found the Popular Democratic Party (PPD) in 1938. She was named the President of the PPD's San Juan Committee in 1940, the same year she wed Jenaro A. Gauthier, an attorney, and the PPD's secretary-general. In 1944, she was approached to run for Mayor of San Juan, and due to her husband's and father's resistance to her candidacy, she declined the opportunity. Still, when Mayor Roberto Sánchez Vilella resigned in 1946, Doña Fela accepted the appointment as mayor of San Juan.

Mayor Doña Fela called her political philosophy "benevolent maternalism." Since her time registering voters, Doña Fela worked to distribute food and shoes to poor children. In addition, she also established centers for elder care and legal aid for low-income residents programs. She also began the renovation of the San Juan Municipal Hospital, making it the first hospital on the island to receive full accreditation from the American Hospital Association. Soon, she paved the way for the School of Medicine in 1950. One of her most celebrated accomplishments was the "Maternal Schools" in 1949. These were preschool/childcare centers that the Head Start program in the United States was modeled after.

Under her leadership, the city constructed schools and housing projects for its expanding population, and San Juan grew from about 180,000 to 500,000. There was an open house every Wednesday at City Hall throughout her time in office, and the community could come and share their concerns or seek help. Doña Fela remained an ally of Governor Muñoz Marín. Earlier, she had favored independence for the island, but her views changed, and she supported the Constitution of the Commonwealth that went into effect in 1952. She consistently kept the commonwealth status for Puerto Rico.

There was a time when Doña Fela hosted a conference, and the owner of Eastern Airlines wanted to give her a gift for her work. Doña Fela refused, he pushed, she declined, and he continued. Finally, she asked for snow. Planeloads of snow arrived to the joy and amazement of the San Juan children. It came for several years, and at the same time, she distributed Christmas gifts.

Doña Fela was devoted to protecting the cultural heritage of Puerto Rico. Her administration created the Historical Monument Commission, which preserved much of the colonial architecture in the historic section of the city, known as El Viejo San Juan ("Old San Juan"). Her conservation work led San Juan to receive the "All American City Award" from the National Civic League in 1959. No surprise, but Doña Fela was reelected four times and served as mayor of San Juan until January 13, 1969.

After she stepped down, she remained politically active and served as a delegate to Democratic Party nominating conventions. In 1992, her last convention was at the age of ninty-five. Doña Fela was the oldest delegate in attendance. She served on a committee for urban rights. She also served as a Goodwill Ambassador to countries around the globe. Doña Fela was presented with many awards and honors from states, civic groups, and religious organizations worldwide.

Doña Fela died of a heart attack in San Juan on September 16, 1994, at the age of ninety-seven. She is buried in the Cementerio de la Capital in San Juan, Puerto Rico.

Christine Granville

b. May 1, 1908
Warsaw, Poland

d. June 15, 1952
London, England

Born **Krystyna Skarbek** in Warsaw, Poland, on May 1, 1908. She was the daughter of Count Jerzy Skarbek, a Polish aristocrat, and the granddaughter of a wealthy Jewish banker in the Goldfeder family. She was educated at a convent in Warsaw and, at age seventeen, participated in a beauty contest and was crowned Miss Poland. I'm trying to imagine the swimsuit competition and the bathing suit she would have brought from the convent.

Krystyna married briefly but divorced soon after. She then married Georg Gizycki, a writer who was twice her age. After they wed, they moved to Africa for Georg to work on his book. The move was near the same time Nazi Germany invaded Poland in 1939. The couple decided quickly and traveled to Britain, where Krystyna volunteered to work with British intelligence services. At the same time, Georg joined the Free Polish Services and was killed in combat.

Krystyna was brought into the Special Operations Executive (SOE) branch of British intelligence. Due to her intellect and fluency in several languages, she fit this elite team. She was given the name Christine Granville by SOE, and she used it for the rest of her life. With specialized training in espionage, Christine was assigned to work with a resistance group in Poland as they fought the Nazi invasion.

When she arrived in Budapest, Christine worked under the cover of being a journalist. Her real purpose was to aid Polish refugees in escapes across the border. Luckily, she was an excellent skier, which helped with the downhill portion of the Tatra Mountains crossing into Poland. This was where Christine would retrieve escaped Polish prisoners of war and lead them out. She established several escape routes to help the Polish refugees flee to England.

Catherine also was trained in parachuting while she was in Cairo, Egypt. She executed numerous jumps into Nazi-occupied France. If that wasn't risky enough, she was assigned to gather information on German troops and armaments. She traveled to England and Poland to deliver this information. On one trip to Poland, she was stopped by German soldiers. Catherine reportedly pulled the pins out of two live grenades and told the soldiers that she would drop them if they attempted to take her into custody. The soldiers allowed her to pass.

Another time, Catherine was stopped at a different border and had dumped incriminating evidence into a river beforehand. Unfortunately, she was still held because of a large sum of money which she wouldn't explain. Thinking quickly, Catherine told the guards to take the money and let her and her comrades through, or she would turn everything over to their superiors. The guards knew the senior officers would keep the cash, so they took the money and let them cross. Still another border occasion, when stopped, she convinced them that she and her companions were simple farm peasants on their way to have a picnic.

When arrested by the Hungarian police, Christine bluffed her way out by convincing them that she was related to Admiral Horthy, Regent of Hungary. They released her, and when she returned to England, she had hidden photos documenting the German troop buildup.

It was 1944, still deep in the war, when Catherine parachuted into southern France. She used the name Pauline (and sometimes Jacqueline) Armand. She delivered messages and materials that could not be transmitted by radio or telegraphed to Cairo.

In her spare time, Catherine worked to spread propaganda, insisting that England would not abandon Poland in its fight against Nazi Germany. She was able to convince some Italian troops to desert their German allies. Two of her new allies were captured in Digne and imprisoned as spies. Christine reported a meeting with the Nazi commandant, and she convinced him that the approaching Allied forces would shoot him if he did not release the men immediately. They demanded that she write a statement clearing them of collaboration with the Nazis and demanded monetary payment, both of which she accommodated.

When the war ended, Christine was released from her intelligence duties. It became necessary to find a new job as soon as possible. She worked as a switchboard operator at the India Hotel in London. She then pulled a gig as a saleswoman at Harrod's department store and later an attendant at the Paddington Hotel.

In 1951 she took a job as an attendant on the Winchester Castle Ocean Liner, which sailed between England, Australia, and South Africa. Her supervisor on the liner was a steward named Dennis Muldowney. Muldowney suffered from schizophrenia and was obsessed with Catherine. He declared his love for her, and she rejected his advances. Catherine had to quit the job, and she returned to London. Muldowney left his job to follow her there. He again professed his love, and Catherine made it clear that this would not happen and told him to leave her alone.

After the final rejection, Muldowney began to stalk Catherine, although quitting the liner and showing up was a good indicator of trouble. On June 15, 1952, Muldowney spotted her walking down the stairs in her hotel, and he rushed over and stabbed her.

Muldowney was sentenced to death for the murder and was hanged in September 1952 at Pentonville Prison in London, UK.

Krystyna/Catherine was buried with the French Croix de Guerre, a medal from Poland, the George Medal for Special Services, the Order of the British Empire, and the French Resistance badge.

Shirley (Mum Shirl) Smith

b. November 22, 1924   d. April 28, 1998
New South Wales, Australia

Coleen Shirley Perry Smith, better remembered as **Mum Shirl**, was born on November 22, 1921, in Erambie Mission, an Aboriginal community in New South Wales. Diagnosed with epilepsy at an early age, Shirl dedicated her life to community activism that resulted in social reform for Aboriginal Australians and other minority communities throughout Australia. Mum Shirl lived in Sydney for most of her life.

After her brother Laurie was arrested, Shirl visited him at Sydney's Long Bay Correctional Complex. She then started to see other Aboriginal inmates. When the guards stopped her and asked how she was related to the prisoners, Shirley said, "I'm their mum" – and her title was born. Her work was not only at the prisons, and Shirl gave as much to the many organizations she started and inspired.

Shirl was a prominent Wiradjuri woman, social worker, and humanitarian activist committed to justice and the welfare of Aboriginal Australians. Shirl founded the Aboriginal Legal Service, the Aboriginal Medical Service, the Aboriginal Tent Embassy, the Aboriginal Children's Service, and the Aboriginal Housing Company in Redfern, a suburb of Sydney.

"Many people have told me they think I'm an exception," she wrote in her autobiography. "I'm not... There are many fine Aboriginal people who, with half a chance, would be doing what I am now doing."

In her work, Shirl traveled a great deal throughout Australia to educate Australians on issues affecting the Aboriginal communities. In her eloquence and ongoing humanitarian work, she was recognized as a National Living Treasure by Australia's National Trust in 1998. Mum Shirl was severely injured in a car crash, followed by a heart attack, and hospitalized for seven months.

Mum Shirl died on April 28, 1998. She was survived by her daughter Beatrice, her sister Harriet and her brother Joe, grandchildren, great-grandchildren, nieces and nephews, great-nieces and nephews, great-great-nieces and nephews, and many who live were educated and helped by her work.

Phoolan Devi

b. August 10, 1963
Uttar Pradesh, India

d. July 25, 2001
New Delhi, India

Born into a poor family in rural Uttar Pradesh, **Phoolan Devi** endured poverty, child marriage that turned abusive, and escaping to a life of crime. At age eleven, Phoolan was married off to a man three times her age. Her life is a story of the ancient caste system and the status of women in modern India. Her husband paid a cow and a bicycle for her, which permitted him to beat and rape her. She was a member of the Dalit (Untouchable caste), and even in this modern era, the division in India's society was a vast chasm.

After a year of marriage, she ran away, traveling further than the width of Texas to her parent's home. I'm sure she wished for that bicycle her husband had paid for her. The family was so disgraced by her impertinent action; her mother suggested she commit suicide. A woman that has left her husband has a status no better than a prostitute. Phoolan didn't follow that advice and matured into an intelligent, beautiful, and accomplished woman. She still had to fight the caste as a low-status woman and was still humiliated and raped by men of the upper classes.

It is almost impossible to escape India's caste system, as it defines all Indians. Phoolan acknowledged that it was assumed that the daughters of the poor are for the use of the rich. When she was twenty-one years old, she was imprisoned for placing a complaint to the village authorities. After her release, bandits (dacoits) invaded her parent's home and kidnapped her. There is a question if her upper cast cousin may have paid for this abduction. She was taken to the hideout and raped by the leader for three days. Finally, on day four, Vikram Mallah, a low-caste man, took pity on her, shot the leader, and took over the gang. Clearly, calling 911 was not a valid option. He and Phoolan became lovers. He taught her to shoot and negotiate through the Indian badlands during this time. He told her, "If you are going to kill, kill twenty, not just one. If you kill twenty, your fame will spread: if you kill only one, they will hang you as a murderess."

Over the following years, they wandered about India, robbed some trains, stole from the upper caste, and killed a number of their enemies. She always prayed to Durga (the mother goddess) before every action. Before long, her fame spread, and she was considered a reincarnation of Durga by the lower caste women. Songs were written about her, and the legend expanded.

In 1980 Vikram was shot while they camped in the jungle; he died with his head in her lap. His killers were upper-class dacoits avenging the leader's death that Vikram had killed to rescue Phoolan. She was bound and taken to the village of Behmai, inhabited by many Thakurs, one of India's highest castes. As much as the lower castes celebrated her, the upper cast feared and hated her. She was held for three weeks, and every night she was raped. Eventually, she was forced outside to be paraded through the village naked before a laughing crowd of upper-class men.

This time Phoolan was rescued by a priest from a neighboring village. Many never recover from less horrifying experiences, but Phoolan did. She started her own gang, and she earned a good/bad reputation similar to a female Robin Hood. Although her morality was questioned, Phoolan didn't let the reputation issue hold her back.

On February 14, 1981, she and her gang entered Behmai, and they dragged thirty Thakur men from their homes and demanded that they turn over the original kidnappers. Refusing to do so, they were marched to the river, forced to kneel, and twenty-two were shot dead. Phoolan avenged her kidnapping and rapes, which resulted in a $10,400 price on her head.

In 1983, Indira Gandhi, the prime minister of India, instructed the police that they must do anything possible to bring her in. They included the outrageous action of negotiation. Phoolan made a deal with the government and turned herself in during a public ceremony, and it was witnessed by a crowd of eight thousand cheering her on. She was imprisoned for eleven years and was finally pardoned. The same year a movie was made about her life, to which she voiced her objection. Phoolan stated she had not been consulted and disapproved of her depiction.

So, Phoolan did what all victims/bandits do, and in 1996 she released her autobiography. At the same time, she was elected to the Indian Parliament by a landslide. Her campaign was based on eliminating the caste system and improving the status of women. In this busy year, Phoolan married Umed Singh, a high-caste realtor.

Phoolan continued to receive death threats while in the high-profile public position: the Bandit Queen turned Member of Parliament. Three men assassinated Phoolan Devi outside her residence in New Delhi, India, on July 25, 2001. She died, but her legend survives.

Scientists

"Certain people – men, of course – discouraged me, saying [science] was not a good career for women. That pushed me even more to persevere."
– Francoise Barré
Virologist and winner of the
2008 Nobel Prize in Physiology or Medicine

"I hadn't been aware that there were doors closed to me until I started knocking on them."
– Gertrude B. Elion
Biochemist, pharmacologist,
and winner of the 1988 Nobel Prize
in Physiology or Medicine

Hypatia

b. *circa 355*   d. *March 415*
Alexandria, Egypt

Hypatia (pronounced hy-Pay-shuh) was born in the second half of the 4th century, probably between 350-370 AD, in Alexandria, Egypt. Hypatia spoke Greek like most educated people of the time. Her name means 'supreme.' Not a Motown singer, but a mathematician, astronomer, and philosopher who lived in a very turbulent era in Alexandria's history. She is the earliest female mathematician whose life and work documentation exists.

    Hypatia was the daughter of Theon, a mathematician and astronomer and the last attested member of the Alexandrian Museum. Theon is best remembered for the part he played in the preservation of Euclid's *Elements*. In addition, he wrote extensively, commenting on Ptolemy's *Almagest and Handy Tables*. I haven't read any of those books in English or Greek. No details of Hypatia's mother survive. Her math mainly was of the multiplying ilk. Her dad's student edition of Euclid's *Elements* has been the go-to version for over a thousand years. Hypatia continued his program, which was essentially a determined effort to preserve the Greek mathematical and astronomical heritage.

She is credited with commentaries on Apollonius of Perga's *Conics* (geometry) and Diophantus of Alexandria's *Arithmetic* (number theory), as well as an astronomical table (possibly a revised version of Book III of her father's commentary on the *Almagest*). All of her works have been lost, but there have been attempts to reconstruct them.

In her time, she was the world's leading mathematician and astronomer, even though she was a woman. She was an honored teacher and lecturer on philosophical topics. Hypatia had many loyal students and drew huge audiences. Her philosophy was Neoplatonist and was considered "pagan." This was a time of bitter religious conflict between Christians, Jews, and pagans. Philostorgius, another Christian historian and contemporary of Hypatia, stated that she excelled over her father in intellectual pursuits and teaching skills.

If that wasn't enough, our gal Hypatia was known for driving her own carriage, which was extraordinary for any woman.

Nothing is known of her physical appearance, but Damascius was taken with her and wrote that Hypatia was "*exceedingly beautiful and fair of form.*" Damascius went on to state that Hypatia remained a lifelong virgin and didn't stop there; he described an incident when a man approached her at a lecture and tried to court her. She tried to reject him by simply playing the lyre. When he refused to abandon his pursuit, she rejected him, showed him her bloody menstrual rags, and declared, "*This *is what you really love, my young man, but you do not love beauty for its own sake.*" According to Damascius, that rejection worked and surely would work in modern times too, and I don't mean the lyre part.

In the religious divide of this era, violence and fighting were rampant. We can still witness this, but around 412 C.E. was the razing of Serapeum, the temple of the Greco-Egyptian god Serapis. This quite likely involved the end of the Great Library of Alexandria at the same time. It was well known that Serapeum housed several library collections. Hypatia was known to have studied there.

As this was the early beginning of Christianity, there was a lot of violence, not the peace and love we like to imagine. Hypatia didn't conceal her paganism, which infuriated the local Christians. The bishop, Cyril, made it his mission to eliminate the pagans' influence, especially our revered, influential idol-worshipping female philosopher and astronomer.

The bishop accused Hypatia and called her an idol-worshipper. It didn't take long before a mob of monks took to the streets. They kidnapped Hypatia and pulled her through the streets. They reported that they found it necessary to resort to torture which included scraping her flesh with oyster shells as they dragged her to the church. This wasn't enough as the monks then stripped her naked, gave her a lashing, then tore her limbs from her body. Once dead, they further dismembered her and threw her parts into a fire.

Hypatia's life continues to be fictionalized by historians and authors worldwide. Over the centuries, her truth has become a mixture of fact and fiction. Her ideas about philosophy, the stars, and space were ahead of the times. She earned the respect of many, and her achievements survived. Hypatia is a powerful female symbol and a figure for illustrating genius in the face of ignorance and prejudice. Her intellectual accomplishments and teaching are sufficient enough to remember her. But, the horror of her death adds to the drama of her life.

Maria Sibylla Merian

b. 1647
Germany

d. 1715
Netherlands

Maria Sibylla was born in 1647 in Frankfort am Main, a city now in Germany. Maria Sibylla enjoyed a privileged childhood that wasn't limited to the traditional "girls" education. She learned alongside her brothers and could paint and print books. Her brothers were allowed to travel to Europe to finish their instructions, and Maria was kept home because of, you know, her sex.

Not to be held back, Maria found her inspiration. Around age thirteen, she began to collect and study insects, especially how they metamorphized over their lives. Her fascination started with a collection of silk worms thanks to her uncle, a silk manufacturer. Maria developed a study that included descriptions and drawings of their life cycle. Maria's family was surprised and impressed by her work and encouraged her art and studies, but not travel.

When Maria was eighteen years old, she married John Andreas Graff, her stepfather's apprentice. Three years later, she gave birth to their first daughter, Johanna. The family moved to Nuremberg in 1670, which was her husband's hometown. Maria's reputation as an artist spread quickly, so she started teaching the local young women how to paint and draw. Maria continued with her studies of plants and insects.

In 1675, her husband published Maria's first book. It was a collection of flower and plant illustrations intended as models and patterns for other art and embroidery. It was extraordinary for a woman to have a published book. Maria didn't rest on her laurels but continued on other projects.

In 1679, just a year after the birth of her second daughter, Dorothea, Maria published her next book, *The Wonderful Transformation and Singular Flower Food of Caterpillar*. The images were painted and engraved in copper. Each picture illustrated an entire life cycle from egg to larvae for the caterpillars and then from pupa to butterflies and moths. Each one had a background of the insect's primary food source, and Maria included text describing the process. More than a book of illustrations, the project intended to educate. The male scientists and educators recognized the value of Maria's work, adding significantly to the relatively new field of entomology, the study of insects.

In 1685, Maria took her daughters to join a radical Christian community. Her husband chose to divorce her rather than join them. Maria and her girls stayed with the community for six years, but she was frustrated that they did not value education and scientific exploration.

It was the 1690s, and Amsterdam, Netherlands, was a center for intellectuals in Europe. Maria took this opportunity to re-establish herself as an artist and entomologist. With a need to earn money to support her family, Maria began selling her artwork and teaching.

When her eldest daughter, Johanna, married a local merchant, Maria used this opportunity to utilize the new son-in-law's business connections. This made it possible for her to travel. Maria traveled to the Americas to collect specimens and observe the entire life cycle of her studies in their natural habitat. It was 1699. Marie sold everything and used the money to book passage to the Dutch colony of Suriname in South America.

This decision was unheard of at the time a woman traveling alone, especially a trip of that distance. Most scientists would share an excursion of that magnitude, but not Maria. Once in Suriname, Maria and her youngest daughter traveled into the jungle daily to study and collect the insects.

Word got around the local area quickly, and soon many of the native enslaved people began to bring her exciting plants and insects. In their meetings, Maria would speak with the people at length. She was driven to learn everything the locals knew about the specimens. Maria often said she learned more from the community than the white colonists. She condemned the merchants' treatment of enslaved people and worked with the enslaved in her research. This unnamed person's work enabled interactions with the colony's aboriginal natives and African slaves, which helped accelerate her research.

Maria also took an interest in agriculture and lamented the colonial merchants' resistance to plant or export anything other than sugar. She later showcased the vegetables and fruits found in Suriname, including the pineapple.

After two years in Suriname, Maria returned to Amsterdam due to illness, which was probably malaria. This was when she began to organize her research and started her book about her discoveries. While trying to earn a living, she opened a shop and sold specimens she had collected and her engravings of plant and animal life in Suriname.

Using the skills she learned from her stepfather and her husband, Maria self-published her most important work, *The Metamorphosis of the Insects of Surinam – Metamorphosis Insectorum Surinamensium*. Her book allowed European scientists to learn about a completely different ecosystem. Maria's status grew as one of the most influential scientists in Amsterdam.

For the rest of Maria Sibylla Merian's life, people came from all over Europe to buy her art and learn from her techniques. In 1715, Maria suffered a stroke, and despite being partially paralyzed, she continued to work. On January 13, 1717, she died in Amsterdam and was buried four days later at Leidse kerkhof.

After she passed away, her daughters took up her work. Her daughter Dorothea published *Erucarum Ortus Alimentum et Paradoxa Metamorphosis*, a collection of her mother's work. Maria Sibylla Merian is remembered today as one of the essential woman scientists of the Enlightenment.

Caroline Herschel

b. March 16, 1750 *d. January 9, 1848*
Hanover, Germany *England*

Caroline Lucretia Herschel was born in Hanover, Germany, on March 16, 1750. She was the eighth child and fourth daughter of Issak Herschel, a self-taught musician, and Anna Ilse Moritzen. Her father was the bandmaster in the Hanoverian Foot Guards, which kept him away from the family due to his regimental duties. He became ill after the Battle of Dettingen and never recovered, suffering chronic pain and asthma for the remainder of his life. Not much information is available on her mother.

The oldest of their daughters, Sophia, was sixteen years older than Caroline. They were the only girls to survive to adulthood. Sophia married and left home when Caroline was five, and Caroline was tasked with much of the household chores as the only girl. Caroline and her brothers were taught to read and write and little else. Her father attempted home schooling, but Caroline received the least education on top of her other duties. Later, Caroline described her youth life in Hanover, Germany, as the "Cinderella of the family."

At the age of ten, Caroline was struck with typhus, which stunted her growth, and she was never taller than 4 feet 3 inches. That wasn't all. Caroline also suffered vision loss in her left eye. The family members assumed that she would never marry, and her mother felt it was best for her to become a household servant, which benefited momma the most with that "women's work" thing. Her father wanted to educate Caroline, and in her mother's absence, he would tutor her or include her in her brother's lessons when possible. Caroline did learn to play the violin and dressmaking. A neighbor taught her needlework, but her time was limited due to the long hours of household chores. To prevent her from becoming a governess and earning any independence, she was forbidden to learn French or more advanced needlework that would have provided some tools for a future.

After her father's death, her brothers William and Alexander proposed joining them in Bath, England. It took a while, but after the brothers intervened with mom, Caroline eventually left Hanover in August 1772. On her trip to England, she was first introduced to astronomy by way of the constellations and optician's shops.

Once settled in Bath, Caroline ran William's household and began learning to sing at the church. Brother William was the organist for the Octagon Chapel in Bath, and Caroline became a singer for William's church performances. He became the choirmaster of the Octagon Chapel, ever busy with his musical career and organizing public concerts. He also started teaching music at 19 New King Street, Bath (now known as the Herschel Museum of Astronomy).

Caroline did not blend in with the local society and made few friends, which isn't surprising with her mom's little household drudge background. It took a while, but Caroline was finally able to indulge her desire for education. She started with singing and learning English. Not to be stopped, Caroline's brother taught her arithmetic, and she learned some dances from a local teacher. Before long, Caroline could play the harpsichord and became even more important to William's musical performances. Gaining recognition as a vocalist, Caroline was offered an engagement for the Birmingham festival. She declined to sing for any conductor but William, and after a performance of Handel's Messiah, her career as a singer began to fade. Soon, she was replaced by distinguished soloists from outside the area.

This was when William wished to spend less time with rehearsals to focus on astronomy. Caroline followed. She stated in her Memoir, "*I did nothing for my brother but what a well-trained puppy dog would have done, that is to say, I did what he commanded me.*"

It didn't take long, and Caroline became interested in astronomy and enjoyed her work. William started to build his telescopes from lenses he had ground which was an improvement over the lenses he could buy. As usual, Caroline would cook and read to him as he worked. She readily turned her back on the musical career.

She became a significant astronomer in her own right due to her collaboration. The Herschels moved to a new house in 1781. Caroline was tending the stock on March 13. That was the night William discovered the planet Uranus. Initially, he mistook it for a comet, but his superior self-made telescope made it possible to detail. Caroline and William gave their last musical performance in 1782 when her brother accepted the position of court astronomer for King George III.

While assisting William in his observations and building telescopes, Caroline spent many hours polishing mirrors and mounting telescopes to maximize the amount of light captured. She learned to copy astronomical catalogs and other publications that William had borrowed. She also learned to record and organize her brother's astronomical observations. While working in support, Caroline became a brilliant astronomer in her own right.

Many nights Caroline sat by a window as William shouted his observations, and she recorded. This was not a simple clerical task. She would have to use John Flamsteed's catalog, which was organized by constellation, and identify the star William used as a reference. Before long, Flamsteed's record became less valuable. So, Caroline created her own reference, organized by north polar distance. Each morning she would go over the previous day's notes and write them into final reports; she called this task "minding the heavens." Caroline spent time with her own telescope and discovered a nebulae and star clusters. She was the first woman to discover a comet, and eventually, she would be credited with eight.

William persuaded the king to reward his assistant, Caroline, with an annual salary, making her the first British woman to get paid for scientific work. Caroline was also the first woman to have her work published by the Royal Society.

After William died in 1822, Caroline retired back to Hanover. There she continued her astronomical work. After Caroline introduced her nephew, John Herschel, to astronomy, she showed him the constellations in Flamsteed's Atlas. He took over his father's position.

Caroline added her final entry to her observing book on January 31, 1824, about the Great Comet of December 29, 1823.

Throughout her later years, Caroline remained physically active and socialized with other scientific luminaries. She finally found some friends. She spent her retirement writing her memoirs and lamenting her body's limitations.

Caroline Herschel died peacefully in Hanover, Germany, on January 9, 1848. She is buried at the cemetery of the Gartengemeinde, next to her parents, with a lock of William's hair. Her tombstone inscription reads, "The eyes of her who is glorified here below turned to the starry heavens."

The King of Prussia presented her with a Gold Medal for Science on her ninety-sixth birthday (1846), just before her death at the age of ninety-seven. With her brother, she discovered over 2500 astronomical objects over twenty years. The asteroid 281 Lucretia (discovered 1888) was named after

Caroline's middle name, Lucretia, and the crater C. Herschel on the Moon is named after her.

Adrienne Rich's 1968 poem "Planetarium" celebrates Caroline Herschel's life and scientific achievements. Additionally, she is honored with a place setting in The Dinner Party art display (see Judy Chicago under artists). Caroline accumulated multiple firsts, and I can only imagine what she could have done with a supportive mother that encouraged her education over her ability to sweep and dust.

Ada Byron Lovelace

b. December 10, 1815   d. November 27, 1852
London, England

Ada Byron was born December 10, 1815, to the Romantic poet Lord Byron and Anne Isabelle Milbanke. Her parents separated a month after Ada was born, and four months after that, Byron left England forever. Ada never met her father (who died in Greece in 1823). Her mother, Lady Byron, struggled between emotion and reason, subjectivism and objectivism, poetics and mathematics. She suffered from ill-health and bursts of energy. It sure sounds like a case of bipolar, not that I'm a doctor.

Lady Byron did what she could to prevent Ada from taking after her father. Ada was seriously educated, with math tutors and music teachers, most anything that could defeat any poetic tendencies. Ada's difficult childhood shined when she produced the design for a flying machine in 1828, seventy-five years before the Wright Brothers took off.

Ada and her mother lived among London's high society, not the politicians or religious leaders, but a gathering of intellectuals more likely to spend time and money pursuing botany, geology, or astronomy. In the early 19th century, the term scientist didn't exist yet, and William Whewell first coined the word in 1836. As usual in so many eras, women were not encouraged to pursue this type of education.

Ada was fortunate to meet a pending scientist, Charles Babbage, and they became lifelong friends. He was a professor of mathematics at Cambridge University and was remembered as the inventor of the Difference Engine, the elaborate calculating machine. Ada was seventeen when they met in 1833, and they would discuss and correspond for years; it wasn't limited to mathematics and logic but expanded to anything and everything.

In 1835, Ada married William King, who was ten years her senior. Her husband inherited a noble title three years later. They became the Earl and Countess of Lovelace. They had three children, and most of their lives, including finances, were controlled by her mother, Lady Byron, which adds to the story of Lord Byron's hasty escape. Fortunately, Ada's husband rarely opposed Lady Byron's dominance.

Her friend Charles Babbage's work on a second calculating machine started before Ada's wedding. This Analytical Engine was presented to his Parliamentary sponsors, and they refused to support it since he had not finished the original project. In 1842, Babbage found some interest from an Italian mathematician, Louis Menebrea, and published a memoir in French on the subject of the Analytical Engine. Since she had worked with and discussed this with Babbage, Ada was enlisted as the translator for the memoir. During nine months in 1842-43, she worked feverishly on the article and added a set of Notes. These are the source of her enduring fame.

Ada referred to herself as an Analyst & Metaphysician, and she used this title in the added Notes. She understood the plans for the device every bit as well as Babbage. But Ada was superior in her ability to articulate its potential. She saw it as what would be called a general-purpose computer, and it was suited for developing and tabulating any undefined function of any level of generality and complexity. Her Notes anticipate future results, including computer-generated music, but there is no mention of Pong or Mortal Kombat.

Ada died of cancer in 1852, at the age of thirty-seven. She was buried next to Lord Byron, the father she never knew. Her contributions to science have recently become recognized, and she is often referred to as Babbage's "Enchantress of Numbers."

Annie Jump Cannon

b. December 11, 1863　　　d. April 13, 1941
Dover, DE, USA　　　　　Cambridge, MA, USA

Annie Jump Cannon was born on December 11, 1863, in Dover, Delaware. Her father, Wilson Cannon, was a state senator, while her mother, Mary Jump, taught Annie the constellations at a young age, inspiring her to pursue science. Annie would often open the trapdoor to the roof so they could watch the stars in the small observatory they had built together.

Although Annie suffered from hearing loss, she continued to excel in her physics and astronomy studies at Wellesley College. While at Wellesley, she had the privilege to study under a pioneer in the field, Sarah Frances Whiting. Later, Annie wrote Whiting's biography for the Popular Astronomy journal. Not stopping when she graduated in 1884 as valedictorian, Annie continued her passion for astronomy for two years at Radcliffe College. However, after graduation, she returned home to Delaware and focused on photography. Annie took pictures of her travels and, in 1893, published her book of photography. It was used as a souvenir for the Chicago World's Fair.

After the death of her mother in 1894, Annie returned to science. She became a junior physics teacher at Wellesley College as she worked on her graduate degree. She took the opportunity to enroll as a "special student" at Radcliffe College and studied astronomy. Radcliffe was the women's college connected to the all-male Harvard College. Two years into her tenure at Radcliffe, Annie was hired by the Harvard College Observatory to work with Edward Pickering.

In 1896, Annie participated in the first x-ray experiments in the country. In addition, she became a part of a group of women at the observatory called "computers" and often as "Pickering's girls." They were to catalog and classify various stars. The women completed the Henry Draper Catalog of stars by categorizing all the stars visible to them in the sky. The women were paid as little as fifty cents an hour, which was worth more in 1896. However, Annie's passion didn't interfere with making significant scientific discoveries.

Before receiving her master's degree from Wellesley College in 1907, Annie published her first catalog of stars in 1901. She developed a new classification system based on temperature. Known as the Harvard spectral classification system, Annie's sequence is still studied by astronomers today. Using a mnemonic device, . Using this, astronomers can organize stars according to their characteristics.

Annie's remarkable work did not stop there. In 1911, she was appointed as the Curator of Observational Photographs at Harvard's observatory, probably with a raise in pay. Known for her speed at classifying stars, Annie ranked five thousand stars per month from 1911 to 1915. By the end of her career, Annie had recorded approximately 350,000.

In 1921, Annie became the first woman to receive a Doctor of Astronomy Degree from Groningen University. Within a year, the International Astronomical Union adopted her method as the official spectral classification system.

In addition to her scientific work, Annie was also dedicated to fighting for women's rights and suffrage as a National Women's Party member. In 1923, Annie was voted one of the twelve greatest living women in America by the National League of Women Voters. She became the first woman to receive an honorary degree from Oxford University and the first woman to be awarded the Henry Draper Medal of honor from the National Academy of Sciences.

After decades of hard work and accepting honors, Annie was appointed to a permanent faculty position as Curator of Astronomical Photographs for the Harvard College Observatory in 1938, two years before her retirement. She published catalogs of variable stars. Her career spanned more than forty years, during which women in science won some acceptance.

Annie Jump Cannon died April 13, 1941, in Cambridge, Massachusetts. She was seventy-seven years old. She was buried at Lakeside Cemetery in her hometown of Dover, Kent County, Delaware, USA.

Lise Meitner

b. *November 7, 1878*
Vienna, Austria

d. *October 27, 1968*
Cambridge, UK

Elise Meitner was born November 7, 1878, into an upper-middle-class Jewish family in the Leopoldstadt district of Vienna. She was the third of eight children born to Hedwig and Philipp Meitner. Her father was one of the first Jewish lawyers admitted to practice in Austria. All eight of the children pursued an advanced education. Elise's father was a confirmed freethinker, which explains her excellent education. As an adult, Elise and two of her sisters converted to Christianity; this was when she adopted the shortened name of Lise.

Lise was drawn to mathematics and science and started research at the age of eight. She kept a notebook of her records under her pillow. Her first studies were of colors in an oil slick and reflected light. Even though women were not allowed to attend public higher education institutions in Vienna until 1897, she completed her final year of school in 1892. When Lise Meitner finished school at age fourteen, she was barred from higher education, as were all girls in Austria.

Besides being a wife, mother, and domestic, the only career available to women was teaching, so she trained as a French teacher. Inspired by the discoveries of William Röntgen and Henri Becquerel, she was determined to study radioactivity. When she turned twenty-one, women were finally allowed into Austrian universities. Two years of tutoring preceded her enrollment at the University of Vienna; she excelled in math and physics and earned her doctorate in 1906. The same year, her thesis was published as *Wärmeleitung in inhomogenen Körpern* ("*Thermal Conduction in Inhomogeneous Bodies*").

Paul Ehrenfest asked her to investigate an article on optics by Lord Rayleigh. He had described his experiment and some of the results he could not clarify. Lise not only was able to explain what was going on, but she also expanded further and made predictions based on her understanding and demonstrated her ability to carry out independent and unsupervised research.

When working on this particular research, Lise was introduced by Stefan Meyer to radioactivity, a new field of study. She dove in, initially studying alpha particles. Soon Lise expanded to a beam of alpha particles and discovered that scattering increased with the atomic mass of the metal atoms in her experiments. Her work led to Ernest Rutherford and the nuclear atom.

Lise wrote to Marie Curie, requesting an opportunity to work with her, but there was no room. So, Lise made her way to Berlin. This was where she began a collaboration with Otto Hahn on the study of radioactive elements. As an Austrian Jewish woman (all three qualities were strikes against her), she was excluded from the main labs and lectures and only allowed to work in the basement. Not someone to be held back, Lise moved to a new university and better lab facilities. Her partnership with Otto Hahn was split physically when she fled Nazi Germany, but they continued the collaboration.

Lise took her work to Sweden. Otto discovered that uranium atoms were split when bombarded with neutrons, and Lise calculated the energy released in the reaction. They named this phenomenon "nuclear fission." Their discovery eventually led to the atomic bomb. In 1945 Lise said, "You must not blame scientists for the use to which war technicians have put our discoveries," Otto Hahn won the Nobel Prize in 1944, and The Nobel committee overlooked Lise.

Lise received many awards and honors late in her life. But being excluded from the 1944 Nobel Prize in Chemistry for nuclear fission was an insult, and several scientists and journalists have called her exclusion "unjust." According to the Nobel Prize archive, she was nominated nineteen times for Nobel Prize in Chemistry between 1924 and 1948 and twenty-nine times for Nobel Prize in Physics between 1937 and 1965. Despite not being awarded the Prize, Lise was invited to attend the Lindau Nobel Laureate Meeting in 1962, but still no plaque and check. However, Meitner received many other honors.

Lise was invited to work on the Manhattan Project, but she refused the work stating, "I will have nothing to do with a bomb." Element 109, discovered in 1997, was named in her honor, Meitnerium.

Never married, her primary recreation besides fission was walking. In addition, Lise loved music and regularly attended concerts. In 1960, after suffering a broken hip, she moved to Cambridge, UK, to be near her nephew Otto Frisch and his family.

Lise Meitner died at the age of eighty-nine in Cambridge on October 27, 1968, after being weakened by a second broken hip and several small strokes. She was buried in the churchyard of St James Church, Bramley, close to where her youngest brother had been buried a few years previously.

Villains

Bad girls, bad girls – what cha' gonna do when they come for you?

Erzsébet (Elizabeth) Báthory

b. August 7, 1560 *d. August 21, 1614*
Nyírbátor, Hungary *Castle Čachtice (Slovakia)*

Countess Erzsébet Báthory is often called Elizabeth, but personally, Erzsébet fits better, is much more exotic, and doesn't sound like anyone I know. August 7, 1560, is the date of her birth on a family estate near the Carpathian Mountains, Nyírbátor, Royal Hungary. Her father was Baron George VI Báthory. Andrew Bonaventura Báthory, a high-ranking official of Transylvania, was her brother, and her mother was Baroness Anna Báthory, the daughter of Stephen Báthory of Somlyó. Her uncle, also a Stephen, was an official or warlord of Transylvania, the king of Poland, grand duke of the Polish–Lithuanian Commonwealth; oh, he was also a prince of Transylvania. Her older brother served as a judge royal of Hungary. Her other uncle, Christopher, was the prince of Transylvania. One more cousin was the Prime Minister of Hungary. Now back to our gal, Erzsébet, considered the most beautiful, intelligent, and politically savvy woman in Europe. Being born into one of the most powerful families in Europe added to her popularity. She grew up living the privileged life of nobility.

Additionally, if it wasn't enough, one of her ancestors worked with Vlad Dracula when he claimed the throne. Her ancestors and relatives included several cases of insanity and general cruel behaviors. Clearly, her "family" had been genetically polluted by incest, alcoholism, murder, sadism, politics, and Satanism, and Erzsébet seems to have learned from them all.

Erzsébet was a difficult child, and there were reports that she may have suffered from "fits" or seizures. She definitely had rages and a severe case of impulse control. She was promiscuous, maybe because her first baby was born when she was fourteen. After the birth, her family immediately betrothed her to Count Ferencz Nadasdy de Nadasd of Fogarasfold. He was a great soldier and politician known as the "Black Hero of Hungary." It seems this was a match made in politics. Both families had certified histories of madness, and the bride and groom were both known for their cruelty. Erz had shown signs of her inclinations since childhood, and The Count's influence seems to have fine-tuned the propensity. He moved his bride to Castle Csejthe in Hungary, where portions of the castle still stand. Ferencz was often gone for extended periods of war, leaving Erz to run the place.

After fathering four children with Erzsebet, the Count fell ill in 1601 and died in 1604, leaving her a widow at the age of forty-four. There is some suggestion that she poisoned him (poisoned, murdered, stabbed, put him in a dumpster, as gossip becomes history.) Some of her children were "shipped off," one son was lucky (?) enough to hang around the castle with mom.

There is a story about a young servant girl brushing Erzsébet's hair, and in some disciplinary action, the chambermaid began to bleed from her nose. When the blood landed on Erzsébet, she believed it made her skin look fresh, almost as peachy as the young bleeder. Her trusted employees were called, and they bled the young wench to death, filling a tub with her blood for a soak. This is what kicked off her full-blown perversion. She developed a torture toolbox containing: needles, pins, branding irons, whips, pokers, scissors, freezing temperatures, starvation, water, and cooperative employees to assist her. The surrounding community feared what could happen if they complained, but as the young women disappeared, they gathered up rakes and torches when she started bringing in the lower nobility. The King arranged for an intervention led by her cousin Count Thurso on Christmas in 1610.

The group of men crept into her castle to investigate the complaints about missing young women and children. It is hard to tell precisely what they found, as it was deemed too monstrous to be put on her permanent record. We must all remember that Erzsebet was part of the ruling family and personally very powerful. However, they found over fifty young women dead and dying, apparently tortured and drained of blood.

After further investigation, it was discovered this had been going on for maybe as long as ten years. There was no report on how old Erzsebet looked. The records of the court proceedings indicate she was charged with killing eighty people, but her diary outlines 650. The staff members practically knocked each other over to testify, hoping for a plea agreement. They told tales of degradation and horror and made suggestions of devil worship, sorcery, and a rigorous beauty regime.

The servants alleged that she bathed in the blood of virgins to make her skin more beautiful. This went on for ten years until one of her intended victims escaped and alerted the authorities to her evil ways. Her castle was raided on December 30, 1610, and at least fifty dead bodies were exhumed. It is estimated that as many as 650 girls were murdered. Elizabeth was sealed inside her bed-chamber at the castle by stone masons, with only a small opening left to pass food. She had eliminated almost all of the "common" girls who had no rights. Still, when she overstepped into the young nobility promising etiquette lessons but no graduations, that forced the scales of justice. There was a trial, but Erz was never convicted of any crime.

Countess Erz was placed under house arrest and sealed into her suite within the castle. She died in this room in 1614, four years after she was first imprisoned.

Her employees did not fare as well; one had her eyes plucked out, and fingers cut off, then burned at the stake. One was beheaded. If you have ever questioned if privilege had its benefits, remember this terrifying "lady" – one of the few documented women of history associated with such monstrous actions.

She was buried in the church of Čachtice on November 25, 1614, but due to the villagers' uproar over having "The Tigress of Čachtice" buried in their cemetery, her body was moved to her birth home at Ecsed, where it is interred at the Báthory family crypt.

It is believed that her story was the inspiration for the novel Dracula by Bram Stoker. Dark.

Anne Bonney
and
Mary Read

b. 1702   d. 1782   b. 1685   d. 1721
County Cork, Ireland   Plymouth, England
Place of deaths still open for speculation

Anne Bonney and **Mary Read** are two of the infamous women pirates of history, and they were the only ones known to have sailed in the new world.

Anne Bonney was born March 8, 1702 (it wasn't International Women's Day then) in County Cork, Ireland. She was the daughter of lawyer William Cormac and his wife's housemaid. The happy couple relocated to a plantation near Charleston, South Carolina, to escape the shame of their daughter and the wrath of Mrs. Cormac.

Anne grew up as a headstrong girl with a known ferocious temper. She eloped with a young sailor/pirate James Bonney when both were young. There is some question that her father drove them away, which is not in the Ford Bronco sense. Bonney took his new bride on honeymoon in the Bahamas, not the resort area we know now, but a haven for pirates. James picked up a temp job as an informant, and

Anne, disgusted with his cowardice, proceeded to fall for Captain Jack Rackham, *a.k.a.* Calico Jack.

Disguising herself as a male, she sailed with Calico Jack on his sloop, the Vanity. Anne was now sailing under the famous skull-and-crossed-daggers flag. Anne is believed to have become pregnant by Jack and returned to shore only long enough to have her baby and leave it with friends in Cuba before rejoining him on the high seas.

Now, Mary Read was born in Plymouth, England, about 1685. Her mother's husband was a seafaring man who went to work and never returned. He had left her mother pregnant, and she gave birth to a son who soon died. Not long after, his illegitimate half-sister, Mary, was born. Her mother decided to disguise Mary as her dead son in financial distress, hoping to receive monetary support from her late husband's mother. Granny was known to love little boys and hate girls.

It worked; granny gave them just enough support. Then it worked further with scores of others after granny died. When Mary was a teenager, she was hired out as a footboy, and she was growing bolder and bolder, looking for a bigger adventure. She signed onto a man-of-war ship and the military, moving her male persona into a career of distinction. You know how intriguing a man in uniform can be, especially to a cross-dressing young woman, and she revealed her sex to a fellow sailor/soldier. Since he did not appear to have a problem with her fashion sense, they married. The happy couple became innkeepers, owning the Three Horseshoes near the castle of Breda in Holland.

Mister died, and money became scarce, so Mary donned her work clothes. She knew that job opportunities in 1700 were much easier for a man (hum – how things have changed), and Mary returned to the sea on a Merchant ship. Sailing off to the Caribbean, her ship was commandeered by English pirates. Bad news for some and a promotion for Mary. Later her ship was taken by Calico Jack and his pirates; she quickly submitted her resume. Anne Bonney was already part of the crew, and they quickly discovered each other's secret (probably at the Tampax machine in the women's bathroom). They had much in common, and they became close friends, possibly very, very close friends. Anne and Mary may have been lovers who could have included Calico Jack, another pot of stew.

Anne and Mary were known for their violent tempers, savage fighting and were often called "fierce hell cats." The crew members knew that no one else was more ruthless and bloodthirsty in times of action than these two. Calico Jack was one heck of a pirate, but he is remembered more for his involvement with the women. Unfortunately, Calico Jack did not take Anne's flirtatious nature well, and his authority waned. He sought comfort in rum while Anne and Mary assumed the actual leadership of the ship. No longer did they hide their true gender.

In October 1720, they were anchored off Point Negril, Jamaica, for a hard-drinking celebration of recent victories. A British sloop surprised them, sending the drunken men scampering below deck to hide. Anne and Mary were left to defend the ship, and yelled at

* more than a footnote

their mates to "come up, you cowards, and fight like men." They angrily raged against the crew, killing one and wounding several others. It made little difference; the two women were left to fight the Brits alone.

The British Navy was victorious, and every survivor was taken to Jamaica. Jack and the male crew were tried and sentenced to hang. Anne was allowed to visit him before his execution, and she wasn't one for sentimentality; her words live in history as *"Had you fought like a man, you need not have been hang'd like a dog."*

One week after Calico's execution, Anne and Mary were tried and found guilty. The judge allowed them to speak at the sentencing, and they both replied, *"M'lord, we plead our bellies.*" Both claimed pregnancy, and since British law forbade killing an unborn child, their sentences were stayed – temporarily.

Mary is said to have died of a violent fever in the Spanish Town prison in 1721, before the birth of her child (or during childbirth, per the History Channel.) Another theory suggests she feigned death and sneaked out of prison under a shroud.

There is no record of Anne's execution. Some say that her father bought her release, and she settled down into a quiet family life on a small Caribbean island. There is another belief that she lived out her life in England, owning a tavern and telling long tales of the sea and adventure.

Choice number three says that Anne and Mary moved to Louisiana, where they raised their children together and were non-traditional to the end.

Cheng I Sao

b. *circa* 1775   d. 1844
Xinhui, Guangdong, Qing China

Once upon a time, a sixteen-year-old prostitute **Shi Yang**, *a.k.a.* **Shi Xianggu**, became the most successful pirate of all recorded history. Her career on the high seas started when she was a young teen. She was just a local girl growing up in a coastal community along the South China Sea, earning a few yuan. In 1801, she met and married a successful businessman (actually more of a mobster/pirate) named **Cheng Sao**. Her name became "**Cheng I Sao**" (wife of Cheng Sao).

The resourceful couple immediately adopted a fifteen-year-old son named Pao and grew the business to about four hundred ships with nearly eight thousand sailors. They made a livelihood of ransoming captives and extorting payment from the good people along the coast. The Chengs all lived happily together for about six years when tragedy struck. In 1807, a gale storm was said to have washed Mr. Cheng Sao overboard, ending the honeymoon and leaving Cheng I, the pirate-widow, entirely in charge of the business.

This was no problem as Cheng I was a resourceful, powerful, and cunning young girl of the streets. She took the business to the next level as she increased the fleet into a powerful federation of two thousand ships, managed as six individual fleets. She appointed her adopted son Cheng Pao to be the leader of the Red Fleet, one of the six divisions in the Federation, and then she married him. Isn't that just like a Pirate?

Her business model was to establish a strong code of conduct, harsh punishments for breaking the code, and generous pay for following it. This practice is how she was able to control such a large company. The code was made for an army of pirates motivated by their pay and loyalty to their boss.

Each obedient pirate received a generous 20% cut from the plunder. Anyone who disobeyed an order or issued a command without proper authorization was beheaded. Anyone stealing from the common booty (petty cash included) was beheaded. Deserters lost an ear and were paraded through the community. The first offense for concealing any part of the loot was flogging, and the second offense was death. If a male employee raped a female captive, he was executed. If the sex was consensual with the prisoner, they were punished along with him. They often tied the women's legs together, added weights, and threw her overboard.

The Chincsc Imperial Navy tried to destroy the pirates, but by 1808 they had lost sixty-three vessels, many of which were confiscated by the pirate Federation, which further improved Cheng's advantages. Captured officers were usually beaten and often butchered. The local villages created militias to repel the land raids, proving futile. The pirates' strength was in their code. They were very good to communities that helped them and very bad to those who opposed them.

As you can imagine, this type of business brings aggressive competition much more interesting to watch than that of reality TV. Her army's growth eventually brought about strong retaliation by the Chinese Government, which built alliances with various foreign governments whose ships were also being attacked and stolen.

By 1810, her legacy had established Cheng I as the most powerful pirate of all written history, but it had run its course. The Government alliances were working, and Cheng I suffered capital losses by ambushes from her unified rivals. She began to fear the punishment that she would receive in defeat. So, Cheng I, decided it was an excellent time to get while the getting was good. As any good businesswoman in the midst of a corporate raid, she had an exit strategy and timed it perfectly. She retired! By negotiating terms of amnesty with the Governor-General of Canton, less than four hundred pirates were punished, banished, or exiled. 126 were thrown under the bus and executed, and the remaining 17,318 surrendered their weapons and junks to the Navy. They were allowed to join the Chinese army and even keep their fortunes. Cheng Pao, her husband/son, chose to take a comfortable government job; he entered the Navy as a lieutenant and commanded a fleet of twenty junks.

In retirement, Cheng I settled down with her husband/son and gave birth to a son/grandson, started a brothel and a gambling house, and maybe even ran a quiet ring of smugglers for her pin money.

348   * more than a footnote

At the age of sixty-nine, she died a wealthy woman with thousands of stories to tell. What cannot be denied is that she was brilliant, ruthless, and had earned her place in this book!

Belle Paulsdatter Gunnes

b. November 11, 1859
Norway

d. Unkown
USA probably

Brynhild Paulsdatter Storset was born in Norway and immigrated to the US in 1881. She Americanized her name to Belle or Bella. She is credited with being the first "Black Widow" in the United States.

At the age of twenty-five, Belle married Mads Sorenson in 1884; they opened a Confectioner's shop, which burned in 1897. They also lost a couple of homes in rapid succession to fire. It appears that at this point, Belle discovered the natural wonder of Insurance. In 1886 her daughter Caroline died; in 1898, her son Axel also passed. They were both diagnosed with acute colitis, and there was no suspicion of poisoning at that time. In 1900, her husband followed the children, she admitted to giving him a "powder" to help his cold, but the death was ascribed to natural causes. And she picked up another insurance check.

In 1902 she wed Peter Gunness, and he wasn't as hearty as Mads and died eight months later when a sausage grinder fell on his head, as they are known to do. Three years later, her foster daughter, Jennie Olsen, vanished, and it was reported she went to a finishing school. Either way, she was finished.Belle started hiring drivers and placing lonely hearts ads in Norwegian language newspapers. She "entertained" several prospective husbands who seemed to disappear. On April 28, 1908, her homestead was destroyed by fire. When the authorities were digging through the rubble, they found four bodies, three children and a headless woman, and they assumed to be Belle. Her handyman, Ray Lamphere, was charged with arson and murder. He professed his innocence and said that he had taken Belle to the train station after helping set the fire.

They continued to investigate the homestead to find sixteen known bodies and twelve additional possibilities. They found ten men buried in the hog pen and two females in the garden patch. There was a multitude of bone fragments and "parts." There was concern that Belle, the inventor of online dating, had faked her death with the headless female corpse. Her dental plate was found, and the authorities ignored the unanswered questions, convicting Roy Lamphere of the arson. He credited her with netting more than a hundred thousand dollars in insurance claims between 1903 and 1908 and committing forty-nine murders. He swore that the headless woman was someone he had hired that evening, apparently for a "cookout."

There were several possible sightings of Belle as late as 1935. If she did fake her death, she would be one of the few killers who had been identified with a strong case and was able to evade arrest and live out her life. If the internet had been operational, her dating heading would have been the rhyme that lasted longer than her relationships.

There's red upon the Hoosier moon
For Belle was strong and full of doom:
And think of all those Norska men
Who'll never see St. Paul again.

2008 Update: The discovery of Gunness' dentures in the house fire led the coroner to declare Belle dead in the arson fire. But when her casket was recently exhumed, the remains of two unidentified children were inside. One theory is that Gunness faked her death and fled to California under an alias, where she continued her killing spree.

Gunness placed the following advertisement in the matrimonial columns of all the Chicago daily newspapers and other large Midwestern cities:

"Personal – comely widow who owns a large farm in one of the finest districts in La Porte County, Indiana, desires to make the acquaintance of a gentleman equally well provided, with view of joining fortunes. No replies by letter considered unless sender is willing to follow answer with personal visit. Triflers need not apply."

Jane Toppan

b. 1857　　　　　　　　　　　　　　　　d. 1983
　　　　　Massachusetts, USA

"Jolly" Jane Toppan was a serial killer in Massachusetts in the late 1800s. Toppan claimed her life goal was to "have killed more people – helpless people – than any other man or woman who ever lived." As we know from previous chapters, that was a challenging goal. She was born as Honora (Nora) Kelley around 1857 in Boston, the youngest of four girls in a poor Irish immigrant family. Her mother died of tuberculosis when she was a year old. Her father, Peter Kelley, a tailor, lost his mind and was said to have sewn his eyelids shut. Known as 'Kelley the Crack,' he tried to raise the girls, but he was suspected of abusing them.

In 1863, Kelley took eight-year-old Delia and six-year-old Honora to the Boston Female Asylum orphanage in the city's South End. The Asylum was where unwanted female children were often abandoned. Nora and her sister, Delia, were raised in the BFA with over a hundred other children. Nora was fostered out as an indentured servant to a widow, Ann Toppan. Toppan changed Nora's name to Jane. Her sister, Delia, was not as lucky and was sent to the streets for prostitution when she was of age. "No exact numbers for legal hooker age."

Toni Kief

Jane was freed of her duties when she was eighteen and given fifty dollars. She chose to work for the family as a servant until Ann passed and Ann's daughter married and left home. Jane then attended Cambridge Hospital in Boston to train to be a nurse.

Jane worked as a student nurse and got along well with her patients. She even falsified their medical records to keep them in the hospital for more extended stays to get to know them. Jane had strong feelings toward elderly patients, thinking them useless and not worth keeping alive. She killed at least a dozen people while working as a student nurse – she would dose her elderly patients with opium to see how they would react to the drug, upping the dose to watch them suffer and ultimately die. She began poisoning with other medications. Occasionally, she would stage a sickness with poison and nurse them back to a "miraculous recovery."

Scoring a private nurse position, Jane worked for families around Boston. She stayed for years without detection. Jane specialized in the older family members and then stole their belongings. She even killed her landlords, fellow doctors and nurses, and friends as she got bored of their company. She wasn't caught until she used a metallic-based poison on a victim, which finally sparked an investigation.

In court in 1902, Jane was found not guilty. She told her attorney that she killed more than a hundred people and sometimes got into bed with her victims as they convulsed from the poison. She was immediately scheduled for another trial and sentenced to life in an asylum.

When she arrived at the asylum, she refused to eat, afraid that her food may be poisoned – which the newspapers gloated as ironic revenge. She stayed in the asylum until she died in 1983 at the age of eighty-one. There was a media resurgence of the story after her death, claiming her to be America's first serial killer, which is extremely doubtful.

Laura Bullion
aka
Della Rose

b. October 4, 1876
Knickerbocker, TX, USA

d. December 2, 1961
Memphis, TN, USA

Laura Bullion could have been born in Knickerbocker, Texas, around 1876 to a German mother and maybe a Native American father. Although the actual date of her birth is unknown, Laura's death record indicates October 4 as her birthday. And Henry Bullion as her father and Freda Byler as her mother. Data in the 1880 and 1900 federal census suggests a Laura might have been born on a farm in the township of Palarm near Conway in Arkansas and might have grown up in Tom Green County, Texas. Other sources claim Laura was born in Kentucky in 1873, and the only consistent location is the USA. She seems to have a birth story with every identity she claimed.

When Laura was a young teen, she met William Carver and Ben "The Tall Texan" Kilpatrick, local outlaws. The town of Knickerbocker was a haven of outlaws, and since Laura's claimed father was a bank robber, her dating pool grew. It was no surprise when she stumbled into the life. She was almost

356   * more than a footnote

fifteen years old when the romance with Will Carver began. He had been married to her aunt, who had recently died. Carver often worked with Black Jack Ketchum, robbing trains before moving to Utah to hook up with Butch Cassidy and the Wild Bunch. Laura, the romantic, followed him. At some point, Laura's affections turned to Ben Kilpatrick, who was also a member of the Wild Bunch.

Laura often helped the gang by fencing goods and making money for them. By then, the guys called her Della Rose, and she was often called the "Rose of the Wild Bunch." Her buddies at the hideout were a wealth of western bad guys and movie inspirations, Butch Cassidy, Sundance Kid, "Black Jack" Ketchum, and Kid Curry. Her affiliation seemed to have stayed with Ben Kilpatrick, a friend of her father.

Having taken part in several train robberies with the Wild Bunch, Kilpatrick and Laura took off for Texas with William Carver, and he was ambushed. In the confrontation, he killed two lawmen and escaped. Which led to Laura and Kilpatrick making another quick move to St. Louis, Missouri.

On or about November 1, 1901, Ben Kilpatrick and Laura arrived in St. Louis by train and checked into the Laclede Hotel using the aliases Mr. & Mrs. J.W. Rose. At 11:50 pm on November 5, Ben Kilpatrick was arrested at Josie Blakey's resort on Chestnut Street. The authorities found a key to a room at the Laclede Hotel in his pocket. The following day, they entered the hotel lobby, where Laura was in the process of checking out with her luggage. In her suitcase, they discovered $8500 in unsigned banknotes taken in the Great Northern train robbery. She was arrested on federal charges for "forgery of signatures to banknotes."

In an arrest report following the train robbery, dated November 6, 1901, Laura is identified as "Della Rose," Her aliases are "Clara Hays, Laura Casey, and Laura Bullion." This appears to be the shortlist of her names of choice. The arrest report lists her profession as a prostitute, probably more of a woman's place instead of a robber. According to a New York Times article, she was "masquerading as 'Mrs. Nellie Rose' at the time of her arrest; The Times went on to write a suspicion that she, "disguised as a boy," might have taken part in a train robbery in Montana. The paper cites Chief of Detectives Desmond: "I wouldn't think helping to hold up a train was too much for her. She is cool, shows absolutely no fear, and would readily pass for a boy in male attire. She has a masculine face, which would give her assurance in her disguise."

Laura was convicted of the Great Northern train robbery and sentenced to five years in prison. Kilpatrick was found guilty of robbery and sentenced to fifteen years in prison. After three years and ten months, Laura was released from the Missouri State Penitentiary at Jefferson City, Missouri. She never saw her lover Ben Kilpatrick again. When he was released in June 1911, he had returned to his previous profession, and while trying to rob a Southern Pacific express near Sanderson, Texas, on March 13, 1912, he was killed with an ice mallet.

Laura settled in Memphis, Tennessee, in 1918, posing as a war widow and using – surprise – an assumed name. Laura, *aka* Freda Lincoln, supported herself as a seamstress and later as a drapery maker, dressmaker, and interior designer.

Laura was the last surviving member of the infamous Wild Bunch. On December 2, 1961, she died of heart disease at the Shelby County Hospital in Memphis, Tennessee, and was buried in Memorial Park Cemetery in Memphis. Her tombstone reads, "Freda Bullion Lincoln – Laura Bullion – The Thorny Rose."

Warriors

"A woman is like a tea bag – you can't tell how strong she is until you put her in hot water."
– Eleanor Roosevelt

"Courage is like a muscle. We strengthen it by use."
– Ruth Gordon

Fu Hao

circa 1200
China

Fu Hao was born around 1040 B.C.E., in the late Shang dynasty period. No parental information is readily available. The Shang dynasty was the second oldest dynasty in Chinese history and was the era that developed the earliest form of writing. In Fu Hao's youth, she was trained in the military and educated in the most advanced arts of war.

King Wu Ding of Shang's strategy for expanding his Kingdom was to have a woman from each nearby tribe enter his harem. He had a total of sixty-four women waiting for his attention. One of these young women was Fu Hao. She quickly became his favorite by giving birth to a son, Xiao Yi, who became the heir apparent. With this accomplishment, Fu became the most powerful of the King's three queens. She was a loyal wife and a caring mother, and it was her loyalty that the King trusted her to command his troops on the battlefield. This assignment makes me appreciate modern times. She broke with tradition by serving as a high priestess and military general.

Historians speculate that Queen Fu died young due to a hunting accident. Her only son, Xiao Yi, preceded her in death. Yet, Queen Fu's story did not end with her death. Instead, she moved into goddess status. The King feared that his Queen Fu would be alone in the afterlife; he married her to Shang's highest god, Di, and his ancestors, including his father. King Wu wasn't kidding when he said she was a favorite. He frequently sought her blessing for future battles.

One of the most extraordinary modern Chinese archaeological excavations was the unearthing of her tomb in Anyang in 1976. To this day, it is open to the public, and it is known to be the most significant preserved tomb from the time of the Shang dynasty. Her remains were buried beneath the royal residence, which protected her from robbery and careless plowing.

If a historian could name Queen Fu Hao's roles in her lifetime, the list would be a multiple-page spreadsheet. According to inscriptions on oracle bones from the time, Fu Hao led many military campaigns, commanded thirteen thousand soldiers, and was considered the most powerful military leader of her time. The many weapons found in her tomb support Fu's status as an honored warrior. We learned from the tomb that she also controlled her own fiefdom on the outskirts of her husband's empire. Queen Fu played so many notable roles that very few women in history have sought to emulate her. In one battle, she commanded the largest recorded army in Shang history and led them to victory against the Qiang. Apparently, King Wu Ding didn't wed all of the royal daughters. Queen Fu is the first recorded female general in Chinese history, and she is also the only woman who had both the rights of royal sacrifice and military command. She also played the role of priestess, conducting many religious rituals. Fu was one of the most powerful women in the Shang dynasty.

    While Queen Fu Hao lived a short life, she was a prominent historical figure in the Shang Dynasty era. Queen Fu Hao has been largely forgotten, but archaeologists and historians are slowly putting her life back together for us to remember and celebrate her being more than wife number one out of sixty-four.

Triệu Thị Chinh
aka
Lady Triệu

b. *circa* 226   d. *248*

Vietnam
Vietnamese: Bà Triệu, Sino-
Vietnamese: 趙嫗 Triệu Ẩu.

Triệu Thị Chinh is also known as **Triệu Thị Trinh**, although her actual name and parents' identities are unknown. She was born sometime around 226 C.E. in a small village in Vietnam. Trieu was orphaned as a toddler and lived with her brother, Triệu Quoc Dat, and his wife. The records indicate that Mrs. Brother was a cruel, violent woman. At the age of twenty, Triệu killed her sister-in-law, supporting that accusation of cruelty. I must imagine what built up to this relationship breakdown, as history and myth aren't always precise.

It is told that Triệu said, *"I'd like to ride storms, kill orcas in the open sea, drive out the aggressors, reconquer the country, undo the ties of serfdom, and never bend my back to be the concubine of whatever man."*

Then she went to the mountain.

366   * more than a footnote

Triệu was strong, brave, intelligent, and driven. While on the mountain, she gathered a band of a thousand followers, where she trained them for battle. Her brother tried to intervene and stop her rebellion, but our Lady told him: "*I only want to ride the wind and walk the waves, slay the big whales of the Eastern Sea, clean up frontiers, and save the people from drowning. Why should I imitate others, bow my head, stoop over and be a slave? Why resign myself to menial housework?*"

She seems to have a thing about wind, water, and whales.

Before the age of twenty-one, Lady Triệu successfully fought in more than thirty battles against the Chinese with her rebel army. According to legend, she was over nine feet tall, with a voice that sounded like a temple bell, and rode into battle on an elephant, wearing golden armor and carrying a sword in each hand. The Chinese were said to be afraid of her fierce gaze, reporting it would be easier to fight a tiger than to face Lady Triệu in battle. Trieu proclaimed herself to be Nhụy Kiều Tướng quân (The Lady General clad in Golden Robe).

Lady Triệu led her troops to join her brother's rebellion. Triệu Quoc Dat soldiers accepted her as their leader because of her courage and boldness.

The battle with the Giao Châu Inspector Lục Dận lasted for six months. At that time, Lady Triệu lost her troops and fought alone. She finally accepted defeat and fled to Bồ Điền, a commune. This was where twenty-two-year-old Lady Triệu committed suicide by throwing herself in the river at Hậu Lộc District, Jiuzhen, Jiaozhou. She was buried at Tùng mountain (Triệu Lộc Commune, Hậu Lộc District, nowaday Thanh Hóa province). No whales were involved in her death.

Later, the Nam Đế, the Southern Emperor of the Early Lý dynasty, praised her as a brave and loyal person and ordered his followers to build a temple. He bestowed her with the title of "Bật chính anh hùng tài trinh nhất phu nhân" (Most Noble, Heroic and Virgin Lady). The temple still stands in present-day in Phú Điền commune.

Today, Lady Triệu is a hero in Vietnam. A national holiday celebrates her bravery, and streets are named in her honor throughout the country, all before she turned twenty-three.

Jeanne des Armoises

aka Jeanne d'Arc?

b. *1407*   d. *circa 1457*

France

There were several **Jeanne D'Arc** (Joan of Arc the Maid) imposters, and **Jeanne des Armoises** was the most genuine. Was she an imposter, or was she the honest St. Joan? These were challenging times, and the Maid battled for France and was immortalized on May 30, 1431, when burned at the stake for being a heretic and wearing boy's clothes.

Jeanne of Purcelle fought for France with distinction and commanded a battalion of troops for two years. She was the mother of two children and was reprimanded for impurity at one time. She responded, *"My value is not dependent on virginity."* Who among us has not made that cry? Five years after the execution, she appeared in Orleans with her knighted husband. The brothers of The Maid accepted this Jeanne and spent a lot of time, drink, and money with her. As of 1436, Orleans stopped celebrating the death of Jean, and apparently, they accepted the new Jeanne.

Now, this Jeanne was either inspired by or maybe was the Maid. There was always hope that Joan had escaped the pyre, and there was a rumor that a young imposter had replaced Joan at the stake. There are no drawings of the Maid and no photos in the Enquirer. The town of Orleans should have known her, and her brothers should recognize their sister. It appears Jeanne partied down and cranked out a bunch of letters all over the place. She was receiving a pension from the government. M. Anatole France offers a theory that the brothers were really after money and saw what they wanted to believe. When they met Jeanne, she told them she was their sister, and that was good enough.

Ten years after the execution, her death was still in question. Jeanne visited the King, and as there was speculation, the officials tried to present an imposter as the king. Jeanne was not fooled. The story continues that the King and Joan had a secret that they shared with no one else, and it involved a prayer. Jeanne knelt, confessed her sin, and cried for mercy when he asked for the secret.

She was sent to prison for five years and released in February 1457, with the stipulation that she bear herself honestly in dress and other matters, as a woman should do.

A legend states that far from being burned and her ashes thrown into the Seine, she is actually buried in Pulligny sur Madon castle. In 1871, two portraits were discovered when the plaster was removed from a 15th century chimney. The village mayor confirmed that his great-great-grandfather covered the portraits on the orders of Monsieur des Armoires (sound familiar) before the French Revolution and that they were of Joan and her husband, Robert des Armoises. Several books have been published on this theory

There is a document from an inquisitor dated 1440 speaking regretfully about the one who got away. Was that Joan or the imposter Jeanne?

Queen Nanny

or

Nanny

b. *circa* 1685
Ghana

d. *circa* 1755
Jamaica

According to Maroon legend, **Nanny** was born into the Akan people about 1686 in what is now Ghana, West Africa. Nanny is referred to as Granny Nanny, Grandy Nanny, and Queen Nanny but is confirmed to be a Maroon leader and Obeah woman in Jamaica. There are several versions of her early story, and it is not clear which one is accurate. In one story, she came as a free woman who may have been a slave owner (I vote no on that one). In another, she came to Jamaica as an enslaved person but escaped, perhaps even jumping off the ship while it was offshore (Maybe). A third version states she was of African royal blood and came to Jamaica as a free woman (no opinion, but it doesn't seem to fit).

It has been accepted that she came from the Ashanti tribe of present-day Ghana. Going with the most likely story, Nanny and her brothers ran away from the plantation and hid in the Blue Mountains. She may have married a Maroon man named Adou, but there were no known children. Maroons were enslaved in the Americas and had escaped and formed independent settlements. They were responsible for several revolts across Jamaica.

Queen Nanny was a well-respected, intelligent, spiritual leader who was instrumental in freeing enslaved people. For over thirty years, Queen Nanny helped more than a thousand people settle into the various Maroon communities of Jamaica. Despite repeated attacks from the British soldiers, Grandy Nanny's settlement, called Nanny Town, remained under Maroon control for years. Now Nanny wasn't the only leader in the Maroon community; her four brothers had also escaped from their plantations into the mountains and jungles of Jamaica. Nanny and one brother, Quao, founded a village in the Blue Mountains in the east of Jamaica, known as Nanny Town.

Nanny Town was placed in the mountains away from European settlements. Due to the location, it was difficult to assault and thrived. Nanny limited attacks on plantations and European territories, preferring to encourage farming and trade with neighbors. As much as she encouraged peace, she did make numerous successful raids to free the enslaved.

While Nanny lived, Nanny Town and the Windward Maroons thrived and grew. The British felt threatened by the Maroons, and the plantation owners were angered over their losses. In addition to the theft of equipment and burned crops. The Plantation owners demanded that colonial authorities act.

Soon the Jamaican jungles were filled with hunting parties made up of the British soldiers, militia, and mercenaries, sometimes including members of the free black community.

The war itself lasted from 1720 until a truce was declared in 1739. During one of the bloody engagements, Captain William Cuffee, often called Captain Sambo, is credited with killing Nanny in 1733.

During the Maroon War, Cudjoe, one of Nanny's brothers and a leader, was the driving force behind the treaty. After Nanny's death, many of the Windward Maroons moved across the island to Jamaica's more sparsely inhabited western side. Nanny Town was eventually captured by the British and destroyed in 1734.

The Government of Jamaica has recognized Nanny's life and accomplishments. She has been honored as a National Hero and awarded the title of "Right Excellent." Currently, there are only seven such National Heroes, and Nanny is conspicuous as the only woman. On the Jamaican $500 note, a modern portrait of Nanny is the largest banknote in circulation.

Bartolina Sisa Vargas

b. *circa* 1750
Peru

d. *September 5, 1782*
Bolivia

Bartolina Sisa was born around 1750 in the indigenous community of Q'ara Qhatu (Caracoto in Spanish), Viceroyalty of Peru, now Bolivia. She was the daughter of José Sisa and Josefa Vargas. She was still a young child when her family moved to Sica Sica. Her family traded coca leaves and made and sold woven goods. It was a common means of survival for peasant families of the region.

As Bartolina grew, she traveled across the Altiplano, selling the goods her family produced. During her travels, Bartolina witnessed the violence and maltreatment of the indigenous population by the Spanish.

According to the Franciscan friar, Matías Balderrama, Bartolina was thin, medium height, of a comely appearance, and had great intelligence. In her home village, she met Julián Apaza, later known as Túpac Katari. They married and, in time, had four children. Due to her awareness of the injustice she had witnessed, she joined her husband as he led an indigenous militia across the Altiplano to resist colonial rule.

In 1780 Tupac led an insurrection of mostly Aymara and Quechua peoples against the colonial rulers of the Viceroyalty of Peru. During this uprising, Bartolina earned a vital leadership role. She led around forty thousand, primarily Aymaran women, in numerous revolts against the Spanish rulers.

Alongside her husband, she participated in the organization of indigenous military camps that took part in the siege of La Paz. This was when she was betrayed and turned in to the Spanish authorities.

September 5, 1782, Bartolina was publicly humiliated in La Paz's Main Square (now Plaza Murillo), beaten, raped, and hanged. Once she was dead, the Spanish cut her body into pieces. Her head was displayed in public to intimidate the other natives, and they sent her limbs to be exhibited in different villages. Like the live violence and "humiliation" weren't enough.

In 1980 the Bartolina Sisa Confederation was named in her honor. It is the primary union of peasant women to improve the participation of indigenous and rural women in the political, social, and economic decisions of Bolivia.

In 1983 the Second Meeting of Organizations and Movements of the Americas gathered in Tiwanaku and decided to Honor Bartolina and celebrate the International Day of the Indigenous Woman every September 5, the same day of her execution.

Mary Ludwig Hays
aka
"Molly Pitcher"

b. October 13, 1754   d. January 22, 1832
Pennsylvania, USA

Molly Pitcher is a symbolic figure in the American Revolutionary War. Many women followed the camps at that time. Martha Washington was the most famous camp follower and an example of the countless other women who traveled with their husbands during the war. The camp followers did the cooking, washing, and other domestic chores in the soldiers' camps and acted as de facto nurses, tending to the wounded.

Historians say that "Molly Pitcher" is a fictional woman who represented the many women working on the battlefields. There is historical evidence that Mary Ludwig Hays was likely to be the "Molly Pitcher" at this battle.

Mary Ludwig Hays was born on October 13, 1754, in Philadelphia, Pennsylvania, or New Jersey. Her parents were German immigrants, and she grew up in humble circumstances. Mary would have had minimal education, if any. She wed William Hays, a barber.

William Hays enlisted in the 4th Pennsylvania Artillery during the Revolutionary War and served in the Continental Army. It was common for soldiers' wives to follow their husbands when they served at those times. Mary had joined her husband at the camp, and she undertook the tasks of washing the husband's clothes and preparing food if possible. It was common for the troops to refer to these women as "Molly Pitcher." Molly was a nickname for Mary, a most common woman's name, and Pitcher would refer to the containers they would carry for water and other tasks during battle.

History states that on June 28, 1778, Mary Hays enlisted to serve with Captain Francis Proctor's company in the Pennsylvania Artillery. There was a suggestion that some of the men who knew Mary described her as an illiterate, pregnant woman who smoked and chewed tobacco and swore as much as any of the men. She gained respect by being a dedicated, hard worker and showed bravery under fire. On that particular day, the soldiers were as likely to die from heat exhaustion and dehydration as from battle wounds. It was documented that Mary went back and forth in the battle carrying water and tending to the wounded.

The story suggests in the Battle of Monmouth, William Hays was a cannoneer and was wounded. Mary, his wife, was there carrying water for the line. She took his place at the cannon with virtually no hesitation and continued the battle. The legend continued suggesting that George Washington later asked about the courageous woman on the battlefield and promoted her to a non-commissioned officer.

William Hays died in 1786 from his wounds. When he died, he left a substantial amount of land to Mary. Some years later, Mary married John McCauley. He was also a veteran of the Revolutionary War, but it is told that he spent her inheritance and then disappeared sometime after 1807.

Hays lived the rest of her life in Carlisle, Pennsylvania, working as a domestic servant. In 1822, the Pennsylvania State Legislature awarded Hays a pension of $40 per year for her service and heroism in the war. On January 22, 1832, she died and was buried in the Carlisle Old Graveyard.

Her burial site is marked "Molly McCauley," with a cannon and a statue of "Molly Pitcher" above her tombstone.

Margaret Cochran-Corbin
aka
"Molly Pitcher"
Part 2 of many

b. November 12, 1751   d. January 16, 1800
Pennsylvania, USA

While doing research, I also discovered **Margaret Corbin**. She was born in western Franklin County, Pennsylvania. Margaret was the daughter of Scots-Irish immigrant Robert Cochran and Sarah, his wife. When Margaret was five years old, in 1756, her parents' farm was raided by Native Americans. Her father was killed in the melee, and her mother was kidnapped, never to return. Most likely, her mother was sold to the French in Canada, a common occurrence at the time. A few would return to their homes in the Colonies, but most did not, especially if no one was left to pay a ransom. Margaret and her brother John had escaped the raid and stayed with their uncle.

When Margaret was twenty-one, in 1772, she married James Corbin, a farmer from Virginia. The Revolutionary War began a few years after their marriage, and John Corbin enlisted. He became part of the First Company of Pennsylvania Artillery and served on the cannon crew. Margaret, in her concern for her husband, followed him to war. She took on domestic and nursing duties in the camp.

As was typical, Margaret was referred to as "Molly Pitcher." a typical camp follower nickname given to women who served in support of the soldiers. (I wonder if they called Martha Washington Molly?) They also often cooled the cannons during battle and any other tasks so the men could be free to fight the war.

Margaret's fame began on November 16, 1776, at Fort Washington in Manhattan, where her husband's company was stationed. He was part of a small garrison George Washington had left behind to guard the island while he and the rest of the Continental Army retreated to White Plains, NY. Once most of the troops were gone, the British attacked Fort Washington. Margaret's husband, John, was firing the cannon at the top of a ridge. John was hit and killed during the battle, leaving the cannon unattended. Margaret had been by his side during the fighting and witnessed him fall.

Margaret knew the cannon was needed, and she had watched her husband use it. With little hesitation, she jumped into the battle and started firing the gun at the British. She stayed at the cannon, being wounded multiple times by enemy fire until she could not continue. Margaret had sustained wounds to her arm, chest, and jaw during the fight. In the end, the British won the battle of Fort Washington, and Margaret had to surrender along with the male soldiers. She was considered an enemy combatant since she had fired on the British. Once the company surrendered, the last place in New York City held by Americans fell. Even though Margaret was not an official part of the Army and was wounded as a combatant, she was treated and released on parole by the British, which was the practice for injured prisoners of war in that era.

Margaret went to Philadelphia after being paroled; her wounds completely disabled her. She was never to recover completely. Margaret never remarried as men at the time wanted a wife who could care for a household. Life was a struggle for Margaret, and she could barely take care of herself. However, the new government of the United States recognized her contribution to the patriot cause, and the Executive Council of Pennsylvania granted her a gift of thirty dollars to take care of herself. On July 6, 1779, the Board of War of the new Congress learned of her case, and due to her bravery and service, they granted Margaret a pension equal to half that of a male soldier (pay equity isn't a modern issue). The pension was paid monthly and included either a new set of clothes or its equivalent in cash.

Margaret Corbin was the first woman to receive a military pension from the United States in the new nation. She was included on Congressional military rolls after this and until the war's end. Congress enrolled her in the Corps of Invalids, which became part of the garrison at West Point in 1781. Her official discharge from the Continental Army was in 1783, and she received her military pension from Congress for the rest of her life.

In 1926, the New York State Chapter of Daughters of the American Revolution recognized Margaret's service to her country and verified her military records. They located her neglected grave, had her body exhumed, and examined by a physician, who confirmed it was her. On April 14, 1926, she was re-interred with full military honors in the cemetery behind the Old Cadet Chapel at West Point. Margaret was one of the two Revolutionary War soldiers to be buried there. The Daughters of the American Revolution then erected the Margaret Corbin Monument to commemorate the bravery and patriotism of this remarkable colonial woman.

WARM SPRINGS APACHES
Two who rode together

Lozen

b. *circa 1840*   d. *1898*
Warm Springs, New Mexico

Lozen, an amazing indigenous woman, was born into the Cheyenne, Warm Springs Apache band in the 1840s. She was the sister of Chief Victorio, who described her as, "Lozen is my right hand . . . strong as a man, braver than most, and cunning in strategy, Lozen is a shield to her people." She never married, knowing that she had no interest in women's work early in life. At the age of eight, she started training physically, and at her Puberty ritual, she was given the power to find enemies.

    She began fighting the Mexican soldiers and scalp hunters when she was a child. By the time she came of age, the "Americans" had arrived in her homeland, and she fought in the campaigns to save her people for the rest of her life. She showed incredible military knowledge, and her instincts had many who believed spirits spoke and protected her. She fought against

384   * more than a footnote

the Mexicans for her homeland until they were confined to the Arizona San Carlos Reservation.

She inspired not only warriors but also women and children. James Kaywaykla, the son of Gouyen, reported seeing a "magnificent woman on a beautiful horse – Lozen, sister of Victorio – Lozen, the woman warrior!" He remembered she held her rifle high above her head as she led the frightened women and children across the raging Rio Grande, saving them from the US Military. She then told his grandmother to take charge, and she returned to help the warriors as they battled on.

Another time she left a campaign to escort a mother and her newborn infant across the Chihuahuan Desert. She set out through Mexican and US Calvary strongholds with limited supplies and a rifle. Fearing a gunshot would betray their location, she killed a longhorn with a knife and butchered it for the meat they needed to survive. She also stole two cavalry horses for them to ride, escaping through a hail of bullets. She not only got away with two horses but also was able to snag a saddle, rifle, ammunition, blanket, canteen, and even the soldier's shirt. Upon delivering everything, she learned that her brother was ambushed by the Mexican and Tarahumara Indian forces on October 15, 1881. The Apaches had almost fought to the last man, and Victorio, holding to Apache tradition, fell on his knife rather than be taken by the Mexicans. Most of the Apache women and elderly were killed in this battle, and around a hundred young women and children were enslaved.

Knowing that the survivors needed her, she rode out alone. Lozen rejoined the decimated band, now being led by the seventy-four-year-old patriarch Nana. Lozen fought with this handful of warriors in a two-month campaign of vengeance across New Mexico. Nana said, "Though she is a woman, there is no warrior more worthy than the sister of Victorio."

In 1885 in the last campaign of the Apache wars, she and Gouyen joined with Geronimo after he broke out of the San Carlos reservation.

It is told that she used her powers to locate enemies. According to Alexander Adams in his book Geronimo, she would stand with her arms outstretched, chant a prayer, and turn around. She would then feel the location of the enemies, even their number. She was photographed with Geronimo several times, and you would never know that she was a woman. She had no concern for appearance and the ways of women; she not only dressed but lived like a man. Lozen devoted her life to the service of her people. She was the only Apache woman allowed to ride in a war as a warrior without a husband at her side.

She had eluded capture until she finally surrendered with Geronimo and this last group of free Apaches in 1886. She died of tuberculosis in 1898 at the Mount Vernon Barracks in Mobile, Alabama as a prisoner of war.

WARM SPRINGS APACHES
Two who rode together

Gouyen

b. 1855   d. 1903
Oklahoma, USA

Her life is so sacred that the Apache does not utter her given name. They refer to her as Gouyen, which means "the one who is wise."

Gouyen was born around 1855 into Chief Victorio's Warm Springs band of Apaches. Before 1880, a Comanche tribe raided the community, killing her husband. After this, she lost her baby daughter, and more than three-quarters of her tribe had perished during this series of battles. As the legend is told, Gouyen became so lost in grief that she had to be watched day and night.

One night, Gouyen gained enough strength to sneak out of camp. She gathered her buckskin puberty ceremony dress and left the camp, carrying only water, dried meat, a bone awl, and sinew. She could not get a weapon, but that did not stop her.

Gouyen was on a mission to find the Comanche chief who had killed her man. After a couple of days of searching, she came upon a Comanche celebration and found him there. She watched as he danced for victory around a bonfire with her husband's scalp hanging from his belt. She smoothed her hair, put on her dress, and slipped into the circle of dancers. The chief was described as "staggering drunk" as Gouyen approached him, looking hot in her ceremonial best. She easily led him alone into the dark, where, without weapons, she leaped upon him like a mountain lion, ripping his throat with her teeth. After he fell to the ground, she stabbed him to death with his knife and took his scalp.

Not completely satisfied, Gouyen cut off the chief's beaded breechcloth, took off his moccasins and headband, and then she *jacked his ride*. She returned to her camp on his horse and presented it to her in-laws with the scalp, clothing, and horse to prove her vengeance against her husband's killer. Little did she know that through her actions, she avenged the deaths of her brothers and sisters and built a reputation that would give her honor beyond her life.

At first, Gouyen worried that her behavior would be inappropriate to tradition and contrary to the Apache rules of wifely conduct. Instead, her impressed chief called her a "brave and good woman" who had taken a bolder action than any man. As it turned out, Gouyen's brutal revenge became an extraordinarily important step in restoring pride and energy to this Apache tribe.

388   * more than a footnote

While it was common for women to participate in a war during these violent times, Gouyen's power shined above the rest. She was believed to be protected during battle by Spirit Forces, which is partly why her given name is guarded with such reverence. Gouyen was part of Victorio's band during their final days, evading U.S. and Mexican troops along the border. On October 14, 1880, the group was resting at Tres Castillos, Mexico, when they were surrounded and attacked by Mexican soldiers. Victorio and seventy-seven other Apache died, and many were taken, prisoner. Only seventeen escaped, including Gouyen and her young son Kaywaykla.

Gouyen married a second time to an Apache warrior named Kaytennae. He was one of the few who escaped. Later, Kaytennae joined the Nana and Geronimo's band during the early 1880s. He and Gouyen escaped with Geronimo from the San Carlos Reservation in 1883. During their maneuvers to evade capture, a man was trying to ambush her husband, and Gouyen saved Kaytennae's life by killing the sniper.

In 1886, Gouyen and her family were taken prisoner by the U.S. Army and others in Geronimo's band. They were held as prisoners at Fort Sill, Oklahoma. The U.S. Army transferred indigenous prisoners from all over to Fort Sill, where most died of tuberculosis, typhoid, or other infectious diseases that raged through the captives. Gouyen died in 1903, seventeen years after being taken. The details of her death don't appear to be recorded.

In her son's words, Kaywaylka, "...*my mother's place was at Kaytennae's side. She prepared food, dressed wounds, and, when necessary, fought beside him as bravely as any man.*"

One of these amazing women could be a movie, but Gouyen and Lozen together – show us actual superheroes!

Maria Bochkareva

b. 1894 *d. May 15, 1920*
Russia

From 1914 to 1917, **Maria Bochkareva** was a Russian national war hero whose information was removed from Russian History by the men who ran the Communist party. She was the historical commander of the "1st Russian Woman's Battalion of Death." She was a Dangerous Dish, who got knocked down, but she got up again, and they never could keep her down. Her story is deep and exciting, filled with aspects of strength, honor, determination, and personal interactions with the leaders of the free and the communist worlds.

She was born to an abusive alcoholic who beat her regularly. She married an abusive alcoholic, who beat her regularly, divorced, and remarried a man who eventually proved to be a thief. After being caught and exiled twice, he became an abusive alcoholic and beat her regularly.

Maria eventually found herself drawn to military duty and discovered the violence of battle to be a place where she could flourish. And flourish she did. When Maria first decided to join the military, they weren't interested in her because she was just, you know, a dumb, fragile girl. So, she used her last few pennies to send a telegram to Tsar Nicholas II, asking him to let her join. She received his personal permission, and in November 1914, at the onset of World War I, she enlisted into the 25th Tomsk Reserve Battalion of the Imperial Russian Army.

At first, she had to endure the typical battering that so many women have had to put up with from the boys on the team. They continually harassed and belittled her for being female. But Maria was a warrior at heart who eventually proved herself and gained their respect. While in battle, she fought hard and smart. She was wounded a few times, but after recovery, she jumped right back into the foxholes, where she not only earned the respect of the male soldiers but taught herself to read.

By 1917 the war was going badly for Russia. The Tsar had been overthrown, the soldiers were exhausted and losing their motivation to fight, and the Russian Front was collapsing. Now a three-time decorated lieutenant, Maria was ordered to establish the "1st Russian Woman's Battalion of Death." She was given two thousand volunteers who joined out of stylish patriotism, but her training program boiled those numbers down to three hundred dedicated and worthy soldiers. The strategy from the top was to put women on the battlefield to shame the men into fighting harder, and Maria simply welcomed the opportunity to contribute, fight, lead, and remain in the war. These women proved to be a formidable force on the battlefield. By October of 1917, as the war effort collapsed, the women's battalion had found themselves to be the last line of defense at the headquarters of the Petrograd Winter Palace. At about 9 pm one evening, Lenin's Bolsheviks seized power. Maria had been wounded and was sent back to Petrograd for recuperation. The war had changed color to become the Russian Civil War.

Maria, whose heart desired a unified Russia, refused to take sides in the civil war. Meanwhile, the 137 remaining women of the battalion were disbanded because the Russian men didn't appreciate their femme success. Only Maria was detained. Her status was of such importance that Lenin and Trotsky interrogated her. They spoke to her with admiration for her courage, and she was offered work with the Bolsheviks. Maria refused.

Then one day, Maria received a telegram ordering her to carry a message to General Lavr Kornilov, commander of the White Army. Almost immediately, the Red Army of the Bolsheviks called again. They arrested her, charged her as an enemy of the state, and stood her before a firing squad. Luckily one of the executioners recognized her and remembered that she had saved his life on the German front. He put down his gun and stood beside her, vowing to die at her side. This action stopped the execution and led to her release.

She was eventually allowed to leave the country, and so she shipped out to San Francisco and then made her way to Washington DC. Maria was able to get a meeting with the President of the United States of America. Boy, when this woman wanted something, she just went right to the top. On July 10, 1918, on her knees pleading, she was able to draw tears out of President Woodrow Wilson, who promised to see what he could do to intervene in the perils happening to her people in Russia.

She then left Washington, turning northeast for Great Britain. Maria bypassed the Prime Minister and secured a meeting with King George V. He bankrolled her return to Russia. She tried to organize another woman's battalion, but this time with no success. Maria then formed the Women's Medical Attachment. Before she could complete the unit, the Bolsheviks arrested her again and sentenced her as an enemy of the state, and this time they executed her for real on May 16, 1920. She was thirty-one years old.

"Come with us in the name of your fallen heroes. Come with us to dry the tears and heal the wounds of Russia. Protect her with your lives. We women are turning into tigresses to protect our children from a shameful yoke – to protect the freedom of our country."

– Maria Bochkareva

Milunka Savić

b. August 10, 1888   *d. October 5, 1973*
Serbia

It is challenging to identify Milunka Savić's birthday. There are multiple dates in the research, and I picked the one that made her a Zodiac Leo. Either way, she was born in the village of Koprivnica, Serbia, in 1888. Details of her early life and childhood are not recorded.

In 1912-1913, her brother received call-up papers for mobilization for the First Balkan War. Accounts vary as to whether she impersonated her brother or simply accompanied him, but she joined the Serbian army disguised as a man. If Milunka decided to go in his place, there must be more to that story and decision. She cut her hair and donned men's clothing, and signed up. Within weeks, she saw combat and earned a medal and a promotion to Corporal for taking part in repeated assaults during the nine-day Battle of Bregalnica.

During the tenth assault, Miulunka was wounded by a Bulgarian grenade, and while being treated in hospital, her gender was revealed. Everyone, except Milunka, was shocked due to her immediate and exemplary service in the battles. Unwilling to punish her due to her valor on the battlefield, Milunka's commanding officer offered her a transfer to a nursing division. Milunka arose, stood tall at attention, and insisted she would only serve her country as a combatant. It was reported the officer told her he would have an answer the next day, and Milunka responded, "I will wait," and remained standing at attention in front of him. It only took about an hour for him to relent and allow her to return to her infantry unit. 1914, in the early days of World War I, Milunka was awarded her first Karađorđe Star with Swords. She received her second Karađorđe Star with Swords after the Battle of the Crna Bend two month long battle between the Bulgarian and the Entente armies. This was when our soldier captured twenty-three Bulgarian soldiers single-handedly.

A year after the Balkan Wars, Europe was torn apart by World War I, and Milunka continued to serve. The war didn't go well for Serbia, and Milunka fought for the French as they reformed the Serbian army.

Milunka's career as a soldier spanned two Balkan Wars and World War I. She was wounded no less than nine times during her service. By the end of WWI, she had received medals from France, Russia, and Britain for her bravery.

After WWI, Milunka turned down a military pension in France to return to Serbia, and she found a job as a postal worker. In 1923, she married Veljko Gligorijević. They were divorced right after the birth of their daughter Milena, and Milunka went on to adopt and foster other children. She worked several menial jobs until she found employment as a cleaning lady in the State Mortgage Bank around 1927. Eight years later, she was promoted to cleaning the offices of the general manager.

In peace, Milunka was nearly forgotten. During the German occupation of Serbia in World War II, she was taken prisoner and sent to the Banjica concentration camp. She refused to attend a banquet with German officers, claiming she operated a hospital to treat wounded partisans. She was spared execution and eventually released by a German officer who recognized her as a war hero.

Milunka died of a stroke in October 1973, aged eighty-five. She was buried with full military honors, and a street in Belgrade is named for her. She is the most decorated woman soldier in history so far.

Sarah Keyes-Evans

b. 1929
Washington, NC, USA

Sarah Louise Keyes was born in rural Washington, North Carolina, in 1929, the second oldest of seven children. Upon graduation from Mercy Catholic High School, she enrolled in the Perth Amboy, New Jersey Hospital School of Nursing in 1948 and moved to New York. Sarah stayed at the Franciscan Handmaids of Mary Convent in Harlem for Career Girls and remained in New York for two years before enlisting in the Women's Army Corps in 1951.

On August 1, 1952, Sarah was on leave and was traveling home. She had bought a ticket for a through bus with no scheduled stops other than her destination. Around midnight, there was an unanticipated driver change in Roanoke Rapids, NC. The new driver woke her up and asked Sarah to give up her seat for a white Marine. He suggested she move to the rear of the bus. She was aware that in 1946, buses originating in the North, with no changes, did not have to adhere to local Southern laws. Understanding her rights, Sarah refused to give up her seat, stating she was comfortable where she sat.

The driver ordered all the other passengers off the bus except for Sarah. Unsure of what was happening, she went to the bus station to inquire. Sarah reported that the clerk dropped the curtain and dimmed the lights at the window. It is evident that there was more to this than expected.

A short time later, the local police arrived and accused her of being belligerent and using profanity, which she denied. This was when Sarah was arrested and held in custody for thirteen hours. At one point, an officer asked if she was wearing a uniform, and she proudly asked if he was unable to recognize the attire of the Woman Army Corps.

She was ordered to pay a $25 fine (over $250 now) for disorderly conduct when she was released. Sarah was taken to the bus station, given an assigned seat, and told not to move until she reached her destination. Her proud stance led to a three-year legal battle culminating in the historic ruling that outlawed segregation in interstate bus travel."

Claudette Colvin was just fifteen when she and other students were asked to give up their seats on March 2, 1955, and it was on December 1, 1955, that Rosa Parks took the same stance in Montgomery, Alabama.

With the help and encouragement of her father, Sarah Keys took her case to the lower court, where she lost. She then turned to the National Association for the Advancement of Colored People (NAACP) for help. They assigned Dovey J. Roundtree and Julius Robertson to the case. The new team presented her case to the Interstate Commerce Commission (ICC) and won. The Keys vs. Coach Company case was settled on November 7, 1955.

Also, in November of 1955, the Interstate Commerce Commission reversed the "separate but equal" policy that ruled that Black passengers who paid the same amount for rail and bus fares as White passengers must receive the same service. They were no longer to be moved to seats reserved for blacks.

Sarah's brave action and perseverance resulted in many well-deserved honors. Her contributions to America's civil rights movement earned an award from the New York State Beauty Culture Association and the Martin Luther King, Jr. Living the Dream Award.

Sarah L. Keys married George C. Evans, Jr., a native of Beaumont, TX, in 1958, and she has lived in Brooklyn, NY, since 1954. She was invited to speak at the 1997 Dedication of the Women in Military Service for America Memorial. In 2020, Roanoke Rapids declared August First as "Sarah Keys Evans Day" and dedicated a mural depicting her story, sixty-eight years after its police arrested the twenty-three-year-old Black Women's Army Corps private.

Dolores Fernandez-Huerta

b. 1930
Dawson, NM, USA

Born on April 10, 1930, in Dawson, New Mexico, **Dolores Fernandez** was the second of three children born to Alicia and Juan Fernandez. Her parents divorced when Huerta was three years old, and her mother moved to Stockton, California, with the children. Dolores maintained contact with her father, who had developed from coal miner to migrant laborer and then a union activist. Juan Fernandez was elected Representative in the New Mexico state legislature in 1938 and only then graduated college. Dolores' grandfather helped raise the three children, while her mother juggled jobs as a waitress and cannery worker. In time, she was able to buy a small hotel and restaurant. With her parents' work and exposure to community activism, Dolores developed a drive for compassionate treatment of workers.

With her dynamic parents, discrimination also played a part in shaping her path. Dolores told of a schoolteacher, obviously prejudiced against Hispanics, accusing her of cheating because her papers were too well-written. Then in 1945, at the end of World War II, white men brutally beat her brother for wearing a Zoot-Suit, a famous Latino fashion of that era.

Dolores obtained an associate teaching degree from the University of the Pacific's Delta College. She married Ralph Head while attending the university, and they had two daughters before the marriage failed.

Subsequently, Dolores married Ventura Huerta, a fellow activist. They had five children before the marriage ended in divorce. Dolores Huerta briefly taught school in the 1950s, but seeing so many hungry farm children coming to school, she was convinced she could do more. This was when she began organizing farmers and farm workers.

Her new career as an activist began in 1955. Dolores co-founded the Stockton chapter of the Community Service Organization (CSO). She worked with voter registration drives and fought for economic improvements for Hispanics. Then Dolores went on to establish the Agricultural Workers Association. With a meeting with César Chávez, the American labor leader and civil rights activist, her interest in organizing farm workers kicked off. In 1962, Delores and Chávez founded the National Farm Workers Association (NFWA), the predecessor of the United Farm Workers' Union (UFW). Dolores served as UFW vice president until 1999.

Despite ethnic and gender bias, Dolores organized the 1965 Delano strike of five thousand grape workers. She led the negotiations in the workers' contract that followed. Her life has been dedicated to organizing workers, negotiating contracts, healthcare, and workers' safety. She was instrumental in addressing the worker's conditions and elimination of harmful pesticides. Dolores' grape boycotts in the late 1960s led to a successful union contract by 1970.

In 1973, she developed an additional grape boycott that resulted in the ground-breaking California Agricultural Labor Relations Act of 1975. This Act allowed farm workers to form unions and bargain for better wages and conditions. Throughout the 1970s and 1980s, Dolores worked as a lobbyist to improve workers' legislative representation. Not one to rest, during the 1990s and 2000s, she worked to elect more Latinos and women to political office and has championed women's issues.

Dolores Huerta has been awarded multiple honors, including the Eleanor Roosevelt Human Rights Award in 1998 and the Presidential Medal of Freedom in 2012. As of 2015, she was a board member of the Feminist Majority Foundation, the Secretary-Treasurer Emeritus of the United Farm Workers of America, and the President of the Dolores Huerta Foundation.

Writers

"I told you in the course of this paper that Shakespeare had a sister; but do not look for her in Sir Sidney Lee's life of the poet. She died young – alas, she never wrote a word. She lies buried where the omnibuses now stop, opposite the Elephant and Castle. Now my belief is that this poet who never wrote a word and was buried at the crossroads still lives. She lives in you and in me, and in many other women who are not here tonight, for they are washing up the dishes and putting the children to bed. But she lives; for great poets do not die; they are continuing presences; they need only the opportunity to walk among us in the flesh."

— Virginia Woolf
A Room of One's Own

Enheduanna

or

Enheduana, En-hedu-Ana

circa 2350-2250, B.C.E.
City of Ur, Sumer (Sumeria)

Enheduanna is the earliest discovered author and poet in the world. She was the daughter of the great Mesopotamian king, Sargon of Akkad, Akkadian, and her mother was possibly Queen Tashlultum. Enheduanna's name translates as 'High Priestess of An' (the sky god) or 'En-Priestess, wife of the god Nanna.' Her parents had high expectations with their naming choices. She came from the northern city of Akkad and would have had a Semitic birth name, but with her high assignment and moving to Ur, the heartland of Sumerian culture, she took a Sumerian official title, *Enheduanna*: 'En' (Chief Priest or Priestess); 'hedu' (ornament); 'Ana' (of heaven)".

Enheduanna's responsibilities in the region of Sumer would have been to keep the populace in check through religion. Enheduanna's contributions to literature include several personal devotions to the goddess Inanna and a collection of hymns known as the "Sumerian Temple Hymns." Additional texts are attributed to her. This makes Enheduanna the first-named author, male or female, in world history. She didn't have to deal with editors or Amazon reviews.

There is no mention of husbands, children, or romance, but she was the first known woman to hold the title of EN, a role of great political importance that was usually only assigned to royal daughters. Enheduanna was appointed by her father to be the priestess of the temple of Nanna, the god of the moon in the Mesopotamian religions of Sumer, Akkad, Assyria, Babylonia, and Aram. His position as the moon god was to the perceived similarity between Nanna's bull horns and the crescent moon, and he was also associated with cattle. The temple was located in Ur, the largest city and center of her father's empire. As a priestess, Enheduanna would have been free to travel to other parts of the kingdom.

Enheduanna helped her father solidify his political power and unite the Sumerian city-states. She accomplished this by merging the worship of many local city goddesses into the Sumerian goddess, Inanna, raising her to a superior position over other deities.

As a break from the constant demands of her multiple positions, Enheduanna wrote three hymns to Inanna, which survive and illustrate three different themes of some ancient religions. Her works are Inninsagurra, Ninmesarra, and Inninmehusa, which translate as 'The Great-Hearted Mistress,' The Exaltation of Inanna,' and 'Goddess of the Fearsome Powers,' all three are powerful hymns to the goddess Inanna, later also known as Akkadian/Assyrian

Ishtar, the Hittite Sauska, the Greek Aphrodite, and the Phoenician Astarte, among others. Enheduanna did have a scribe to handle her dictation and tablet carving. Imagine working with a sack of styli and a bucket of clay – then take dictation!

In Inninsagurra, Inanna is a ferocious warrior goddess who defeated a mountain despite other gods refusing to help. The second hymn celebrated Inanna's role in governing civilization and overseeing the home and children. In the third, Enheduanna calls on her relationship with the goddess for help in regaining her position as the priestess of the temple against a male usurper (sound familiar?). The lengthy text of the hymn tells the story of Inanna and the belief by a few scholars to be mistakenly attributed to Enheduanna, but the overall consensus is that it is hers.

At least forty-two, perhaps as many as fifty-three, other hymns survive attributed to Enheduanna, including three hymns to Nanna, and other temples, gods, and goddesses. The surviving cuneiform tablets with the hymns are copies from about five hundred years after Enheduanna's death, and they attest to a continued study of her poems in Sumer. It is believed that Enheduanna's prayers influenced the psalms of the Hebrew Bible and Homeric and Christian hymns. Experts have noted that the Sumerian gods seemed more compassionate and embraced all people after Enheduanna took to tablet.

Because we don't know how the language was pronounced, we cannot study some of the format and style of her poetry. The poems seem to have eight to twelve syllables per line, and many lines end with vowel sounds. She also uses repetition of sounds, words, and phrases.

Her father, Sargon of Akkad, ruled for fifty-five years and appointed her to the high priestess position late in his reign. When he died, his son, Rimush, and Enheduanna continued to rule. When her second ruling brother died and Enheduanna's nephew Naram-Sin took over, she again continued in her position. No telling exactly when her long poems were written; some may have responded to parties that attempted rebellion.

Enheduanna remains an important figure, perhaps even attaining semi-divine status. Although her poems are not on Amazon, several books about her are.

From Wikipedia, I found Hymn 26, translated by Betty De Shong Meador:

Temple Hymn 26 The Zabalam Temple Of Inanna
O house wrapped in beams of light
wearing shining stone jewels wakening great awe
sanctuary of pure Inanna
(where) divine powers the true me spread wide
Zabalam
shrine of the shining mountain
shrine that welcomes the morning light
she makes resound with desire
the Holy Woman grounds your hallowed chamber
with desire
your queen Inanna of the sheepfold

that singular woman
the unique one
who speaks hateful words to the wicked
who moves among the bright shining things
who goes against rebel lands
and at twilight makes the firmament beautiful
all on her own
great daughter of Suen
pure Inanna
O house of Zabalam
has built this house on your radiant site
and placed her seat upon your dais
Did you hum along?

    Now try to get that tune out of your head for the rest of the day.

Murasaki Shikibu

b. 978　　　　　　　　　　　　　　d. 1014
　　　　　Kyoto, Japan

Murasaki Shikibu is a descriptive name; her personal name is unknown, but she may have been Fujiwara no Kaoriko (藤原 香子), as was mentioned in a 1007 court diary as an imperial lady-in-waiting. We will refer to her as Murasaki Shikibu. She was born around 978 in Kyoto, Japan, to a lesser branch of the Fujiwara family. The exact dates of Lady Murasaki's life are unknown, as is her real name. "Shikubu" may have been a reference to her father, who served in the Ministry of Ceremonies. The name Murasaki translates to "Violet." It could be a reference to the heroine in the *Tale of Genji* or to the first element of her maiden name. Her mother is unknown. Her great-grandfather was a poet, and her father, Fujiwara Tamatoki, was a scholar and a poet. As a child, Murasaki was brilliant and learned faster than her brother. Her father once said, "If only you were a boy, how happy I should be!"

　Lucky for the world, her father allowed Murasaki to study with her brother, which included studies in Chinese and Buddhist classics. At the time, that was considered improper for females. You know that delicate head thing.

In her early twenties, Murasaki married a distant relative. Her only daughter was born in 999. Her husband died in 1001, near the time her father became governor of the province of Echizen, about eighty miles from the capital. The imperial family learned of her writing talent and intellectual capacity. Murasaki was invited to court, and soon she was promoted from guest to lady-in-waiting serving Akiko (Empress Shoshi).

Murasaki was not fond of court life, which she found frivolous, and she was often withdrawn. In 1008, Murasaki began writing a diary about her life at court, which she continued for two years. When Emperor Ichijo died in 1011, Empress Shoshi retired with her ladies-in-waiting. During this time of turmoil, her father retired as governor and entered a monastery, but still no mention of her mother.

All of the moving around leads us to Murasaki's book, considered the world's first novel, *Genji Monogatari* (*The Tale of Genji*). This book is often referred to as the greatest work of Japanese literature. It concerns the life of charismatic Prince Genji and his descendants. It is a subtle and thorough depiction of the complex society of the time. It was intended to be read aloud, as education was for the few. The book contains fifty-four chapters and is twice the length of *War and Peace*. The various storylines in the novel are remarkably consistent, following the romantic involvements and the court intrigues surrounding Prince Genji. It ends (spoiler alert) with a gloomy psychological analysis of unrequited love. Murasaki is believed to have started writing the novel around 1003, and it may have been still incomplete at her death. Three works are attributed to Murasaki: *The Tale of Genji*, *The Diary of Lady Murasaki*, and *Poetic Memoirs*, a collection of 128 poems. Her work reflected the creation and development of Japanese writing.

Almost nothing is known about Murasaki's later life other than writing and editing. She may have retired from court, run off with Matt Damon, or entered a convent around the age of fifty. Her writings suggest that she was sensitive to the approaching political changes that would permanently affect her privileged lifestyle towards the end of her days. It is believed that Murasaki died around 1031C.E. Murasaki Shikibu's tomb is located in Kyoto, just south of the Kitaoji-Horikawa intersection.

Murasaki's legacy as a novelist and poet was memorialized in many Japanese paintings from the time. Her daughter Kenshi also entered court service and became a famous poet.

Margaret Lucas Cavendish
Duchess of Newcastle-upon-Tyne

b. 1624
Colchester, England

d. December 15, 1673
Welbeck, England

Margaret Lucas was born in 1624 in Colchester, England. She was the youngest of eight children of Thomas Lucas, a wealthy landowner, who had been exiled after a duel that led to the death of "one Mr. Brooks." He was pardoned by King James, who apparently didn't like Mr. Brooks either. Her father returned to England in 1603. Margaret's mother, Elizabeth Leighton (Knollys), also known as Lady Leighton, was the daughter of Sir Francis Knollys and Catherine Carey. She held a royal position as the Chief Lady of the Bedchamber. Her father died in 1625, and since Margaret was only about a year old, she didn't know him well.

The Lucas family moved to the royalist, or pro-monarchy, town of Oxford south of London. She did not receive a formal education, but she had access to libraries and tutors. She became an avid reader, which goes a long way toward being educated. Margaret began to put her ideas to paper at an early age, and even though it was considered improper at the time, she didn't let this stand in her way. Her close relationship with her middle brother, John, enhanced her education. John was already a well-established scholar: a student of law, philosophy, and natural science, he was fluent in Hebrew, Latin, and Greek. In time John would become a founding member of the Royal Society.

In an attempt for independence, Margaret applied to serve Queen Henrietta Maria in 1643. Her brother and mother's high positions probably added to her resume. Margaret was appointed maid of honor at the court of the Queen. After two years of service, Margaret accompanied the queen into exile in Paris, France. Around 1645, while in Paris, Margaret married William Cavendish, Duke of Newcastle, an English courtier and supporter of the arts. He was a renowned royalist military hero, horse breeder, writer, and patron of the playwright Ben Jonson. William was part of the intellectual group known as the Welbeck Circle. Oh, and he was thirty years older than Margaret.

Her husband's station and connections allowed Margaret to do more than serve tea in the Cavendish circle. The Circle was a collection of intellectuals, philosophers, and creative geniuses. Margaret also could visit the all-male Royal Society, the prestigious scientific organization. Some of the critics pointed out her apparent lack of formal training. After all, Margaret didn't speak any foreign or dead languages and had no classical education. Margaret met with constant ridicule because of her prolific papers.

It was in 1651 when Margaret and William moved to Antwerp, Belgium, after being exiled by the incoming administration. The powers-that-be came and went and made it possible for Margaret to return to England. She traveled with her brother-in-law, Charles Cavendish, to seek payment for William's estate, and even though her request was denied, she remained in England for nearly two years. This was when Margaret published her first works, *Poems and Fancies and Philosophical Fancies*, in 1653.

After returning to Antwerp, she wrote four more books, beginning a productive, twenty year career. They returned to England in 1660 when King Charles II took the throne at the beginning of the Restoration. They settled at William's estate, Welbeck, in Nottinghamshire, where Margaret continued to write.

Margaret is best known today for *The Description of a New World Called the Blazing World*, published in 1666. I assume you haven't read this, so in brief, it tells the story of a young lady who is abducted by a foreign merchant and taken by ship. The merchant and the crew froze during the passage into the new world, and they would thaw out once they arrived and spread corruption. The same young woman transforms into a warrior queen. She rules over the Blazing World, fighting rebellions and commanding armies of bird-men, worm-men, bear-men, and other assorted warrior-men in a series of fantastic adventures.

Often referred to as "Mad Madge," her contemporaries viewed Margaret as being rather eccentric. Known for her unusual sense of fashion, Margaret was extravagant, flirtatious, and accused of using speech full of 'oaths and obscenity.' This reputation survives today, and she drew attention by dressing unconventionally, often in a combination of women's and men's clothing – kind of like the outfit I have on now.

Margaret was very prolific in her writing and published under her own name. She produced a more significant body of work than any other mid-17th century woman. Not limited by genre, she wrote poems, plays, literary critiques, volumes of observations, and even works on natural philosophy. Her writings received a mixed reception – more negative than positive, and this was before Amazon reviews and the cursed five stars.

While she may have been only a minor literary figure in the late 1600s, her works gained serious attention from literary scholars, historians, scientists, and women's studies during the 20th century. Scholars have recently studied her as a fantasy, autobiography, and biography writer.

Blazing World is often referred to as one of the first science fiction novels. Many 20th century scholars also regard the book as a daring exploration of women's power.

Margaret Lucas Cavendish continued to write until her sudden death in 1673, at age fifty. Her body is interred next to her husband at Westminster Abbey, London, England. The graves are marked with a black and white marble monument to William Cavendish, Duke of Newcastle (1593-1676), and his wife Margaret (1623 -1673). The recumbent effigies show the Duke in his robes lying on a rush mattress wearing the Order of the Garter chain. Margaret holds an open book, a pen case, and an inkhorn to immortalize her prolific literary output.

Olympe de Gouges

b. *May 7, 1748*
Quercy, France

d. *November 3, 1793*
Paris, France

Olympe de Gouges, born **Marie Gouze**; May 7, 1748 in Montaubaun, Quercy (southwestern France). Her mother, Anne Olympe Mouisset Gouze, was the daughter of a middle-class family with an upper-class name. Her father may have been her mother's husband, Pierre Gouze, or maybe she was the illegitimate daughter of Jean-Jacques Lefranc, Marquis de Pompignan. When Marie/Olympe was older, she encouraged rumors that Pompignan was her father, and their relationship is considered plausible but unverifiable since no one was doing DNA in the 1700s. Another tale in the 18th century suggested Louis XV was her father. Her middle-class mum must have run in some exciting crowds.

The primary support for the identification of Pompignan as Marie/Olympe's father is found in her semi-autobiographical novel, *Mémoires de Madame de Valmont*, published after Pompignan's death. Some suggest she fabricated the story to raise her prestige and social standing when she moved to Paris, and besides, it helped with sales.

Marie/Olympe began her career as a playwright in the early 1780s. At the same time, the political tension was rising in France, and she became increasingly involved in politics and law, which is reflective in some of her work.

Her play *l'Esclavage des Noirs*, was staged at the famous Comédie-Française in 1785, and it helped her name gain notoriety. In 1788 she published *Réflexions Sur Les Hommes Négres*, which demanded compassion for the plight of enslaved people in the French colonies. Olympe firmly believed there was a direct link between the autocratic monarchy in France and the institution of slavery. She was known to argue that *"Men everywhere are equal... Kings who are just, do not want slaves; they know that they have submissive subjects"*. During the same time, she began writing political pamphlets. In her *Declaration of the Rights of Woman and the Female Citizen* (1791), she challenged the practice of male authority and the notion of male-female inequality. As a playwright and political activist, her feminist and abolitionist writings reached large audiences.

Olympe was one of the first women to fight for equal rights. She wrote her famous *Declaration of the Rights of Woman and the Female Citizen* shortly after the French Constitution of 1791 was ratified by Louis XVI and dedicated it to his wife, Queen Marie Antoinette. The French Constitution marked the birth of the short-lived constitutional monarchy and implemented status-based citizenship. To be considered a citizen, it was necessary to be a man over twenty-five, "independent," and have paid the poll tax. Only these chosen few had the right to vote.

Additionally, to hold a public office, a man had to be a voting citizen and deemed fit for office. To be afforded any rights of active citizenship, women were excluded as well as the men who could not pay the poll tax, children, domestic servants, rural day laborers, enslaved, Jews, actors, and hangmen. Louis would regret the stuff about executioners.

This was followed by Olympe's *Contrat Social* ("*Social Contract*," named after a famous work of Jean-Jacques Rousseau), proposing marriage be based upon gender equality. Her profound humanism moved her to oppose discrimination, violence, and oppression in all forms.

Denied a place in the influential circles of the day, Olympe didn't let that silence her political voice. She wrote an astonishing number of pamphlets and posters that she freely disseminated around Paris. Her writing illustrates her battles against injustice and inequality and her belief that solidarity and cooperation should predominate. In addition, her hatred of dictatorships and the corrupting influence of power topped off with her profound pacifism and respect for humankind, love of nature, and, of course, her desire that women be allowed a beneficial role in society. She spoke against slavery and the death penalty, dreamed of an equal society and proposed intelligent taxation plans to enable wealth to be more fairly divided. She called for a form of welfare state, trial by jury, and fair divorce laws to protect women and children from poverty. Believing in the power of drama to encourage political change, she wrote several plays that ingeniously highlight contemporary concerns. Many of her battles continue today.

Olympe never allowed the prejudices of her time, her critics, or the danger of being outspoken during the times of terror to silence her. For having expressed her opinions on democracy, she was considered a threat by those in power during the last years of the French Revolution.

Olympe de Gouges was executed by guillotine on November 3, 1793, during the Reign of Terror (1793–1794). She was charged with attacking the Revolutionary government's regime and her association with the Girondists to be a dangerous agitator. She was buried at Cimetière de la Madeleine, Amiens, Departement de la Somme, Picardie, France.

Carolina Louisa Waring Atkinson

b. *February 25, 1834*
Sutton Forest, NSW, Australia

d. *April 28, 1872*

Carolina "Louisa" Waring was born February 25, 1834, in Oldbury near Berrima, New South Wales, Australia. She was the daughter of James Atkinson and Charlotte Waring. Her father had arrived in Sydney in May 1820; he succeeded Michael Massey Robinson as principal clerk in the colonial secretary's office. He wrote *An Account of the State of Agriculture & Grazing in New South Wales* (London, 1826). In 1829 he published in Sydney, *On the Expediency and Necessity of Encouraging Distilling and Brewing from Grain in New South Wales*. He died when Louisa was nearly a year old, leaving a literary legacy.

Louisa lived most of her life in Kurrajong Heights in a home called Fernhurst that her mother built. Louisa was educated privately, primarily by her mother, a former teacher. Her mother was also an artist and deeply interested in natural history. The freedom from formal education and her mother's influence guided Louisa into interests in geology, botany, and zoology. Her interest expanded as she aged. Her widowed mother married George Bruce Barton.

As Louisa grew, she became an active member of the community, operating as an unpaid scribe for people of the district and an aid to the elderly and the sick. Louisa, to this day, is still regarded as a ground-breaker for Australian women in journalism and the natural sciences. She has been recognized for her consideration of the Aboriginal Australians in her writings and her promotion of conservation. In the forested area of her home and during her travels around Australia, Louisa expanded her plants and natural wildlife studies. She published several articles and added many admirable drawings. In addition, Louisa collected specimens and submitted them to the eminent botanists of that day. She was honored with her name being applied to several new species. Her knowledge of birds and insects extended into taxidermy, too.

Due to her life and research demands, she was influential in women's clothing reforms. There was quite the scandal as Louise wore trousers to ride and explore, as skirts were a nuisance in the outback. She was either ahead of her time or a leader to a modern era. By the 1860s, Louisa was aware of the impact of European agriculture on native flora. She wrote about this on several occasions, voicing her concerns. She was quoted, *"It needs no fertile imagination to foresee that in, say, half-a-century's time, tracts of hundreds of miles will be treeless."* She wasn't wrong.

Louisa became the first woman in Australia to have a long-running article series in a major newspaper and the first woman born in Australia to publish a novel, *Gertrude the Emigrant: A Tale of Colonial Life (by an Australian Lady)* in 1857. Her subsequent books were *Cowanda, the Veteran's Grant*, and *The Author of Gertrude*. Louisa's writing was described in both books as a simple moral tone with descriptive passages. This point also applies to a number of her other fictional works, which appeared as serials in the Sydney Morning Herald and Sydney Mail between 1861 and 1872.

Louisa and her mother returned to her home in Oldbury. in 1865. Her mother passed away after a few years. On March 11, 1869, Louisa married James Snowden Calvert. He was a survivor of Leichhardt's expedition of 1844–5 and had a strong interest in botany. When they met, James was the manager of Cavan station at Wee Jasper near Yass. Cavan was a sheep and cattle grazing district.

Only eighteen days after the birth of her daughter, Louise Snowden, Annie Louisa died. She was buried at All Saints Church Cemetery in the Atkinson family vault forest. Her obituary in the Sydney Morning Herald reported, *"This excellent lady, who has been cut down like a flower in the midst of her days, was highly distinguished for her literary and artistic attainments, as well as for the Christian principles and expansive charity which marked her career."*

Sadly, Louisa's fully illustrated book on the fauna and flora of New South Wales was being prepared in Germany at the time of her death and was never completed. Many of her paintings have vanished. She did, however, provide illustrations of animals and views for her articles in local journals. '*Notes on the Months*', which occasionally appeared throughout the *Illustrated Sydney News*.

Sarah Winnemucca

b. 1844
Nevada, USA

d. 1891
Henry's Lake, ID, USA

Born into the Northern Paiute tribe in or around 1844, **Sarah Winnemucca**'s birth name was **Thocmetony**, which means "shell flower." At the time of her birth, the Northern Paiutes and Washoes were the sole inhabitants of western Nevada.

Later she was quoted, "*I was a very small child when the first white people came into our country. They came like a lion, yes, like a roaring lion, and have continued so ever since, and I have never forgotten their first coming.*" Her grandfather, Chief Truckee, welcomed the arrival of his "white brothers" and also helped General John C. Fremont in the Bear War against Mexicans for control of California. Even with her grandfather's enthusiasm, her father, Chief Winnemucca, did not trust the white people and cautioned his tribe. She was raised with opposing viewpoints in dramatically changing times and lived a life with two cultures.

When Sarah was six, her grandfather insisted she travel with him to California. She was initially frightened but did enjoy the luxury of beds, chairs, brightly colored dishes, and exotic food. When she was thirteen, her grandfather arranged for Sarah and her sister to become Major Ormsby's household members at Mormon Station, now Genoa, Nevada. By the age of fourteen, she had learned five languages, three Native dialects, English and Spanish. Each time she left her tribe, Sarah witnessed multiple incidents of the invaders treating her people poorly.

Sarah's final visit to the white culture was at the age of sixteen, and it fulfilled her grandfather's deathbed request that she and her sister Elma be educated in a convent school in San Jose, California. The two girls were never officially admitted to the school, but she acquired more knowledge and experience with the new culture during their few weeks there. As Sarah reached maturity, the white emigration west continued to encroach on the Paiute territory. Eventually, whites insisted on moving all Natives onto reservations, first the Pyramid Lake Reservation in Nevada, then the Malheur Indian Reservation in Oregon, and finally to Yakima, Washington.

The life of hunting and gathering had ended for her tribe by 1871. She married Lt. E. C. Bartlett during this time, but he abandoned her with nothing. She was able to sue for divorce later and retake her own name after proving she had supported herself by making gloves and sewing. In January 1880, she pled the Indian's cause in Washington, D.C., before Secretary of the Interior Carl Schurz and President Rutherford B. Hayes. Sarah received promises of improvements for her people, which the government later broke. Despite her tireless advocacy, the broken promises caused her community to distrust her. Undaunted,

Sarah still dedicated the remainder of her life to this work. She gave more than four hundred speeches on behalf of the Paiutes.

A small group of the Paiute tribe returned to their native land to defend it against colonization. They lost the war and were forced onto Malheur Reservation. Sarah acted as an interpreter and later became a translator for the United States Army. In 1881 General Oliver O. Howard hired Sarah Winnemucca to teach Shoshone prisoners held at Vancouver Barracks. While there, she met and became close to Lieutenant Lewis H. Hopkins, an Indian Department employee. They married that year in San Francisco.

Sarah voluntarily accompanied them as an official translator when the remaining tribal members were moved to the Yakima Reservation. After observing the deplorable conditions there in 1883, she began a series of lectures across the U.S. to raise awareness of the injustice suffered by Native Americans. That same year Sarah became the first aboriginal American woman to publish a book of her lecture materials, *Life Among the Paiutes: Their Wrongs and Their Claims*. It was a critical step toward recognition of the plight of the Native American people and advocacy on their behalf. The book was a monumental achievement, recording the Native American viewpoint of whites settling the west, told in a language that was not her own, and written and published by a woman when women still couldn't vote.

The book was secondary to her daily work to educate and promote justice across cultures. From

1883 to 1886, Sarah taught at a Paiute school near Lovelock, Nevada. She published a pamphlet in 1886, *Sarah Winnemucca's Practical Solution to the Indian Problem*. She easily could have been in the warrior chapter too.

In 1886 her husband died, and ill herself, Sarah moved in with her sister. Sarah Thocmetony Winnemucca spent her final years retired from public activity. She died of tuberculosis at her sister Elma Smith's home at Henry's Lake, Idaho

Posthumously, she was awarded the Nevada Writers Hall of Fame Award for her book, *Life Among the Paiutes: Their Wrongs and Their Claims*, from the Friends of the Library, University of Nevada, Reno.

In 1994 an elementary school in Washoe County School District was named in her honor, Sarah Winnemucca Elementary.

Mary Johnston

b. November 21, 1870　　　d. May 9, 1936
Buchanan, VA, USA　　Warm Springs, VA, USA

American novelist **Mary Johnston** was born in Buchanan, Virginia, on November 21, 1870. She was the first child of John William Johnston, an American Civil War veteran, and Elizabeth Dixon Alexander Johnston. Due to frequent illness, Mary was educated at home, which encouraged her love of books. Her family was wealthy enough to buy the books, and they allowed Mary to devote herself to writing.

When Mary was sixteen, her father's work with the Georgia Pacific Railroad transferred him and his family to Birmingham, Alabama. Soon after they moved, Mary attended the Atlanta Female Institute and College of Music in Atlanta, Georgia. Her only formal education lasted three months due to her mother's bad health and death.

After her mother died, Mary stayed home to help raise her five younger siblings. The family moved again in 1892 to New York. Then four years later, they returned to Birmingham and then to Richmond, Virginia, in 1902. This was life in the travel industry before flight.

Mary was the first woman to top the best-seller list in the United States. Her historical books and novels often combined romance with history. Her first book, *Prisoners of Hope* (1898), dealt with colonial times in Virginia. Her second book, *To Have and To Hold*, was the best-selling novel in the U.S. She wrote *The Goddess of Reason* (1907) using the theme of the French Revolution, and in *Lewis Rand* (1908), she portrayed political life at the dawn of the 19th century. In 1900, three of her novels were adapted into silent films.

The Long Roll, her novel on the Civil War, told the story of Stonewall Jackson and the troops that fought under him. In modern times her characterization of General Jackson seems sympathetic, but Stonewall Jackson's widow published an editorial in the *New York Times* denouncing the book. Mary published twenty-three novels, numerous short stories, two long narrative poems, and a play during her writing career.

Mary spoke out against lynching, but her view of the confederacy was typical of many Southerners of the time. Her father was a Civil War veteran, and Mary was a friend of Margaret Mitchell, who wrote *Gone with the Wind*. Mitchell once said, "I hesitate to write about the South after having read Mary Johnston."

Her book *Hagar* is considered an early feminist novel, and she lost a lot of her readers. In this book, Mary wrote in support of the women's suffrage movement. She did more than just write; Mary was instrumental in founding the Equal Suffrage League of Virginia. Mary didn't stop there. She spoke before state legislatures in Virginia and Tennessee, supporting women's right to vote.

Mary Johnson died of Bright's disease in 1936 at home in Warm Springs, Virginia. Three Hills, her house at Warm Springs, was added to the National Register of Historic Places in 2013, and her Richmond home was listed in 1971.

Mary was honored by the Library of Virginia as part of its 2005 class of Virginia Women in History. Her name is featured on the Wall of Honor on the Virginia Women's Monument, located in Capitol Square in Richmond. Even though her novels are not widely read now, she's remembered for being a hugely popular woman writer when women were much less likely to get to read, let alone write and be published.

Mary Crow Dog
aka
Mary Brave Bird

b. September 26, 1954   *d. February 14, 2013*
Rosebud Res., SD, USA   *Crystal Lake, CA, USA*

Born **Mary Ellen Brave Bird** in 1954 on the Rosebud Indian Reservation, South Dakota, she was a member of the Sicangu Oyate, also known as the Burnt Thighs Nation or Brulé Band of Lakota. While Emily Brave Bird, her mother, went to Pierre, South Dakota, to attend nursing school, her grandparents stepped in and raised the four children. Mary's grandfather, Robert Brave Bird, was a trapper in the winter and a farmer in the summer. He was a descendant of Pakeska Maza (Iron Shell).

When Mary was five, she was sent to a Catholic boarding school. Even more recently, there was a strong effort to "Americanize" the Native Americans. Mary started young and reported the nuns beating Indian children when they spoke their Native language or practiced Native customs. Her mother was also raised in the Catholic school system, and Mary had not learned much of her ancestral heritage. She describes herself as a half-breed, degraded by both the white and the full blood societies. Mary describes the schools as an American concentration camp that destroyed all hope and community. This is supported by ongoing investigations and the discovery of hidden cemeteries.

The Reservation offered no jobs, no promise, and the knowledge that the Native population did not hold any significant value to South Dakota or the U.S. As a woman, life was valued even less. Women are often beaten by their partners, and many disappear and are murdered with minimal investigation. Mary's sister was forcibly sterilized, not uncommon on the Rez (Reservation). Mary had recognized that in the community, many were murdered, and there would be little to no investigation or repercussions. Like many other people in tough circumstances, Mary turned to alcohol and drugs to numb a bleak outlook.

Mary's life was changed forever by a young hippie from New York who appeared on the Rez in the 1960s. The young speaker carried a message about the civil rights and Indian movements. Shortly after that experience, the American Indian Movement (AIM) blew into town like a plain's tornado. Mary's intelligence and clear understanding of the Native condition was ready for the adventure.

At the age of sixteen, she met Leonard Crow Dog at a powwow. He was a spiritual and political leader of AIM and thirty-one years old. They wed when she was seventeen. Leonard taught Mary the ceremonies, used healing plants, and reconciled her to the role of a medicine man's wife. This involved feeding multitudes of uninvited guests at the feasts following every service. Mary signed on and would participate in the occupation of the Bureau of Indian Affairs building in Washington, D.C. Not stopping there, she was also at the second Wounded Knee action in 1973, where her son would be born during the seventy-one day siege. Wounded Knee had been the site of the 1890 Indian massacre. Leonard was a leader and medicine man, and he felt that Mary did not have the background he believed she deserved. So, he worked double-time, teaching her more than the duties of a medicine man's wife but also political activism. Mary raised seven children. Richard, Ina, and Bernadette were from Leonard's previous marriage, and her four with Leonard, Pedro, Anwah, June Bug, and Jennifer Louise.

    Leonard and AIM would revive the Indian Spirit and ancient religious ceremonies. Through this movement, Mary learned that she was a powerful descendant of a vast history. On September 5, 1975, 180 government agents broke into the Crow Dog home and took Leonard away in handcuffs. After three trials, he was sentenced to twenty-three years in prison for his political activities. After Leonard was arrested and imprisoned, Mary discovered her true ability as a writer and public speaker. She traveled all over the country, drumming up money and support for the movement and her husband's defense. She credits participation in a Sun Dance that brought her fully to being a Native and a woman.

Mary and Leonard divorced, and in 1991, she married Rudy Olguin. They had Summer Olguin in 1991 and later their second child, Rudy Olguin. She had six children and remained active in the Native American Church.

As an author, Mary looks directly at the struggles and complexities of Native life. She acknowledges poverty, discrimination, government, and life as a political activist and some of the violence of change. *Lakota Woman* (1990) and *Ohitika Woman* (1993) are memoirs. *Lakota Woman* was self-published under Mary Crow Dog and won the 1991 American Book Award. It describes her life until 1977.

Fifteen years after her memoir, Mary released another book entitled *Ohitika Woman*. It detailed her life experiences up to 1992 and continued to share ancient myths and traditions of the Lakota people, and added detail to what was written in her earlier book. Her books describe the conditions of the Lakota Indian life and her experience growing up on the Rosebud Indian Reservation in South Dakota and conditions in the neighboring Pine Ridge Indian Reservation under the leadership of tribal chairman Richard Wilson. She covered aspects of the role of the FBI, the U.S. Bureau of Indian Affairs, and the treatment of the Native Americans and their children in the mid-1900s. Her work focuses on themes of gender, identity, and race.

1994 movie *Lakota Woman: Siege at Wounded Knee* was produced by TNT and Jane Fonda. The film starred Irene Bedard as Mary Brave Bird. The movie depicted the events during the 1973 uprising of the AIM (American Indian Movement) organization and their stand-off at Wounded Knee. Mary had a cameo appearance in the film, and she and Leonard also made cameo appearances in the 1991 Oliver Stone film *The Doors*.

Mary Ellen Brave Bird died on February 14, 2013, aged fifty-eight or fifty-nine. She is buried at the Clear Water Cemetery, Rosebud, Todd County, South Dakota, USA.

Her spirit and work live on.

Bibliography

About Famous People
    www.aboutfamouspeople.com

Adventures of Rocky and Bullwinkle (Universal Studios)
    www.rockyandbullwinkle.com

Africa, by Terrie Wright Chrones

All The Women of the Bible, by Edith Deen

Ancient Warriors of Womenhood, by Merlin Stone

Bad Girls, by Barry Yeoman
    Psychology Today 1999
    www.barryyeoman.com/articles/badgirls.html

Bad Girls Throughout History by Ann Shen

Elizabeth Báthory: The Opera by Dennis Báthory-Kitsz
    www.bathory.org

BBC News
    www.bbc.co.uk/news

Bella On Line
    www.bellaonline.com

The Best of Black History on the Net
    www.blackhistorypages.net/

Biography on A & E
    www.biography.com

Bits of Blue and Gray: An American Civil War Notebook
    www.bitsofblueandgray.com

The Book of Women, by Lynne Griffin and Kelly McCann

Bullfinch's Mythology, by Thomas Bullfinch, Untangel Inc. 1998
www.mythome.org/bullfinc.htm

Real Mermaids
www.realmermaids.net

1996-2005 Chicago Reader, Inc. *Bits of Blue & Grey*,
www.bitsofblueandgray.com/october2002.htm

Codrescu, Andrei, *The Blood Countess*, Dell, New York, NY, 7/2/1996

The Columbia Electronic Encyclopedia Copyright 8 2003, Columbia

www.ethelsmyth.org

University Press. Licensed from Columbia University Press. All rights reserved.

Crime Library
www.crimelibrary.com

Encyclopedia of Gods by Michael Jordan

Fatal: The Poisonous Life of a Female Serial Killer by Harold Schechter.

Fearless Girls, Wise Women and Beloved Sisters by Kathleen Ragan

Harvard Education:
140.247.102.177/maria/Apachewomen.html

www.harrietjacobs.org

Hell's Belles by Seale Ballenger

The History Makers https://www.thehistorymakers.org/

Hoover Stanford Education Department
www.hoover.stanford.edu/bios/

Incidents in the Life of a Slave Girl, by Harriet A. Jacobs, 1861

Jewish Virtual Library

Kaywaykla, James, & Ball, Eve, *In the Days of Victorio; Recollections of a Warm Springs Apache*, 1972, Phoenix Az, University of Arizona Press

Native History Association
www.nativehistoryassociation.org/

Wistrich, Robert, *Who's Who In Nazi Germany*, New York, NY Routledge, Frances & Taylor Group, 2002
books.google.com/books?id=PrYwT3eI3wcC&printsec=copyright&source=gbs_pub_info_s&cad=3

Knauss, Sibylle, *Eva's Cousin*: New York, NY, Doubleday, Dec. 2, 2003

Svenn A. Hanssen, Master of Science
www.hanssen.priv.no/svenn/indians/#gouyen

Internet Public Library
www.ipl.org/div/natam/bin/browse.pl/A20

Hornberger, Francine, *Mistresses of Mayhem, The Book of Women Criminals*, Exton, PA, Alpha; 1st edition (March 13, 2002)

Library of Halexandria http://halexandria.org/

Queens through Swedish History, Lelua University
www.luth.se/luth/present/sweden/history/queens
www.historyofroyalwomen.com

www.Royalty.nu

Incidents in the Life of a Slave Girl under the pseudonym Linda Brent.

The Deeper Wrong, by Harriett Ann Jacobs

Spies!: Women in the Civil War. White Hall: Shoe Tree Press, 1992.

www.aboutfamouspeople.com/article1139.html

The Vampire Killers, by Katherine Ramsland

www.trutv.com/library/crime/serial_killers/weird/

That's Not in My American History Book by Thomas Ayres

Unsung: A History of Women in American Music by Christine Ammer

Uppity Women of Ancient Times, Leon, Vicki, 1995, New York, NY, MJF

Uppity Women of the New World, Leon, Vicki, 2001, New York, NY, MJF

Walker, Barbara,: *The Woman's Encyclopedia of Myths and Secrets,* and *The Woman's Dictionary of Symbols and Sacred Objects,* 1988, New York, NY, Harper Collins

Wikipedia
www.wikipedia.com

Wild Women and Books by Brenda Knight

Women Art & Society by Whitney Chadwick

Women & the American Story

Women of the Bible
www.womeninthebible.net

Women of Discovery, Milbry Polk, Mary Tiegreen

Women Healers of the World: The Traditions, History, and Geography of Herbal Medicine by Holly Bellebuono.

Women in World History
www.womeninworldhistory.com

Mickelson, Barbara & David, *Urban Legends* 1995-2003.

Jones, David E., *Women Warriors: A History*, 3/1/2000, Potomic Books

www. Worldhistory.com

MUSEUMS

International Association of Women's Museums (IAWM)
iawm.international/about-us/womens-museums/museums-list/

Museum of Ancient and Modern Art
www.mama.org/exhibits/ancient/goddess/

Florence Kellye at Northwestern University
www.florencekelley.northwestern.edu

The New World Encyclopedia

Australian Women's Museum
wmoa.com.au/herstory-archive/

Women's History Museum
www.womenshistory.org/womens-history

About the Author

Born in central Illinois it took a few moves for her to settle in her mother's hometown north of Seattle, Washington. She intends to stay for the majesty of the trees and mountains. Her father always claimed she was named for a stripper in the 1940s. His stories were always better than the truth, and it was his passion for reading that started her fascination with history.

She raised other women's children who puzzled her, but they never failed to make her proud. Toni marched for civil rights, and shared bread with icons of politics and art. No one has successfully told her how to vote, although some tried. Known as the first to show up for meetings and events with a baked good, she will donate 50 cents of her last dollar to a worthy cause.

Toni was in her sixties when James Johnson dared her to write and it changed her life. She is last to let laugh or cry alone, but she may be taking notes. Toni continues to struggle towards an honest voice, with cats and NPR playing in the background.

Toni is one of the founding directors of The Writers Cooperative of the Pacific Northwest that continues to grow.

www.tonikief.com   www.writers-coop.com
        www.amazon.com/Toni-Kief/e/B01CR8V3RG

Made in the USA
Middletown, DE
22 September 2022